THE SECRET SOURCE

THE LAW OF ATTRACTION
AND ITS HERMETIC INFLUENCE
THROUGHOUT THE AGES

By Maja D'Aoust
Adam Parfrey

The Secret Source:
The Law of Attraction and its Hermetic Influence Throughout the Ages

ISBN: 978-1-934170-32-8

10 9 8 7 6 5 4 3 2 1

Process Media
1240 W. Sims Way Suite 124
Port Townsend WA 98368

www.processmediainc.com

Design by Dana Collins

CONTENTS

{Introduction}

THOUGHTS HAVE WINGS

The greatest discovery of my generation is that man can alter his life simply by altering his attitude of mind.

—William James (author, The Varieties of Religious Experience*)*

I hold it true that thoughts are things;
They're endowed with bodies and breath and wings;
And that we send them forth to fill
The world with good results, or ill.
That which we call our secret thought
Speeds forth to earth's remotest spot,
Leaving its blessings or its woes
Like tracks behind it as it goes.
We build our future thought by thought,
For good or ill, yet know it not.
Yet, so the universe was wrought.
Thought is another name for fate;
Choose, then, thy destiny and wait,
For love brings love and hate brings hate.

—Henry Van Dyke (chaired the committee that wrote the first Presbyterian printed liturgy, The Book of Common Worship*)*

IT WAS IMPOSSIBLE in the summer of 2007 to watch television, browse the internet, listen to the radio, read newspapers or magazines, or go to bookshops without being deluged with a phenomenon paradoxically known as *The Secret*.

A publishing sensation in its hardcover, CD, audio and DVD entities; on the top of *New York Times* bestseller lists, featured on the Amazon.com home page, stacked on the front tables at Barnes & Noble and Borders. Millions of hits on youtube.com, videogoogle.com, news sites, blogs, and a sweeps week cavalcade on *Oprah*, *Larry King*, and *Regis and Kelly*. On everyone's lips at the water cooler and yoga class.

The smog of commercial success that hangs over *The Secret* makes it easy to overlook its essential pitch: that the "greatest people in history" achieved their financial, intellectual and political success due to their knowledge and use of forbidden ancient teachings, despite the attempts of church and state to withhold and destroy these ideas.

Author Rhonda Byrne tells us that she originally discovered *The Secret*'s secret in the obscure century-old book: *The Science of Getting Rich* by Wallace D. Wattles. The practical directives of Mr. Wattles' occult belief system inspired Ms. Byrne to embark on a quick and voracious consumption of other "secret" texts. These included the ancient Hermetic *Emerald Tablet* and later writings from New Thought, a nineteenth-century philosophical movement that says the physical world can be affected and changed through ideas and thoughts, particularly in regard to wealth and health, as expressed by the Law of Attraction.

For more than a century, Hermetic ideas have been filtered down for the American public as New Thought, Prosperity Consciousness, New Age—and most recently as *The Secret*. *The Secret* has re-introduced Hermeticism into mainstream consciousness on a large scale, but this publication merely scratches the surface of a tradition and knowledge that requires no small amount of discipline, experience and rigor to comprehend its truths. Scholars and alchemists have spent lifetimes attempting to understand the meaning of the *Emerald Tablet* alone, which is quoted and lionized at the beginning of *The Secret*.

Hermetic wisdom has infused every major religion and countless schools of thought for over two millennia. The Hermetic tradition comes to us in various guises—Platonism, Py-thagorean philosophy, Sufism and Gnosticism, even in certain Christian principles.

This information has been kept secret for hundreds of years through brotherhoods, not only to retain a fraternal group's sense of exclusivity, but also to guard the information from competing religious and political power structures, and to protect the igno-rant from the power of its implications. If you believe that knowl-edge must be restricted by the directives of church and state, then the idea of the masses becoming aware of these teachings could clearly cause trouble for those in charge; certainly the misuse of some of these teachings could backlash on the user poorly.

"Fragments of a Great Secret," says *The Secret*'s flap copy, "have been found in the oral traditions, in literature, in religions and philosophies throughout the centuries. For the first time, all the pieces of The Secret come together . . . ."

What actually comes together in *The Secret* is just one frag-ment of Hermetic thought which has been otherwise available throughout the centuries in hundreds of books. But *The Secret* art-fully simplifies this fragment of Hermetic Law into the kind of lan-guage that can be easily digested by modern minds, minds that are constantly distracted by the aggressive multimedia bazaar.

Singing its praises, a yoga teacher says, "I know at least three people where *The Secret* has changed their lives. A friend said his life became immediately much better when he realized that when he complained his life became worse. And when he was grateful for what he had, his mental state and his health improved right away."

As a motivational work encouraging readers to reprogram themselves with a more positive frame of mind, *The Secret* is a spectacular success. But in keeping its thesis simple and positiv-istic, with an emphasis on material gain and instant gratification, *The Secret* has also neglected to include adequate instruction to guard against potential missteps and disappointments.

Within its pages, *The Secret* intimates, but does not say overtly, that its principles are drawn from the American New Thought movement that developed in the late nineteenth cen-tury as both a pantheistic and mystical Christian response to a fast-expanding capitalist environment that saw prosperity

13

as a primary goal. Through positive thinking, affirmations, meditation and prayer, the New Thought movement taught spiritually-inclined materialists how to find health, wealth and happiness through mystical principles. *The Secret* is the New Thought's twenty-first century corollary.

An early twentieth century text, *The Kybalion*, attributed to the "Three Initiates," incorporates Hermetic Laws and New Thought movement ideas in a fusion to form the idea of mental transmutation. This mysterious work is thought to have been written by Paul Foster Case (a member of the occult group The Golden Dawn and founder of Builders of the Adytum Mystery School), Michael Whitty and the New Thought movement leader William Walker Atkinson, who is quoted in and given praise by *The Secret*, particularly in respect to his more than a dozen books explaining his use of the Law of Attraction.

The two-dozen talking head "teachers" seen in *The Secret* DVD repeatedly tell the story of their reluctant belief in the Law of Attraction as an immutable spiritual truism, that the Universe is an inexhaustible cornucopia of riches, and that all one needs to do to access them is to believe, be grateful and open to receive. Says "teacher" Joe Vitale, "*The Secret* is like having the universe as your catalogue."

Critics have disparaged *The Secret* as yet another incarnation of mindless hope-peddling for the "power of positive thinking" racket. Considering America's dark history of greedy men profiting from consumer naïveté, this skepticism seems like a completely valid perception. On the other hand, to always comfort ourselves with reflexive nay-saying destroys the essential human component of being able to imagine and discover heretofore unheard-of possibilities.

The open-ended, exploratory beliefs of the New Thought and Prosperity Consciousness movements could only have blossomed in a wild, unformed land like America. Wattles' *Science of Getting Rich*, Atkinson's *The Law of Attraction in the Thought World* and *The Kybalion*, pseudonymously authored by the "Three Initiates," will be excerpted within.

The more commercial guise of Hermetic Laws in New Thought and Prosperity Consciousness movement directives has been showered on the American public for more than a century. But what is *The Secret*'s essential source? What is the true nature and purpose of the messages of Hermes? The basic tenets of Hermeticism have been so intertwined with Christian, Jewish, Islamic and Greek writings that it has become difficult to discover where one ends and the other begins. And how have the new influences of mystical capitalism transformed the Hermetica?

What is the Hermetic literature, or *Corpus Hermeticum*? Who wrote it, and what does it say? What is the history, in all its tragedies and successes, of the Law of Attraction?

Depending upon whose account we read, Hermes Trismegistus could have been an actual God, a wise sage named after Hermes (the dream-bringing messenger from the Gods to humans) or the Egyptian Thoth, the scribe of the Gods. Hermes Trismegistus is said to have been responsible for countless divine or divine-inspired writings (some say as many as tens of thousands), most of which were lost when the Library of Alexandria was burned, according to scholars, when the Roman emperor Theodosius I ordered the destruction of all pagan temples in 391 AD.

The *Emerald Tablet* is a brief and cryptic text of universal laws attributed to Hermes Trismegistus. Though no original copy of the *Emerald Tablet* exists, translations have been passed down by priests and occult initiates through the millennia. An early Latin translation calls it "The Secret of Secrets." Roger Bacon, Albertus Magnus, Isaac Newton and even Aleister Crowley have written their translations and variants. Some are excerpted within this book.

The Ancient Mystical Order Rosæ Crucis (AMORC), commonly known as the Rosicrucians, enticed readers of the pulpy magazines *Fate* and *Popular Science* throughout the twentieth century with illustrated advertisements proclaiming "Thoughts Have Wings: You Can Influence Others With Your Thinking!" and "Magic of Mind: The Greatest Power on Earth!" The reader would be shown "how to use your natural forces and talents to do things you now think are beyond your ability." With its mail-order business of weekly occult lessons, AMORC teaches a more all-inclusive variety of Hermetic and New Thought ideas.

This book aims to guide readers through many Hermetic teachings and history, to examine the folklore of the *Emerald Tablet*, and elucidate the shape-changing aspect of the Hermetic tradition and Hermes himself. You'll learn how large sections of the Christ mythos and Jewish Kabbalistic texts were borrowed from the pages of Hermetic works. We'll also investigate the revival of Hermetic teachings in their Freemasonic, pop culture and New Age reformulations. We'll reveal how many of the get-rich-quick schemes borrow from Hermetic laws, utilizing them for strictly materialistic or ego-oriented goals.

We, the authors of *The Secret Source*, are not gurus, nor are we Inquisitors on behalf of the scientific or theological establishment. We intend to examine the history of the concepts expressed in *The Secret* without imposing our views as to their essential validity.

Perhaps the true attraction of *The Secret* lies in its ability to persuade us of new possibilities in a time of suicidal jihad, 2012 apocalypse and the twilight days of the biosphere. After all, everything is possible, isn't it?

To celebrate this new hardcover edition, the authors have included writings on sex magic by the extraordinary nineteenth century mulatto and Rosicrucian author Paschal Beverly Randolph in addition to further explorations into "Solomon's Secret".

Namaste,

Maja D'Aoust
Adam Parfrey

{SECTION ONE}

HEALTH, WEALTH, AND THE ORIGINS OF THE MIND CURE

IN THE LATE nineteenth century, Americans were moving away from farms and small towns and pouring into cities with millions of new Catholic and Jewish immigrants.

With its doctrine of doom and depravity, hellfire and damnation, Calvinist Puritanism, the primary religion of post-Revolutionary America, seemed increasingly at odds with the large, beautiful, untamed land, with its freedom of church and state and endless possibilities.

The popularity of Freemasonry and other secret societies catapulted in popularity in the late nineteenth century, providing manly drinking clubs and extravagant pomp and ritualism to its members. These deist clubs threatened the Catholic church to such a degree that in 1884, Pope Leo XIII issued the "Humanum Genus," a papal encyclical condemning Freemasonry. Catholics, wishing to join a fraternal order that offered similar insurance programs and quasi-militaristic regalia, were offered instead the ability to join another sort of fraternal organization, The Knights of Columbus, around the same time. In turn, the Ku Klux Klan, a Protestant fraternal order, warned against the influx of immigrants for reasons of job security and its view that Catholics practiced demonic idolatry.

Immigrants to the new land often embraced a less orthodox variety of the European version of their faith. Reform Jews were particularly interested in integrating themselves into society at large, rejecting messianic nationalism and kosher practices. Unlike their Orthodox brethren, Reform rabbis were expected to receive a secular education.

Within the fast-growing cities, a smorgasbord of disparate beliefs started to reveal themselves: Theosophy, Ariosophy, Buddhism, Hinduism, Rosicrucianism, Mystical Christianity, Spiritualism, Mediumism, and hundreds of occult and fraternal orders.

The New Thought movement was created and expanded during this "Gilded Age" of the late nineteenth century, a time of delirious industrialization, of robber barons and shady business practices. During the early 1890s, the world economy tailed into a recession. Banks foreclosed on farms and farmers moved into cities, where they often had to learn the sales trade, and how to convince others to purchase inessential goods.

In America, the old faiths were changing guard, obscure faiths were showing their faces, and new faiths began to grab people's attention.

The revolutionary idea of New Thought was to make God and extraordinary possibilities accessible to all. All one needed to change reality was the ability to change one's mind.

The central concept of New Thought, that thoughts have presence in the material world, is derived mostly from ancient sources, Hermetic sources, that likely predated Christianity. According to Hermetic philosophy, all matter is made either as a thought in the mind of God, or as a word emanating from the mouth of God.

How exactly did this ancient Hermetic knowledge make its way into the New Thought movement? The first avenue was through Franz Anton Mesmer.

Animal Magnetism

We have all heard the word "mesmerized," which owes its origin to Franz Anton Mesmer (1734–1815). Mesmer discovered what he called *magnétisme animal* (animal magnetism), which later became popularly known as "Mesmerism."

Mesmer was born in the village of Iznang, Germany, and studied medicine at the University of Vienna in 1759. While a medical student, Mesmer was impressed by the writings of Theophrastus Philippus Aureolus Bombastus von Hohenheim, commonly known as Paracelsus (1493–1541).[1] Paracelsus was the first European physician to explore the phenomenon of magnetism in relation to the human organism, and his studies in this area were based on the Hermetic principle of interrelationship, namely, "as above, so below." Mesmer's "27 Propositions" are taken directly from the writings of Paracelsus.

The high level of Hermetic penetration into Mesmer's ideals is incontrovertible. Even Isaac Newton, on whose writings Mesmer based his doctoral thesis, was teeming with Hermetic ideology.[2]

---

1   Other Hermetic influences on Mesmer included Robert Fludd, Anasthasius Kircher and von Helmont, one of Paracelsus' students.
2   Dobbs, Betty Jo Teeter, *The Foundations of Newton's Alchemy: Or, "The Hunting of the*

Mesmer adored Newton and, above all, wanted to be considered a physicist on his level. It was for this reason that Mesmer declined to give due accord to God and the high spirit in his writings on the phenomenon of magnetism, even though his Hermetic predecessors always recognized the Divine as the key source of power.

It was under the influence of a friend that Mesmer undertook his magnetic studies. Maximilian Hell (1720–1792), a court astronomer and Jesuit priest, used magnets in the treatment of diseases. Hell believed that everyone possessed a magnetic force which connected all human beings, and he attempted to rationalize a belief in astrological influences on human health as being the result of planetary forces through a subtle, invisible fluid. Later, Mesmer would discredit Hell, and convince the world that it was he, Mesmer, who in fact had the correct answers where magnetic healing was concerned.

In 1766, Mesmer published his doctoral dissertation, *De Planetarum Influxu in Corpus Humanum*,[3] that focused on the influence of the moon and the planets on the human body and on disease.[4] The main influence on this work was astrophysics (rather than astrology) that relied mainly on the theories of Isaac Newton. In the dissertation, Mesmer postulates the existence of a universally distributed but invisible fluid that flows continuously, everywhere. (Newton referred to this fluid as "the Aether" in his writings, as did many others after him.[5]) This cosmic fluid, according to Mesmer, served as a vehicle for the reciprocal influences of heavenly bodies, the earth, and living organisms. Mesmer called his theory of the action of this cosmic fluid "animal magnetism." In a later work, Mesmer described his animal magnetism in the following terms:

> I set forth the nature and action of Animal Magnetism and the analogy between its properties and those of the magnet and electricity. I added "that all bodies were, like the magnet, capable of communicating this magnetic principle; that this fluid penetrated everything and could be stored up and concentrated, like the electric fluid; that it acted at a distance."[6]

Greene Lyon,"
3   *On the Influence of the Planets on the Human Body.*
4   As above, so below!
5   Maxwell, Sagnac, Einstein, etc.
6   Mesmer, Franz Anton, *Mesmerism,*

Mesmer believed that the universe was filled with available energy, and that "the harnessed powers of the cosmic energies" were accessible only to those whose consciousness had risen high enough to perceive them, such as himself. Mesmer believed that sickness and disease were caused by imbalances of the universal fluid within the body. According to d'Eslon, Mesmer understood health as the free flow of the process of life through thousands of channels in our bodies. Illness was caused by obstacles to this flow. Overcoming these obstacles and restoring flow produced crises, which restored health.7 (To us this may sound quaint, but acupuncture is based on this concept, and has been used for thousands of years.)

The action of this power over distance was also very specifically outlined in the Paracelsus material:

> By the magic power of the will, a person on this side of the ocean may make a person on the other side hear what is said on this side . . . the ethereal body of a man may know what another man thinks at a distance of 100 miles or more.[8]

Over time, Mesmer developed varying techniques to put his patients into a sort of trance through the use of touching, stroking, hypnotic stares and the waving of magnetic wands to restore cosmic fluid imbalance. Dr. Mesmer treated his patients while dressed in long, lavish, silken purple robes, brandishing various glass rods which appeared perhaps as magic wands. Really, all he needed was a pointy hat, and voilà! A wizard!

In 1774, Mesmer made what he called an "artificial tide" in a diseased woman, by making her swallow a preparation containing iron and then attaching magnets to strategic spots on her body. The patient said she felt streams of a mysterious fluid running through her body, and was relieved of her symptoms for several hours.

At no point in his studies did Mesmer believe that the magnets were acting on their own to effect cures. For Paracelsus and the Hermeticists, the healing was due to the presence of God acting through the healer; the magnets were only a tool. Mesmer, however, gave

---

7   Ask the Chinese, they have been using Acupuncture based on this concept for thousands of years.
8   Quoted by Hartmann, Franz. *The Life of Philippus Theophrastus Bombast of Hohenheim Known by the Name of Paracelsus and of the Substance of his Teachings,*

himself a more important role. Not only God, but Mesmer himself had some influence on the matter at hand, and no small one at that. Mesmer realized early on that the practitioner himself was key to the healing effects on the patient, and he was very vocal about this:

> That man can act upon man at any time, and almost at will, by striking his imagination; that the simplest gestures and signs can have the most powerful effects; and that the action of man upon the imagination may be reduced to an art, and conducted with method, upon subjects who have faith.[9]

For Mesmer, it was the mind of the healer that did the work, not specifically the fluid. The fluid was the medium that carried thoughts through time and space from one person to the other. The practitioner made himself like a magnet, attracting a healing influence and passing it on to the patient.

The concept that we are magnets and can become attractors is entirely Hermetic, and it can be traced directly from Paracelsus to Ancient Egyptian beliefs:

> Soul, then, is an eternal intellectual essence, having for purpose the reason of itself; and when it thinks with it, it doth attract unto itself the harmonies intention.[10]

It was due to this concept, that thoughts attract things in the world, that the New Thought movement developed the Law of Attraction and Prosperity Consciousness. The authors who most thoroughly developed the Law of Attraction within the New Thought philosophy, William Walker Atkinson[11] and Quimby, drew upon the Hermetic materials for their inspiration.

> We have the power to choose; it is within our power to choose the better, and in like way to choose the worse, according to our will. And if our choice clings to evil things it doth consort with the corporeal nature; and for this cause fate rules o'er him who makes this choice.[12]

---

9   Mesmer, Franz Anton, from *The Proceedings to The King of France*.
10 Stobaeus, Fragment XIX from the *Corpus Heremticum*, as translated by G.R.S. Mead.
11 See the chapter on *The Kybalion* for Atkinson's Hermetic influences.
12 Stoebius, *The Power of Choice*; G.R.S Mead, *Thrice Greatest Hermes*.

Compared with:

> The man or woman who is filled with love sees love on all sides and attracts the love of others. The man with hate in his heart gets all the hate he can stand.[13]

The Rise of Spiritualism

Although Mesmer met with resistance from the scientific community, it is important to note that he did in fact cure thousands of people. The high level of success in healing with the Mesmeric method was undeniable. In the early decades of the nineteenth century, Mesmerism was the most commonly used Western method of surgical pain-relief beyond drinking ethyl alcohol. Americans lapped up the Mesmeric cure eagerly, and Mesmerists touring the country helped cure many legitimately incurable diseases;

> Evidently, Americans felt mesmerism treated the whole person rather than isolated complaints. They believed that the mesmerizing process helped them to reestablish inner harmony with the very source of physical and emotional well-being. While in their mesmeric state, they learned that disease and even moral confusion were but the unfortunate consequences of having fallen out of rapport with the invisible spiritual workings of the universe.[14]

The downfall of Mesmerism, in the eyes of the scientific community, was essentially twofold. Firstly, it was due to a woman, and secondly, it was due to large groups of women.

The first woman involved was Marie Antoinette. At the time of her acquaintance with Mesmer, Marie Antoinette was the wife of King Louis XVI. Marie became enraptured with Mesmer and took to visiting him incessantly for "healing" sessions. She helped fund his institute and provided him with salon audiences of the most prestigious sort in Paris. It wasn't long before the king took offense to his wife's growing interest in this powerfully magnetic

---

13 Atkinson, William Walker, *Thought Vibration: The Law of Attraction in the Thought World.*
14 Fuller, Robert C., "Mesmerism and the Birth of Psychology" from *Pseudo-Science and Society in Nineteenth-Century America*, Arthur Wrobel, Editor, University Press of Kentucky.

individual, and he took actions against Mesmer and his theories. In 1784, King Louis XVI appointed commissioners to investigate animal magnetism. These included the chemist Antoine Lavoisier, the physician Joseph-Ignace Guillotin,[15] the astronomer Jean Sylvain Bailly and the American ambassador Benjamin Franklin.[16] The commission conducted a series of experiments aimed not at determining whether Mesmer's treatment worked, but whether he had discovered a new physical fluid. The commission concluded that there was no evidence of such a fluid, even though in every case the treatments were effective. The committee also concluded that magnetic treatment was hazardous to women, since its effects might destroy their sexual inhibitions, a ruling which was most probably influenced by the involvement of Marie Antoinette in the matter. Mesmer was stigmatized as a deviant and accused of using his powers for the seduction of the fairer sex. He was forced to leave Paris and return to Vienna, lest Guillotin engage the use of his favorite device.

The second group of women who brought about the decline of Mesmerism were the spiritualists and mediums of America. Spiritualism, which tried to communicate with the spirit world through the use of mediums, was a popular movement in America from the 1840s through the 1930s. The spiritual mediums of the day found that once they were put into a Mesmeric trance, or hypnotized, their clairvoyant abilities increased considerably. Once word spread of this phenomenon, every medium adapted Mesmeric practices, claiming them for the spiritualist movement.

Due to the resulting quackery, doctors were forced to abandon the techniques. Before long, no self-respecting doctor in the country would go near a Mesmerist. This is a true tragedy because, at the time, Mesmerism was being studied extensively by the medical community for use as anesthesia during surgeries. Most Mesmerists ended up becoming spiritualists, as that was the fad at the time, and they followed the most plausible source of income.

---

15 Ironically, Lavoisier would later meet his doom on the guillotine, which was invented by his colleague on this board. Marie Antoinette and King Louis XVI would also expire by this device several years later.

16 Benjamin Franklin's involvement here is also ironic because at the end of every healing session Mesmer performed, he would play a song for his patient on a device called a "glass harmonica," which Ben Franklin invented.

When table-turning and spirit-rapping were introduced into this country from America, the Mesmerists soon identified the mysterious force which caused the phenomena with the mesmeric or neuro-vital fluid. A little later, when the trance and its manifestations were exploited in the interests of the new gospel of Spiritualism, many of the English Mesmerists, who had been prepared by the utterances of their own clairvoyants for some such development, proclaimed themselves adherents of the new faith.[17]

The last nail in the coffin of Mesmerism would come not from any of these ladies, but from an actual Mesmerist: Phineas Quimby was ultimately responsible for all but eradicating Mesmerism from America, by transforming it into his own brand of "Mind Cure." There was a time when Quimby was considered the most famous and accomplished Mesmerist in America.[18] When Quimby turned on Mesmerism, the American followers turned with him, investigating instead the Christian Science method of healing.

Phineas Quimby's Mesmeric Adventures
Every phenomenon in the natural world has its origin in the spiritual world.

—Phineas Quimby

It was in 1838 that Quimby learned of Mesmerism by attending a lecture by a Dr. Collyer, and he shortly thereafter set about becoming a Mesmerist. Quimby went through spurts of success and failure with treating patients for many years, until finally he found one individual whom he could influence no matter the situation.

This patient was a young boy named Lucius Burkmar. Lucius appeared not only to be prone to Quimby's influence, but to actually possess clairvoyant abilities of his own. Quimby discovered that Lucius could in fact diagnose the diseases of others with great accuracy.

One day Lucius offered a diagnosis for Quimby himself, who had been suffering considerable back pain that he had never mentioned to Lucius. Lucius told Quimby that his kidney was detaching, and he proceeded to pass his hands over the area, telling

---

17 Podmore, Frank, Mesmerism and Christian Science: A Short History of Mental Healing.
18 Fuller, Robert C., Mesmerism and the American Cure of Souls.

Quimby it was now fixed. Afterwards, Quimby never again felt a pain in this area, and was effectively cured. This lead Quimby to believe that Lucius was reading his mind, and convincing him that his ailment did not exist.

Phineas Quimby's son George wrote about his father's life and curious healing techniques for *New England* Magazine in 1888:

Mr. Quimby was of medium height, small in stature, his weight being about one hundred and twenty-five pounds; quick motioned and nervous, with piercing black eyes, black hair and whiskers; a well-shaped, well-balanced head; high, broad forehead, a rather prominent nose, and a mouth indicating strength and firmness of will; persistent in what he undertook, and not easily defeated or discouraged.

In the course of his trials with subjects, he met with a young man named Lucius Burkmar, over whom he had the most wonderful influence; and it is not stating it too strongly to assert that with him he made some of the most astonishing exhibitions of mesmerism and clairvoyance that have been given in modern times . . .

Mr. Quimby's manner of operating with his subject was to sit opposite to him, holding both his hands in his, and looking him intently in the eye for a short time, when the subject would go into that state known as the mesmeric sleep, which was more properly a peculiar condition of mind and body, in which the natural senses would or would not operate at the will of Mr. Quimby. When conducting his experiments, all communications on the part of Mr. Quimby with Lucius were mentally given, the subject replying as if spoken to aloud. . . .

It should be remembered that at the time Mr. Quimby was giving these exhibitions, the phenomenon was looked upon in a far different light from that of the present day. At that time it was a deception, a fraud, and a humbug; Mr. Quimby was vilified and frequently threatened with mob violence, as the exhibitions smacked too strongly of witchcraft to suit the people.

As the subject gained more prominence, thoughtful men began to investigate the matter, and Mr. Quimby was often called upon to have his subject examine the sick. He would put Lucius into the mesmeric state, [and Lucius] would then examine the patient, describe his disease, and prescribe remedies for its cure.

23

After a time Mr. Quimby became convinced that whenever the subject examined a patient, his diagnosis of the case would be identical [to] what either the patient himself or someone present believed, instead of Lucius really looking into the patient, and giving the true condition of the organs; in fact, [Quimby believed] that he was reading the opinion in the mind of someone, rather than stating a truth acquired by himself.

Becoming firmly satisfied that this was the case, and having seen how one mind could influence another, and how much there was that had always been considered as true, but was merely some one's opinion, Mr. Quimby gave up his subject, Lucius, and began the developing of what is now known as mental healing, or curing disease through the mind.

While engaged in his mesmeric experiments, Mr. Quimby became more and more convinced that disease was an error of the mind, and not a real thing; and in this he was misunderstood by others, and accused of attributing the sickness of the patient to the imagination, which was the very reverse of the fact. No one believed less in the imagination than he. "If a man feels a pain, he knows he feels it, and there is no imagination about it," he used to say.

But the fact that the pain might be a state of the mind, while apparent in the body, he did believe. As one can suffer in a dream all that it is possible to suffer in a waking state, so Mr. Quimby averred that the same condition of mind might operate on the body in the form of disease, and still be no more of a reality than was the dream.

As the truths of his discovery began to develop and grow in him, just in the same proportion did he begin to lose faith in the efficacy of mesmerism as a remedial agent in the cure of the sick; and after a few years he discarded it altogether.

Instead of putting the patient into a mesmeric sleep, Mr. Quimby would sit by him; and, after giving him [an] account of what his troubles were, [Quimby] would simply converse with him, and explain the causes of the troubles, and thus change the mind of the patient, and disabuse it of its errors and establish the truth in its place; which, if done, was the cure.

He sometimes, in cases of lameness and sprains, manipulated the limbs of the patient, and often rubbed the head with his hands, wetting them with water. He said it was so hard for the patient to believe that his mere talk with him produced the cure, that he did this rubbing simply [so] that the patient would have more confidence in him; but he always insisted that he possessed no "power" nor healing properties different from anyone else, and that his manipulations conferred no beneficial effect upon his patient.

He never went into any trance, and was a strong disbeliever in Spiritualism, as understood by that name. He claimed, and firmly held, that his only power consisted in his wisdom, and in his understanding the patient's case and being able to explain away the error and establish the truth, or health, in its place. Very frequently the patient could not tell how he was cured, but it did not follow that Mr. Quimby himself was ignorant of the manner in which he performed the cure.

Suppose a person should read an account of a railroad accident, and see in the list the name of his son who was killed. The shock on the mind would cause a deep feeling of sorrow on the part of the parent, and possibly a severe sickness, not only mental, but physical.

Now, what is the condition of the patient? Does he imagine his trouble? Is it not real? Is his body not affected, his pulse quick, and has he not all the symptoms of a sick person, and is he not really sick?

Suppose you can go and say to him that you were on the train, and saw his son alive and well after the accident, and prove to him that the report of his death was a mistake. What follows? Why, the patient's mind undergoes a change immediately, and he is no longer sick.

It was on this principle that Mr. Quimby treated the sick. He claimed that "mind was spiritual matter and could be changed," that we were made up of "truth and error;" that "disease was an error, or belief, and that the Truth was the cure." And upon these premises he based all his reasoning, and laid the foundation of what he asserted to be the "science of curing the sick" without other remedial agencies than the mind.

Quimby's escapades with Lucius and his clairvoyant abilities had no small influence on spiritualists of the time, and, based upon their performances, many began utilizing the Mesmeric trance to achieve clairvoyant capabilities. It was on account of these unexplainable mind readings that Quimby came to question what was happening in Mesmerism, eventually developing his own system of spiritual healing. In Quimby's teachings, the emphasis was on the action of God, rather than merely the influence of one human mind on another. Quimby was convinced that he had rediscovered the healing method of Jesus. He abandoned his assistant Lucius and developed his own theory of healing, called the "Quimby Method," reintroducing the earlier Hermetic ideas that God was the driving force behind the success of Mesmeric treatment.

"Now for my particular experience," writes Mr. Quimby in an article quoted in *The True History of Mental Science*:

> I had pains in the back, which, they said, were caused by my kidneys, which were partly consumed. I was also told that I had ulcers on my lungs. Under this belief, I was miserable enough to be of no account in the world. This was the state I was in when I commenced to mesmerize. On one occasion, when I had my subject asleep, he described the pains I felt in my back (I had never dared to ask him to examine me, for I felt sure that my kidneys were nearly gone), and he placed his hand on the spot where I felt the pain. He then told me that my kidneys were in a very bad state—that one was half-consumed, and a piece three inches long had separated from it, and was only connected by a slender thread. This was what I believed to be true, for it agreed with what the doctors had told me, and with what I had suffered; for I had not been free from pain for years. My common sense told me that no medicine would ever cure this trouble, and therefore I must suffer till death relieved me. But I asked him if there was any remedy. He replied, "Yes, I can put the piece on so it will grow, and you will get well." At this I was completely astonished, and knew not what to think. He immediately placed his hands upon me, and said he united the pieces so they would grow. The next day he said they had grown together, and from that day I never have experienced the least pain from them.
>
> Now what was the secret of the cure? I had not the least doubt but that I was as he described; and, if he had said, as I expected he would, that nothing could be done, I should have died in a year or so. But, when he said he could cure me in the way he proposed, I began to think; and I discovered that I had been deceived into a belief that made me sick. The absurdity of his remedies made me

doubt the fact that my kidneys were diseased, for he said in two days that they were as well as ever. If he saw the first condition, he also saw the last; for in both cases he said he could see. I concluded in the first instance that he read my thoughts and when he said he could cure me he drew on his own mind; and his ideas were so absurd that the disease vanished by the absurdity of the cure. This was the first stumbling-block I found in the medical science. I soon ventured to let him examine me further, and in every case he could describe my feelings, but would vary about the amount of disease; and his explanation and remedies always convinced me that I had no such disease, and that my troubles were of my own make.

At this time I frequently visited the sick with Lucius, by invitation of the attending physician; and the boy examined the patient, and told facts that would astonish everybody, and yet every one of them was believed. For instance, he told of a person affected as I had been, only worse, that his lungs looked like a honey comb and his liver was covered with ulcers He then prescribed some simple herb tea, and the patient recovered; and the doctor believed the medicine cured him. But I believed the doctor made the disease; and his faith in the boy made a change in the mind, and the cure followed. Instead of gaining confidence in the doctors, I was forced to the conclusion that their science is false.

Man is made up of truth and belief; and, if he is deceived into a belief that he has, or is liable to have, a disease, the belief is catching, and the effect follows it. I have given the experience of my emancipation from this belief and from my confidence in the doctors, so that it may open the eyes of those who stand where I was. I have risen from this belief; and I return to warn my brethren, lest, when they are disturbed, they shall get into this place of torment prepared by the medical faculty. Having suffered myself, I cannot take advantage of my fellow men by introducing a new mode of curing disease by prescribing medicine. My theory exposes the hypocrisy of those who undertake to cure in that way. They make ten diseases to one cure, thus bringing a surplus of misery into the world, and shutting out a healthy state of society . . . . When I cure, there is one disease the less . . . . My theory teaches man to manufacture health; and, when people go into this occupation, disease will diminish, and those who furnish disease and death will be few and scarce.

What really were the differences between Dr. Quimby's methods and those of Mesmer? Quimby studied and practiced Mesmerism for no less than twenty-one years (1838–1859) before establishing his own methodologies. Quimby went to great pains to separate himself from the Mesmerists, most likely due to certain stigma becoming attached to them through the Spiritualism community.

> As my practice is unlike all other medical practice, it is necessary to say that I give no medicines and make no outward applications, but simply sit by the patient, tell him what he thinks is his disease, and my explanation is the cure. And If I succeed in correcting his errors, I change the fluids of the system, and establish the truth, or health. "The Truth is the cure."[19]

Quimby claimed to have "changed the fluids," which is precisely what animal magnetism does. What is the difference between a "spiritual force" and a "cosmic fluid?" What exactly is the difference between mental influence and animal magnetism? The reality is that there is no appreciable difference, despite the different names.

Mesmer was trying to prove that a physical force was at work, while Quimby went about trying to prove that it was a spiritual force. Mesmer removed the word "God" from his Hermetic sources, and Quimby put it back in. Instead of putting the patient into a mesmeric sleep, Quimby himself would go into a trance-like state.

It is important to realize that this method dates back to shamanic traditions. Quimby would sit next to the patient and speak in hushed tones. Sometimes he would lay on hands and massage, after wetting his hands with water. Quimby said that sometimes he ran into resistance from the patient if he didn't touch them, although he asserted that touch was unnecessary to bring about a cure.

> As you have given me the privilege of answering the article in your paper of the 11th inst., wherein you classed me with spiritualists, mesmerisers, clairvoyants, etc., I take this occasion to state where I differ from all classes of doctors, from the allopathic physician to the healing medium. All of these admit disease as an independent

---

19 Quimby, Phineas, *Circular to the Sick*,.republished in *The Quimby Manuscripts*.

enemy of mankind . . . . Now I deny disease as a truth, but admit it as a deception, without any foundation, handed down from generation to generation, till the people believe it, and it has become a part of their lives . . . . My way of curing convinces [the patient] that he has been deceived; and, if I succeed, the patient is cured. My mode is entirely original.[20]

Well, not entirely original, since such faith-healing had in fact been used since the time of Hermeticists and shamans.

There is no small amount of scientific research to support the fact that some form of energy can be transferred from one person to another through the windows of our eyes, the gateways to our souls. Rupert Sheldrake has laid forth his considerable research into this matter in his book *Seven Experiments That Could Change the World: A Do-It-Yourself Guide to Revolutionary Science.* Sheldrake asserts that "Vision may involve a two-way process, an inward movement of light and an outward projection of mental images."

This means that our minds reach out and "touch" the things we see. If this happens, our minds can have some influence on what is within our vision. This is also corroborated by findings of quantum physicists such as Heisenberg, that our observation of electrons alters their behavior. In 1898, the psychologist Edward B. Titchener tested what people can sense when they are being stared at by another person; his findings were later corroborated by several scientists.[21] That we can physically "feel" a stare certainly implies some form of energy exchange. This energy can be either helpful or malicious, according to various folk traditions, especially in the Middle East. The "evil eye" has been used for centuries to send bad energy to people, such as curses and diseases. It fits, then, that if one can send a disease to someone through their eye, they may heal them of it by the same means.

---

20 Quimby, Phineas, *The Portland Advertiser.* The main purpose for copies of this work in present day seem to be for protection against evil. As the text contains many talismans, there are Jews who believe that simply keeping a copy on your person is enough, even if you don't know how to read Hebrew.

21 Coover (1913), Williams (1983), and Braud, Shafer and Andrews (1993).

As shocking as this may sound to some, it is by no means a new concept. The East Indian equivalent of hypnosis is called *sammohan*.

> *Sammohan shakti* has been practiced in India since Vedic times. It can be defined as the power of attraction. *Sammohan* is inborn in every human being. Even while I talk to you, there is a kind of hypnosis where I try to attract and hold your attention, planting subtle suggestions.[22]

In Hermetic literature, the world is thought of as a panoply of mental images, the mental images as contained within the intellect of the adept (and God) and projected upon the world. We "dream the world into being." Once the mind of the adept is aligned with the mind of God, the adept can affect change in the world simply through thought.

Having attained unity with the God whose thought was the universe, a Hermeticist was presumably empowered to work magic by commanding his thoughts. As a rationalization of already existing Hermetic practices of conjuring, Hermetic rebirth may, as Nock suggested, have been "a curious sacrament of auto-suggestion."[23] The *Corpus Hermeticum I* concludes: "This is the final good for those who have received knowledge: to be made god." We become the God-mind once we align ourselves to its thoughts.

Quimby and the Founding of Christian Science

The effectiveness of the mind cure could not be denied. People were being cured of many diseases across the country by these ancient methods. Quimby successfully treated nearly 12,000 people in the last eight years of his life, and subsequently died from exhaustion. Among the many students and patients who joined Quimby and helped him commit his teachings to writing were Warren Felt Evans, Annetta Seabury Dresser and Julius Dresser (the founders of New Thought as a named movement) and Mary Baker Eddy (founder of the Christian Science movement).

---

22 Dr. Ramesh Paramahamsa, Delhi's Institute of Psychic and Spiritual Research.
23 Merkur, Dan, *Stages of Ascension in Hermetic Rebirth, Esoterica I.*

**The less we know or think about hygiene, the less we are predis-
posed to sickness.**

—**Mary Baker Eddy,** *Science and Health with Key to the Scriptures*

Christian Science is a system of mental healing marketed by
Mary Baker Eddy, probably the most famous (and infamous) of
all Quimby's students. The Christian Science movement, which
grew quickly, advocated no treatments by doctors of any kind.
All illnesses could be healed by faith in Jesus Christ as a consciousness, according to the tenets of the church.

Mary Baker Eddy (1821–1910), born Mary Morse Baker,
founded the Church of Christ, Scientist in 1879. Her most note-
worthy published work was *Science and Health with Key to the
Scriptures*, and it was subjected to a still-ongoing controversy
involving Quimby supporters. Eddy was chronically sick with
many ailments, including paralysis, hysteria, seizures and con-
vulsions. At twenty-two, she married her first of three husbands,
George Glover (an avid Freemason), who died within six months
from yellow fever. This led her to explore types of healing that
were outside of the realm of traditional doctors, such as homeop-
athy and Mesmerism. After Glover's death, she became an active
Mesmerist[24] and involved herself in the Spiritualist community.
It was her studies in Mesmerism that drew her to the office of Dr.
Quimby in 1862. In the beginning of her studies of animal magnetism, Mrs. Eddy hailed its treatments. After Quimby passed
away, however, she changed her tune regarding this practice. She
began to refer to it as "malicious animal magnetism" or M.A.M.
She wrote of it in her Church manual as mental malpractice. According to Mrs. Eddy, the M.A.M.s would send evil suggestions
to her, sickening her.

It was said by Quimby supporters that Mary Baker Eddy
came into possession of her healer's manuscripts, and borrowed
their ideas and vilified their author after his death, despite rely-
ing on him exclusively for her treatments while he was alive.

**Mrs. Eddy has for many years persistently denied her indebtedness
to Quimby and asserted the latter was only a Mesmerist, or that he**

---

24 Ruth Tucker, *Another Gospel.*

healed by electricity. She has even claimed that, so far from being in-debted [to him] for her own writings, it was she who corrected his ran-dom scribblings . . . . When Julius Dresser published some of the letters and articles in which Mrs. Eddy had lavished praise upon Quimby as her teacher, she invoked her serviceable fiend, Malicious Animal Mag-netism: "Did I write those articles purporting to be mine? . . . For I was under the mesmeric treatment of Dr. Quimby from 1862 till his death . . . my head was so turned by Animal Magnetism and will-power, under treatment, that I might have written something as hopelessly incorrect as the articles now published in the Dresser Pamphlet."[25]

Later she would even deny that she had ever been Quimby's stu-dent, though it was Quimby himself who coined the phrase "Chris-tian Science." When her third husband, Asa Gilbert Eddy (a noted spiritualist and clairvoyant) died of heart disease, she claimed that he had been mentally poisoned with arsenic by a Malicious Ani-mal Mesmerist. The autopsy returned no trace of arsenic in his sys-tem, but Mrs. Eddy maintained that there would be none, since the poisoning had been mental. Mrs. Eddy eventually went so far as to hire a team of virgins to stand vigil over her twenty-four hours a day, in order to protect herself from these malicious influences.[26] It is interesting to note that one of Mrs. Eddy's main ailments upon her first visits to Quimby was "hysteria." When asked why she had to wear glasses, Mrs. Eddy's reply: the M.A.M.s. When asked why she was addicted to morphine, her reply: the M.A.M.s. When asked why she visited a dentists, her reply: M.A.M.s.

In 1879, the Church of Christian Scientists was assembled, and Eddy was ordained as the pastor. By this time, the controversy surrounding the split between New Thought and Christian Sci-ence was characterized by the dispute between Mary Baker Eddy and Annetta and Julius Dresser, who continued to attack Eddy throughout the rest of their lives.

Some of the shenanigans of the Christian Science movement have attracted quite a bit of attention over the years. Mark Twain relates several stories in his book *Christian Science*, along with his passionate opinions on the subject, some of which are included here:

---

25 Podmore, Frank, *From Mesmer to Christian Science*.
26 Ibid

Among other witnesses there is one who had a "jumping tooth-ache," which several times tempted her to "believe that there was sensation in matter, but each time it was overcome by the power of Truth." She would not allow the dentist to use cocaine, but sat there and let him punch and drill and split and crush the tooth, and tear and slash its ulcerations, and pull out the nerve, and dig out fragments of bone; and she wouldn't once confess that it hurt. And to this day she thinks it didn't, and I have not a doubt that she is nine-tenths right, and that her Christian Science faith did her better service than she could have gotten out of cocaine. . .

No one doubts—certainly not I—that the mind exercises a powerful influence over the body. From the beginning of time, the sorcerer, the interpreter of dreams, the fortune-teller, the charlatan, the quack, the wild medicine-man, the educated physician, the mesmerist, and the hypnotist have made use of the client's imagination to help them in their work. They have all recognized the potency and availability of that force. Physicians cure many patients with a bread pill; they know that where the disease is only a fancy, the patient's confidence in the doctor will make the bread pill effective.

Faith in the doctor. Perhaps that is the entire thing . . . . Genuine and remarkable cures have been achieved through contact with the relics of a saint. Is it not likely that any other bones would have done as well if the substitution had been concealed from the patient? When I was a boy a farmer's wife who lived five miles from our village had great fame as a faith-doctor—that was what she called herself. Sufferers came to her from all around, and she laid her hand upon them and said, "Have faith—it is all that is necessary," and they went away well of their ailments. She was not a religious woman, and pretended to no occult powers. She said that the patient's faith in her did the work. Several times I saw her make immediate cures of severe toothaches. [Once] my mother was the patient . . . . Within the last quarter of a century, in America, several sects of curers have appeared under various names and have done notable things in the way of healing ailments without the use of medicines. There are the Mind Cure, the Faith Cure, the Prayer Cure, the Mental Science Cure, and the Christian-Science Cure; and apparently they all do their miracles with the same old, powerful instrument—the patient's imagination.

33

From the very start, the New Thought movement was unique among religious movements of the late nineteenth and early twentieth centuries, for having women play a prominent role in its leadership. The first graduation ceremony of the New Thought movement's Emma Hopkins College of Metaphysical Science in 1889 had twenty-two graduates, twenty of whom were women.

Conspicuous among the many women involved New Thought and Prosperity Consciousness movements were two: Emma Curtis Hopkins, who edited the *Mind Cure Journal* after being excommunicated by Mary Baker Eddy from Christian Science for not being Jesus-centered enough, and Elizabeth Towne, who in 1910 started the widely read New Thought magazine *Nautilus*.

While the New Thought movement did a great deal to make an individual feel more responsible for his outcome, it also had the side effect of disconnecting the individual from a greater causality. Not everything can be traced back to personal and individual actions, and there are some things out of the realm of possibility for any individual to change. Take for example slavery in America, or the Armenian Holocaust in Turkey or the Jewish Holocaust in Europe. In his book, *Mesmerism and the American Cure of Souls*, Robert C. Fuller explains how he thinks New Thought ideology separates people from one another:

> As an orientation to life, the New Thought philosophy aggravated rather than assuaged the emotional distance between people. Since the psychological model of human fulfillment New Thought borrowed from the mesmerists completely lacked any interpersonal variables, it couldn't demonstrate the strength-bestowing importance of such traditional virtues as cooperation, compromise, or delay of personal gratification . . . . Thus, the nation's first popular psychology degenerated into an ideology that taught its adherents to systematically exclude the needs or opinions of others as illusory obstacles to self-actualization. The New Thought projected values which ironically prevented confused individuals from coming in touch with the most valuable healing resource of all—each other.

While New Thought reinforces the idea that sickness and poverty reveal the individual's incapacity to connect with a higher purpose, other Christian beliefs taught that Jesus said that sickness had a divine purpose, usually to encourage one's spiritual evolution, and that sickness was not caused by sin alone.

> With the man born blind, Christ gives to his disciples a surprising reply: It was not that this man sinned, or his parents [had], but that the works of God might be made manifest in him. We need not assume that Christ denies that sin is at the root of this blindness too. However, he reveals here another aspect of sickness. . . . Every sickness has two aspects: one of the past, the cause; one of the future, [which] meaning shall be made manifest. The disciples learn to see that this illness, indeed that every illness, is for the manifestation of the works of God. Every illness is given in order that man may grow into a further manifestation of the divine in him.[27]

PROPONENTS OF THE MENTAL CURE
Warren Felt Evans

> All that we know of matter is force, as all its properties are only modifications of force. Its inmost essence may be spiritual, and what we call matter may be only the outward clothing, or ultimation, or external manifestation of some spiritual reality. The properties of matter are reduced to the single idea of force. Mind is a higher and diviner force, approaching many degrees nearer the Central Life. All force, in its origin, as well as all causation, is spiritual. Mind is a manifestation of force entirely distinct from that we call matter. Between color and thought, there is a broad distinction. They are not identical. One belongs to matter, the other to mind. One is a material, the other a spiritual property or force.
>
> —Warren Felt Evans, *The Mental Cure*

Warren Felt Evans was a farmer's son, born to Eli and Sarah Edson Evans in Rockingham, Vermont, on December 23, 1817, the sixth of their seven children. Evans, along with the Dresser family, wrote extensively on the teachings of Phineas Quimby. Evans didn't quite establish a movement like Mrs. Eddy; instead he set up a healing practice in Salisbury, Massachusetts. Evans quickly gained notoriety due to his skill as a healer, and he published sev-

---

27 Heidenreich, Alfred, *Healing in the Gospels.*

eral books that were widely popular. These include *The Mental Cure: Illustrating the Influence of the Mind on the Body, Both in Health and Disease, and the Psychological Method of Treatment* (1869); *Mental Medicine* (1872); *Soul and Body, The Divine Law of Cure* (1881); *The Primitive Mind Cure* (1885); and *Esoteric Christianity and Mental Therapeutics* (1886).

Evans' first work was released three years prior to Mary Baker Eddy's *Science and Health*. Aside from Mrs. Eddy, Mr. Evans was the only person who actually made a cohesive philosophical system of mental healing immediately after Quimby's passing. One of the most interesting aspects of Evans' written works is that he integrated the work of Phineas Quimby and the spiritualist inspiration of Emanuel Swedenborg.

Emanuel Swedenborg

Emanuel Swedenborg (1688 –1772) was a Swedish scientist, philosopher, Christian mystic and theologian. Swedenborg had a prolific career as an inventor and scientist, and was another in the line of Hermetic prophets who claimed to receive information from angels. According to Swedenborg, he had developed a technique which allowed him to converse with angles clairvoyantly, whenever he wished. This method, which he called "Testicular Breathing"[28] was performed during intercourse.

According to Swedenborg, after a theophanous vision (during sex), he was allowed to enter freely into Heaven and Hell, and communicate with angels, demons, or any other spirit he should happen across. The narratives in *Conversations With Angels* have been ably translated by Swedenborg scholars David Gladish and Jonathan Rose, and have been selected from three of Swedenborg's works, *Conjugal Love, Apocalypse Revealed*, and *True Christian Religion*. The Hermetic inspirations and nature of Swedenborg's writings have been examined by many scholars, but are best made plain in Ethan Allen Hitchcock's *Swedenborg, a Hermetic Philosopher: Being a Sequel to Remarks on Alchemy and the Alchemists*. This work shows that Swedenborg writings may be interpreted from the point of view of Hermetic philosophy.

---

28 Schuchard, Marsha Keith, *Why Mrs Blake Cried: William Blake and the Sexual Basis of Spiritual Vision.*

Along with the New Thought movement, the works of Swedenborg inspired a church of worshippers (The New Jerusalem Church), the Spiritualist movement in America, and such literary figures as William Blake, August Strindberg, Charles Baudelaire, Balzac, Waldo Ralph Emerson (and the Transcendentalist movement), William Butler Yeats and Carl Jung.

Emma Curtis Hopkins

Emma Curtis Hopkins (1849–1925) was a student of Mary Baker Eddy's, and some credit her with founding the New Thought movement. She worked closely with Mrs. Eddy for several years, but eventually had a falling out with the Church of Christian Science and began teaching and lecturing on her own.

Following Eddy, Hopkins conceptualized the Trinity as three aspects of divinity, each playing a role in different historical epochs: God the Father, God the Son and God the Mother-Spirit. Hopkins believed that the changing roles of women indicated the re-emergence of the Mother aspect of God.

Hopkins went on to inspire a good number of New Thought writers and founders of their churches. Two of her better-known students were Charles and Myrtle Fillmore, who founded Unity School of Christianity, the largest denomination with members in the New Thought movement.

Charles and Myrtle Fillmore

The difference between Jesus and us is not one of inherent spiritual capacity, but in difference of demonstration of it. Jesus was potentially perfect, and He expressed that perfection; we are potentially perfect, [but] we have not yet expressed it.

—Charles Fillmore

Charles Fillmore was born to a Chippewa trader on an Indian reservation near St. Cloud, Minnesota, in 1854. His wife, Myrtle, was born in Pagetown, Ohio, in 1845. Like Quimby, Charles suffered from tuberculosis, and as a result of his disease, set out on a quest for healing. Together the Fillmores roamed the West seeking a cure for Charles' illness, until they came across Christian Scientists and Emma Curtis Hopkins. Charles started a prayer group called "Silent Unity." (He had originally wanted to call it Christian Science, after Quimby, but was forced to change the name due to a legal conflict with Mary Baker Eddy.) Around 1891, the prayer group grew into what is known today as the Unity School of Christianity. Christianity here was used in a loose sense of Christ-consciousness; the teachings of the Fillmores were mostly metaphysical and even included reincarnation. In the Unity Church, salvation is attained by "atonement with God," a reuniting of human consciousness with God-consciousness. They taught that if Jesus had attained this, all men could.

Prentice Mulford

Prentice Mulford (1834–1891) wrote humorous pieces for various journals in California before he helped found the New Thought movement. Mulford was also an avid prospector for many years, jumping claims all over California in his search for gold. Much of his writing career focused on the unimportance of money and material things. He often wrote that those who suffered from lack of money were forced to become more intelligent that those that had it: "Poverty argued for us [in] possession of more brains"[29] Mulford played a fairly large role at the beginning of the New Thought Movement with the publication of his popular book, *Thoughts Are Things*. The writing in this book offers New Thought ideals combined with humor.

> The surest way for a young woman to become ugly is to be discontented, peevish, cross, complaining and envious of others. Because in these states of mind she is drawing to her the invisible substance of thought, which acts on and injures her body. It ruins the complexion, makes lines and creases in the face, sharpens the nose and transforms the face of youth into that of the shrew in very quick time.
>
> The more you get into the thought current coming from the Infinite Mind, making yourself more and more a part of that mind (exactly as you may become a part of any vein of low, morbid, unhealthy mind in opening yourself to that current), the quicker are you freshened, and renewed physically and mentally. You become continually a newer being. Changes for the better come quicker and quicker. Your power increases to bring results. You lose

29 Mulford, Prentice, *Prentice Mulford's Story.*

gradually all fear as it is proven more and more to you that when you are in the thought current of Infinite Good there is nothing to fear. You realize more and more clearly that there is a great power and force which cares for you. You are wonderstruck at the fact that when your mind is set in the right direction all material things come to you with very little physical or external effort. You wonder then at man's toiling and striving, fagging himself literally to death, when through such excess of effort he actually drives from him the rounded-out good of health, happiness and material prosperity all combined.[30]

Thomas Troward

Though the laws of the universe can never be broken, they can be made to work under special conditions which will produce results that could not be produced under the conditions spontaneously provided by nature.

—Thomas Troward

Thomas Troward (1847–1916) is said to be the second father of the New Thought movement, after Quimby. He served as a Divisional Judge in Punjab for twenty-five years. A devout churchman and a student of all religions, he formulated a philosophy that explained a creative mental process. Troward, like most New Thought adherents, believed that all people mentally create the world in which they live. He called his philosophy "Mental Science," and lectured on it all over the world. Troward spoke several languages, studied biblical scripture written in Hebrew, read the Koran, and researched the writings of Raja Yoga.

Troward was the author of many highly influential books in the New Thought world, including *The Edinburgh Lectures* (1904) and *The Dore Lectures* (1909). Troward's writings influenced many later New Thought authors, such as Emmet Fox, Ernest Holmes, Paul Foster Case, Joseph Murphy and Bob Proctor (who is prominently featured in Rhonda Byrne's *The Secret*).

Troward considered himself a Rosicrucian, and focused much of his teachings and inspiration on this source. He ends his final published writing with the following quote:

---

30 Mulford, Prentice, *Thoughts are Things.*.

We are as yet only at the commencement of the path which leads to the realization of this unity in the full development of all its powers, but others have trodden the way before us, from whose experiences we may learn; and not least among these was the illustrious founder of the Most Christian Fraternity of the Rosicrucians. This master-mind, setting out in his youth with the intention of going to Jerusalem, changed the order of his journey and first sojourned for three years in the symbolical city of Damcar, in the mystical country of Arabia, then for about a year in the mystical country of Egypt, and then for two years in the mystical country of Fez. Then, having during these six years learned all that was to be acquired in those countries, he returned to his native land of Germany, where, on the basis of the knowledge he had thus gained, he founded the Fraternity R.C., for whose instruction he wrote the mystical books *M.* and *T.* Then, when he realized that his work in its present stage was accomplished, he of his own free will laid aside the physical body, not, it is recorded, by decay, or disease, or ordinary death, but by the express direction of the Spirit of Life, summing up all his knowledge in the words, *"Jesus mihi omnia."*[31]

Troward voraciously studied Rosicrucian teachings, According to Claude Brodeur:

Troward has based his philosophy on the principle of a "Universal Subconscious Mind," and that man's subconscious is no more nor less than universal and infinite God-consciousness . . . . This kind of thinking puts a Rosicrucian stamp on the new religious thinking called New Thought.[32]

THE ROSICRUCIAN AND HERMETIC BROTHERHOODS

Several New Thought authors considered themselves to be Rosicrucians. Most people have a hazy idea that Rosicrucians inhabit secret conspiracy-type organizations, but few realize Rosicrucianism's Hermetic basis, which evolved in Europe in the seventeenth century. Myriad fraternities have formed throughout time (and many still

---

31 Brodeur, Claude PhD, *The New Thought Movement in America.*
32 Ibid.

exist today) that have studied and practiced the Hermetic arts. These groups tend to be secretive, often to avoid persecution from larger religious organizations such as the Catholic Church, but occasionally they expand, sharing their information with a wider audience. The Rosicrucians are one group that shared much of its information with the public. Also known as "The Brethren of the Rose Cross," Rosicrucians are traditionally Christian organizations, but to be certain, they are Christian Hermeticists.

In his *Apology*, Fludd described the Rosy Cross Brothers as true Christians and the spiritual descendants of Hermes Trismegistus. He declared himself a disciple without being a member, and he thought it possible that there was no formal Rosicrucian organization; a community of minds sharing the same spiritual and philosophic goals was quite enough to constitute a movement, in his opinion. "I affirm that every Theologus of the Church Mystical is a real Brother of the Rosy Cross."[33]

The history of Christian Hermeticists goes back to the dawn of Christianity itself, and there have been schools of thought that combine these two philosophies. The Rosicrucians claim their origins date back to the time of Christ, but there is no written evidence of their existence until the early 1600s in Germany. At that time, three Rosicrucian manifestos were anonymously published one year after the other: *Fama Fraternitatis* (1614), *Confessio Fraternitatis* (1615), and the *Chymical Wedding of Christian Rosenkreutz* (1616). This last work is entirely alchemical and Hermetic in its contents, basing its contents on the *Emerald Tablet*. Contained within the pages of these books, particularly *Fama*, is the story of an initiate who undergoes a spiritual revolution. The name of the initiate is given as Christian Rosenkreutz (also known as C.R.C.). There is no small amount of mystery concerning the origins and identity of C.R.C., and many say the entire story is simply to be taken allegorically. However, Rosenkreutz is commonly credited with being the founder of the original Rosicrucian Order. During his lifetime, the Order was said to consist of no more than eight members, all of whom dissipated after his death. The Order picked up again much later, upon the discovery of his tomb:

---

33 *Ancient Wisdom and Secret Sects*, Mysteries of the Unknown series, Time-Life.

In the morning following, we opened the door, and there appeared to our sight a vault of seven sides and corners, every side five foot broad, and the height of eight foot. Although the sun never shined in this vault, nevertheless it was enlightened with another sun, which had learned this from the sun, and was situated in the upper part in the center of the ceiling. In the midst, instead of a tombstone, was a round altar covered over with a plate of brass, and thereon this engraven: "This is all clear and bright, as also the seven sides and the two Heptagoni: so we kneeled altogether down and gave thanks to the sole wise, sole mighty and sole eternal God, who hath taught us more than all men's wits could have found out, praised be his holy name. This vault we parted in three parts, the upper part or ceiling, the wall or side, the ground or floor. Of the upper part you shall understand no more of it at this time, but that it was divided according to the seven sides in the triangle, which was in the bright center; but what therein is contained, you shall God willing (that are desirous of our society) behold the same with your own eyes; but every side or wall is parted into ten figures, every one with their several figures and sentences, as they are truly shown and set forth *concentratum* here in our book."

—from *Fama Fraternitatis*

Rumors had it that the *Emerald Tablet* itself was amongst these texts in the tomb. It is theoretically possible that somehow C.R.C. could have come across it, or that the book copied someone else's interpretation of the *Emerald Tablet*. It was also speculated that some of the texts belonged to other Alchemists such as John Dee:

Inside the tomb there were said to have been alchemical books with a quasi-political overtone, definitely favoring the court of Frederick V, the Elector Palatine. All this was disseminated as gospel in a kind of alchemical Protestant revival. Curiously, these texts, *The Fama* and *The Confessio*, had many doctrinal similarities to Dee's *Hieroglyphic Monad*, so that it appears that Dee's earlier work was used as the model for the Rosicrucian broadsheets by their authors.[34]

It is most likely that Rosenkreutz came upon Hermetic writings as a young boy living at a monastery. According to legend, Rosenkreutz was

---

34 McKenna, Terence, *The Archaic Revival*.

rescued by a monk from a fire that burned his family's castle. The monk happened to be an Albigensian adept from Languedoc, and a specialist in Hermeticism. Rosenkreutz was brought up and educated in the monastery, and, with four other monks in the community, he formed a fraternal group determined to devote themselves to the search for truth.[35] Later in his life, C.R.C. traveled to Arabia where he apparently studied with some Arabic alchemists, learning their deepest secrets.

From the Arabians C.R.C. also learned of the elemental peoples and how, with their aid, it was possible to gain admission to the ethereal world where dwelt the genii and Nature spirits. C.R.C. thus discovered that the magical creatures of the Arabian Nights Entertainment actually existed, though invisible to the ordinary mortal. C.R.C. became an adept n the gathering of medicinal herbs, the transmutation of metals, and the manufacture of precious gems by artificial means. Even the secret of the Elixir of Life and the Universal Panacea were communicated to him. Enriched thus beyond the dreams of Croesus, the Holy Master returned to Europe and there established a House of Wisdom which he called Domus Sancti Spiritus. This house he enveloped in clouds, it is said, so that men could not discover it. What are these "clouds," however, but the rituals and symbols under which is concealed the Great Arcanum?[36]

The publications of these three works caused a huge stir in Europe. Alchemy was both popular and taboo during this time period, so people were looking for any information they could get their hands on. The third and last book in the Rosicrucian trilogy, *The Chymical Wedding of Christian Rosenkreutz*, was infused with the srongest type of alchemical material which focused more on the soul's evolution than the production of gold:

[It was] replete with rich allegorical details, as well as cosmological, alchemical, astrological, magical and chivalric symbols. As the allegory began, Rosenkreutz was preparing for the celebration. All manner of trials, ordeals, and strange initiation rites were put before him, but he triumphed over them in what can be seen as a spiritual

---

35 Magre, Maurice, *Magicians, Seers, and Mystics.*
36 Hall, Manly P., *Lectures on Ancient Philosophy: An Introduction to the Study and Application of Rational Procedure.*

progression. . . . He was invested with the chivalric Order of the Golden Stone, an apparent reference to the legendary philosophers' stone, by means of which base substances could be turned into gold and silver. As in the earlier tracts, the author went to great lengths to indicate that the goal of Rosenkreutz, as well as all the others who received the Golden Stone, was a transmutation of the spirit and not the crasser sort of alchemy.[37]

Much like Christianity, Rosicrucianism has had many different groups who all have their own interpretations of the material. The differences between these organizations can be as pronounced as, say, the Catholic and the Episcopal churches. Some of these groups disseminate the information on a large scale, while others remain secretive and exclusive.

Ancient Mystical Order Rosæ Crucis (AMORC): This group is probably the most widely known, as they do the most advertising and invite all members of the public to join (who are over eighteen). AMORC touts itself as a worldwide mystical, philosophical, educational, humanitarian and fraternal organization devoted to the investigation, study and practical application of natural and spiritual laws.

Harvey Spencer Lewis (1883–1939) founded the organization in 1915 in America, bringing over the Rosicrucian philosophies he had learned while studying in Europe. He set up a Rosicrucian and Egyptian museum (still extant in San Jose, California). Lewis was an illustrator and worked in advertising, so it is no wonder that this particular group was so prolific in this area. Lewis was an extremely productive author and his books are generally available to this day.

AMORC has a special connection to the New Thought movement through William Walker Atkinson. There has been much controversy regarding the sources of some of Lewis' material; some claim he plagiarized it from Atkinson. Under the pen name Magus Incogniti, Atkinson wrote *The Secret Doctrine of the Rosiscrucians*. Then Lewis slapped Atkinson with a lawsuit for revealing the secrets of the Order[38] (though Lewis certainly revealed just as much information in his own works.) The Order

---

37 *Ancient Wisdom and Secret Sects*, Mysteries of the Unknown series, *Time Life*.
38 Melanson, Terry, *Oprah Winfrey, New Thought, "The Secret" and the "New Alchemy"*, http://www.conspiracyarchive.com/Commentary/Oprah_The_Secret.htm

that Lewis was referring to was the Rosicrucians, not AMORC. Atkinson had spent his entire life practicing law before his New Thought endeavors. Lewis did not win his lawsuit.

The Rosicrucian Fellowship: In 1909, a few years before AMORC came on the scene (and having no affiliation with it), a Rosicrucian brotherhood was founded in Oceanside California by Max Heindel. The Rosicrucian Fellowship conducted Spiritual Healing-Services and offered correspondence courses in Esoteric Christianity, Philosophy, Spiritual Astrology, and Bible Interpretation. In the fall of 1907, Heindel traveled to Germany, where he attended several lectures given by Rudolf Steiner, founder of the Anthroposophy movement (similar to Theosophy in intent, but with variants due to the personalities of Steiner and Blavatsky). Steiner was an avid student of Rosicrucianism, and even published his own version of *The Chymical Wedding*.[39] Shortly after attending these lectures, Heindel claims he received his Rosicrucian initiation via an apparition who came to him in a vision. Heindel states in his writings that this entity identified himself as an Elder Brother of the Rosicrucian Order from 1313, and conferred upon him the most intricate secrets of the Order at this time. Additionally, according to Heindel, the Elder Brother gave him directions to an exclusive Rosicrucian temple located on the German border, which he traveled to, studying there with other Elder Brothers of the Rose Cross. The Rosicrucian Fellowship has no affiliation with any other Rosicrucian groups and no ties to any of the fraternities in Europe. After this time, Heindel wrote immense amounts of information on the Rosicrucian cosmology and many books on astrology, most of which are still in print today.

Societas Rosicruciana in Anglia (SRIA): This was one of the most infamous of the Rosicrucian groups of its time, due to some of its celebrity participants. These include John Yarker, P.B. Randolph, E. Bulwer-Lytton, Dr. Wynn Westcott, S.L. MacGregor Mathers, Eliphas Levi, Theodor Reuss, Kenneth Mackenzie, Paul Foster Case and Frederick Hockley. The SRIA was founded in 1860 by R.W. Little, an active freemason. Most of the members of this society were both freemasons and Rosicrucians. Little is said to have been introduced to the material when he came across some Rosicrucian documents from the much

---

39 Faivre, Antoine & Needleman, *Modern Esoteric Spirituality*. Crossroad.

more ancient "August Order," but these were never seen by anyone verifiable. The SRIA spread abroad after infiltrating Canada and the United States. The Scottish Rite Freemason Albert Pike was chartered to head a branch of the organization in the U.S. around 1879, which eventually transformed into the Societas Rosicruciana in America. Today, the S.R. in America have no ties to the original lodges in Europe, reportedly due to the fact that they admit women into their ranks. The original SRIA got into all kinds of trouble on account of sexual issues, and several of its members were tried in court for Sex Magic rituals.[40] The teachings of the Rosicrucians, and the Hermetics for that matter, did include quite a bit of sexual material.

> Hargrave Jennings, a founder of the Societas Rosicruciana in Anglia, "hinted as strongly as he could that these rites and mysteries were of a fundamentally sexual nature, though to make his point in Victorian England he was obliged to resort to some involved and often poetically purple prose. Dancing around the theme of Tantric sex as the basis of the Rosicrucian philosophy, Jennings was almost specific when he pointed out that . . . the Masonic seal of Solomon symbolizes the intertwined triangles of male and female, which in conjunction represent life . . ."
>
> —Peter Tompkins, *The Magic of Obelisks*

Fraternitas Rosæ Crucis (FRC) was founded in 1912 by Reuben Swinburne Clymer. Clymer was a student of the eminent mulatto occultist Pascal Beverly Randolph, and he claimed that Randolph had originally founded the Order in secret in 1856. Randolph was initiated into the SRIA in 1868, and was also a member of the Hermetic Brotherhood of Luxor. For one of Randolph's ethnicity to rise to the ranks he achieved, at his time, was nothing short of astonishing. A good amount of time and effort in Clymer's Rosicrucian career was spent battling with H.S. Lewis of AMORC, who devoted much of his writings to countering and disproving anything and everything Lewis had to say. This created a rivalry between the groups, and is why, if members of AMORC are asked what they think of Clymer of Randolph's writing, they will usually respond negatively.

---

40 Paschal Beverly Randolph, for one.

It is entirely possible to attract, direct and redeem by the thoughts we hold in the mind, those who are inclined to follow destructive tendencies. Our thoughts become magnets, continually attracting to us those things and people toward which our thoughts are turned, thus the nature and quality of Man's thoughts become the ruling power in his life.[41]

Societas Rosicruciana Civitatibus Foederatis: This organization was founded in Pennsylvania in 1879, and the only ones welcome to join were "Master Masons." It received many members from defunct lodges of the SRIA.

The Hermetic Order of the Golden Dawn: This was an offshoot of the original SRIA, and all of its founders were members of this organization. It was started in 1888 by S.L. MacGregor Mathers, William Robert Woodman and Wynn Westcott. This society probably had the most influence on the occult world as it exists today. The writings of some of its members are widely circulated and looked upon as bibles by occultists the world over. Individuals such as Aleister Crowely, Paul Foster Case, William Butler Yeats, Bram Stoker, Israel Regardie and Dion Fortune represent some of the magi who came out of this organization.

Ordo Templi Orientis (OTO) was originally founded by Carl Kellner, Heinrich Klein and Franz Hartmann in 1895. Franz Hartmann's works were particularly popular, and continue to influence students of occult history today. The Order defined itself as Rosicrucian and belonging to the original Knights Templar. The Rosicrucian influence was reinforced when Theodore Reuss became its chief, as Reuss had been a member of the Societas Rosicruciana. Under Reuss' leadership, the organization grew throughout Europe and into the U.S. After Reuss stepped down, he appointed Aleister Crowley to lead the organization.

Collegium Pansophicum: This organization was founded by Heinrich Tranker in 1923 after he left the OTO, upset that Crowley and not himself had been asked to take over. Tranker said that his group was the only one to teach the "true" Rosicrucian secrets, but he worked closely with H.S. Lewis of AMORC in several endeavors.

Ordre Kabbalistique de la Rose Croix (the Kabbalistic order of the Rosy Cross): This group began in Paris in 1888, headed

---

41 Clymer, R. Swinburne, MD., *Occult Science*.

by Count Stanislas de Guaita. Like the Societas Rosicruciana, this group attracted many famous participants and had some crossover with the SRIA, including Eliphas Levi and E. Bulwer-Lytton. H.S. Lewis was also rumored to have been a member of this group at one time. This fraternity worked with another esoteric group in Paris headed by Papus called The Martinist Order.

The Rosicrucians provided a template (and much written material) for the New Thought writers, who further extrapolated and developed the concepts formed by the unification of the Christian and Hermetic philosophies. But how was it that the Rosicrucians came upon this information to begin with? What exactly are the Hermetic teachings and where do they come from?

The Hermetic Origins of the Mind Cure

Mind leads phenomena

Mind is the main factor and forerunner of all actions

If one speaks or acts with a cruel mind,

Misery follows, as the cart follows the horse.

Phenomena are led by the mind.

Mind is the main factor and forerunner of all actions.

If one speaks or acts with pure mind,

Happiness follows, as a shadow follows its source.

—Dharmapada

The idea that the body can be healed by a suggestion of the mind, either one's own or that of another, is an ancient one indeed. In Pharoahnic Egypt, where many place the origins of medicine,[42] the soul and the mind act directly on the state of the body's health. The Aesculapian temples of Alexandria utilized the same healing methodologies of the Mesmerists and even Jesus, predating them by some hundreds of years.

> Old temple disciplines included purification, temple-sleep, and various hypnotic rest states. Bodily processes were aroused and focused through intensities of suggestion, through touching the patient, along with lifting the faith of one who was ill.[43]

---

42 Ayurveda of India and Chinese medical practices also predate Christ and still continue strongly.

43 Jayne, Walter Addison, M.D., *The Healing Gods of Ancient Civilizations.*

Such recommendations and cures have been found on Egyptian papyri dating as far back as 2000 BC. And they always speak of Thoth and Hermes.

> Eventually all the great medical centers were located at the chief capitals along the Nile. These shrines were depositories of medical lore, and the ancient traditions are confirmed by the lists of diseases and their cures. Clement refers to forty-two Hermetic books at the temple of Hermopolis, of which six were medical texts giving formulas and remedies. On the walls of sanctuaries were inscriptions and tablets in commemoration of miraculous cures with statues and steles erected by former patients in grateful recognition of cures effected by the divinity.[44]

The power of the mind as it relates to the higher mind of God is tantamount to Hermetic thought. And this is echoed in the teachings of Phineas Quimby: "Mind is matter in solution and matter is mind in form." From *The Quimby Manuscripts*:

> 1. Mind is changeable "spiritual matter," a receptive, moldable something, susceptible to numerous subtle influences, often erroneous opinions (operating even when one is not consciously thinking about them).
> 2. Man is spiritual and has spiritual senses.
> 3. "Spiritual man can become open to and use spiritual power." That means that man is not to follow his own inclinations, but to pursue Wisdom's way.

All matter is contained in the spiritual mind. The Hermetic God is a mind that is immanent throughout the cosmos. This is stated repeatedly throughout the *Corpus Hermeticum*. In the *Corpus Hermeticum V* we see this concept expressed even in its title, "That God is invisible and entirely visible."

I [am Mind and] I see another Mind, the one that [moves] the soul! I see the one that moves me from pure forgetfulness. You give me power! I see myself! I want to speak! Fear restrains me. I have found the beginning of the power that is above all powers, the one that has no beginning. I see a fountain bubbling with life. I have said, my son,

---

44 Ibid.

that I am Mind. I have seen! Language is not able to reveal this. For the entire eighth, my son, and the souls that are in it, and the angels, sing a hymn in silence. And I, Mind, understand.[45]

FAITH HEALINGS

> The mind is a place of its own. It can make a heaven of hell, or a hell of heaven.
>
> —John Milton

The healing methodologies of the New Testament Christ and those of the Hermetic Egyptians are strikingly similar. Faith healings were carried out long before Yesu arrived on the scene. Belief was used by the ancients to activate the healing powers within the patient. A perfect example of faith healing can be found in the caduceus story of Moses. Moses uses the serpent on the staff to heal his people in the wilderness, and this gesture is more tied to the mind cure than one might think.

> The significance of looking on the bronze serpent and living is that the healing is based on faith, not on the copper serpent itself; this was emphasized later in John 3:14 and 3:15, when Jesus refers to this incident to say that the Son of Man must be lifted up, so that all who believe on Him will have eternal life. The bronze serpent illustrates that the "instrument of judgment becomes the means of deliverance." In this episode, the symbol of pain and death becomes a symbol of healing. [46]

In exorcisms of demons and the devil, Jesus cured a variety of physical ailments that were regarded as demonic possession, including blindness (John 9:2), dumbness (Matt 9:32, Luke 11:14), blindness and dumbness (Matt 12:22), the gout (Luke 13:11), dropsy (Luke 14:2), leprosy (Luke 17:12), palsy (Mark 2:5), fever (Luke 4:38) and dystrophy or paralysis (Mark 3:5). In one instance, not only is the victim not a follower of Jesus, but he rebukes him entirely:

> And there was in their synagogue a man with an unclean spirit; and he cried out, saying, Let us alone; what have we to do with thee, thou Jesus of Nazareth? art thou come to destroy us? I know thee who

45 Robinson, James M., ed., *The Nag Hammadi Library in English*, 3rd ed.
46 Montenegro, Marcia, *The Serpent in Egypt and in the Bible: Evil, Power, and Healing*.

thou art, the Holy One of God. And Jesus rebuked him, saying, Hold
thy peace, and come out of him. And when the unclean spirit had torn
him, and cried with a loud voice, he came out of him. (Mark 1:23)

The majority of the healings were actuated by the faith of the sick,
not the actions of Christ himself. He stated, "Your faith has made
you well." This, importantly, places the power of healing in the
hands of the sick, rather than it being a supernatural act.

Faith healing has been taken to the extreme by some Pente-
costal churches in America, and has come to resemble assembly
lines rather than personal, individual healing sessions. Though they
wouldn't admit this, the churches' faith healing owes a stylistic debt
to the New Thought movement, and therefore the Hermetic ideals:

> It is important to note at the outset that the bulk of [the Faith move-
> ment's] theology can be traced directly to the cultic teachings of New
> Thought metaphysics. Thus, much of the theology of the Faith move-
> ment can also be found in such clearly pseudo-Christian cults as Religious
> Science, Christian Science, and the Unity School of Christianity. Although
> proponents of Faith theology have attempted to sanitize the metaphysi-
> cal concept of the "power of mind" by substituting in its stead the "force
> of faith," for all practical purposes they have made a distinction without
> a difference. New Thought writer Warren Felt Evans, for example, wrote
> that "faith is the most intense form of mental action."[47]

The Catholic church has disparaged the Evangelical movement
as "prosperity gospel," not viewing it as Christian at all. Many
Christian leaders condemn the idea that God will reward the
faithful with health and wealth. We might remember the scan-
dals of popular televangelists of the 1980s who used people's
donations to support their lavish lifestyles. These televangelists—such as Creflo Dollar, Joyce Meyer, Paul Crouch and Kenneth Copeland—encouraged their followers to "sow a seed" of
faith by donating to their ministries in order to recoup prosperity in the future.

---

47 Hanegraaff, Hendrik H., "What's Wrong With The Faith Movement—Part One: E.W. Kenyon and the Twelve Apostles of Another Gospel," *Christian Research Journal*, Winter 1993.

Whether Egyptians, Greeks, or another ancient civilization had a hand in it, the importance of stimulating the patients' own healing energies was understood to be the cause for the miraculous cures which did take place, miracles equal to, and sometimes greater than, those performed by Jesus Christ, as described in the New Testament. The authors are not attempting to state that Jesus was erroneous or insincere in his teachings or practices, simply that a lineage of these traditions existed long before Jesus' existence. The most overt similarities between the healing methods of Jesus and the Hermeticists can be found with Asclepius, a student of Hermes Trismegistus, as suggested by the existence of the *Corpus Hermeticum* writing, "The Asclepiad." The cult of the Asclepians was popular around 300 BC, the same time that Alexandria began to flourish, when Asclepius was adapted by the Greeks and came to be known as the Greek god of healing. Like Christ, Asclepius died and descended to the underworld before being resurrected. Both Asclepius and Christ were the sons of a mortal woman and a god, Asclepius being born to Apollo and Christ being born to Jehova.

Asclepius, like Jesus, used no small amount of faith when healing the sick in his temples:

> Tales of the marvelous cures effected at the healing temples spread the fame of the healing deity, Asklepios, throughout Greece. It was such common knowledge that the sick, in going to these sanctuaries for relief, were probably already imbued with a certain religious fervor, while their imagination was excited by the hope that they also might be the recipient of the divine grace.[48]

In the *Iamata*, Asclepius is recorded as healing such illnesses as paralysis and blindness, some of Jesus' most famous accomplishments. The early Christian church Fathers were not ignorant of these similarities, and went about replacing the Asclepian temples with Christian churches whenever possible. In the Byzantine empire, for example, where the popularity of Asclepius was rampant, the Christian church made quick work of pronouncing him an agent of the Devil, and then converted or killed all of his followers:

---

48 Jayne, Walter Addison, M.D., *The Healing Gods of Ancient Civilizations.*

Despite the institutionalization of Christianity as the state religion of the Byzantine Empire, the popularity of the pagan cult of Asclepius was unshaken. Christianity's inability to triumph provoked resentment on the part of the Church Fathers, which they released in demonizing Asclepius who, according to Lactantius and the *Acta Pilati*, cast out devils in the name of the Devil, and in ostracizing Asclepius' medical disciples—the doctors. The vindictiveness unleashed in the destruction by Christians of Asclepius' shrines, notably at Dor, was the popular expression and outlet of the same frustration. As Asclepius persisted in attracting followers, the Church changed its tactics. It absorbed physically the sacredness inherent in Asclepian sanctuaries by building churches over them, as at Dor, as well as appropriated and Christianized the healing rites of Christ's main rival.[49]

We also find parallels to the miracle "mind cure" healings of Jesus in the Hermetic individual known as Apollonius of Tyana. A contemporary of Christ, Apollonius of Tyana's life was so similar to that of Jesus, many argue that they were the same individual[50]

All through the third century, there is repeated mention of this (Apollonius' teachings). But it was not until Hierocles, in the beginning of the fourth century, boldly charged upon the Christian priesthood their plagiarism of the teachings and works of Apollonius that the latter found it necessary to set every means at work that could in any way help to conceal the great truth that Hierocles proclaimed with such portentous force.[51]

Apollonius became known as a great healer when he spent time in the Asclepian temple of Aegae. Apollonius remained there for years, and he showed an astonishing gift for healing and clairvoyance. If one were to agree with several scholars' suppositions that Apollonius and Jesus were in fact the same person, this would indicate that Christ was directly involved in a lineage to the Hermetic healing arts. Among Apollonius' credits are raising the dead, exorcizing a devil afflicting a boy by writing the devil a threatening letter, and

49 Dauphin, C.M., "From Apollo and Asclepius to Christ: Pilgrimage and Healing at the Temple and Episcopal Basilica at Dor."
50 In 300 AD, Hierocles wrote an emphatic attack on the Christians, called "Lover of Truth," for plagiarizing Apollonius as the Christ figure.
51 Roberts, J.M., *Antiquity Unveiled: Ancient Voices from the Spirit Realms Proving Christianity to Be of Heathen Origin.*

curing a blind man and a man with a withered hand. Apollonius was also resurrected and ascended to heaven in front of witnesses.[52]We cannot confirm that the origins of the mind cure are solely Hermetic, either, as we also find this information in Indian and Chinese healing modalities that predate Egypt. Additionally, shamanic teachings that stretch back to pre-history echo Hermetic procedures.

Giant Fiery Flying Serpents

The origin of the mind cure takes us back to the initial problem of the origins of Hermetic philosophy: giant fiery flying serpents. Can it be coincidental that the serpent is known for hypnotizing, or *mesmerizing*, its prey before ingestion? Or is the mind cure linked to serpent knowledge? In the Hermetic Asclepian temples, healing was always performed while the healers were surrounded by serpents. In all mythological language, the snake is an emblem of immortality. The shedding of its skin makes the serpent a symbol for rebirth and renewal in all cultures.

> All the Logoi of all the ancient religious systems are connected with, and symbolized by, serpents . . . . It was the emblem of the resurrection of Nature, as also of Christ with the Ophites, and of Jehovah as the brazen serpent healing those who looked at him; the serpent being an emblem of Christ with the Templars also . . . . The symbol of Knouph . . . "is represented among other forms under that of a huge serpent on human legs; this reptile, being the emblem of the good genius and the veritable Agathodaemon"[53]

The snake is a powerful archetype of shamans the world over, as the deliverer of healing knowledge. For example:

> Among the Aboriginals of Australia, the most widespread of mythic beliefs has to do with a gigantic rainbow serpent . . . . He (sometimes she) is also the source of magical quartz crystals known as Kimba from which the medicine man derives his own power.[54]

---

52 Ranke-Heinmann, Uta, *Putting Away Childish Things: The Virgin Birth, the Empty Tomb, and Other Fairy Tales You Don't Need to Believe to Have a Living Faith.*
53 Blavatsky, H.P., *The Secret Doctrine* Vol. 1.
54 Munkdar, Balaji, *The Cult of the Serpent: An Interdisciplinary Survey of its Manifestations and Origins.*

Remember that it is the Hermetic serpent on the staff that remains the symbol for healing, testament to the ancient origins of all healing. In Egypt, the serpent is seen as the source of the healing powers, and it was Thoth who brought this knowledge to the Egyptians. Sanchoniathon describes Thoth as the founder of serpent worship in Egypt:

> He taught the Egyptians . . . a religion, which, partaking of Zabism and Ophiolatreia, had some mixture also of primeval truth. The Divine Spirit he denominated Cneph, and described him as the Original, Eternal Spirit, pervading all creation, whose symbol was the Serpent.[55]

One very practical explanation offered lately of the connection of the serpent image and the gaining of this most sacred healing knowledge comes to us through Jeremy Narby in *The Cosmic Serpent*:

> This is the observation that led me to investigate the cosmic serpent. I found the symbol in shamanism all over the world. Why? That's a good question. My hypothesis is that it is connected to the double helix of DNA inside virtually all living beings. And DNA itself is a symbolic Saussurian code . . . . According to my hypothesis, shamans take their consciousness down to the molecular level and gain access to bimolecular information.

Narby offers an extraordinary explanation of how the mind cure is executed, namely, the healer is communicating to the victim's DNA and instructing it to heal the body. The shaman, like the Mesmerist, utilizes a change of perceptual state. Unlike the Mesmerist, who places the victim into a somnambulist state, the shaman also goes into this trance-like state in order to communicate with the patient's DNA directly.

He who conquers the mind, conquers the world.

—Guru Nanak Dev

---

55 As quoted by Hargrave Jennings in *Ophiolatreia*.

In a strange twist of fate, the early usurpation of Hermetic principles by the Christian religion was to be recapitulated hundreds of years later by the New Thought movement, an ironic title for a movement based upon some of the most ancient ideas of the human race.

New Thought borrowed several key Hermetic concepts, including; "as above, so below," and the idea that "God is Mind" and that God is an intelligent force in the physical world, which is also known as pantheism. These Hermetic principles were then applied by the New Thoughters to health and healing, and also to the acquisition of personal wealth. This "new" concept of healing was called by several different names: Mentalism, the Mind Cure, and Christian Science or Mental Science, to name a few. As stated before, healing was one of the main focuses of the Hermetic art, and the most renown Hermetic occultists of old were all doctors, from Asclepius to Paracelsus.

The New Thought movement rekindled these ancient Hermetic healing techniques and principles, bringing them into the mainstream consciousness of the industrial and materialistic mindset of the time. While there were some who acknowledged the pre-Christian and pagan nature of these concepts, most New Thoughters tended to ascribe them to Jesus, or, in some cases, attempted to claim the findings for themselves exclusively. Jesus' role in all this business would be slightly different this time however, because within the New Thought movement, Jesus was primarily understood as a "consciousness" rather than a human being.[56] The Christ of the New Thought movement was an outgrowth of Quimby's philosophy. According to Quimby, "Christ" was an impersonal *Divine Nature* or *Principle*. Jesus was believed to have embodied or appropriated the Christ-principle as no human had before. He had fully realized his Christ-nature. As such, Jesus was not considered a messiah or savior to mankind; he was merely a "way-shower." Salvation for the New Thoughters was based not on Jesus but on the recognition of the Divine within oneself.

---

56 The origin for this concept, it might be added, can be found in the Egyptian Gnostics and the early Platonists, later to be done away with by the Catholic church.

Jesus never said that he—the man—was God; but he strove to teach the people of the existence of a living principle of wisdom to which matter was subject. And this truth, being fully revealed to his mind—he called it the "son of God"—admitting it in every act and never teaching that the flesh and blood of the natural man was God. The dispute between him and the people was not whether he, the man Jesus, was God or Christ or John the Baptist, but whether the man Jesus had any claim to wisdom superior to that of any wise man or prophet. He contended that he had, and in his words he showed a wisdom superior to their own. But they, not understanding how such works as his could be done intelligently, were deaf to his words of wisdom and ascribed to him a mysterious power.[57]

New Thought merged Hermeticism with Christianity to form a sort of "Christian Pantheism" in which Christ-consciousness permeated the universe and was present in the material world as a form of wisdom. The Hermetic nature of this statement can not be underemphasized:

It is nothing more or less, that has given to New Thought, Christian Science, and the various other mental science organizations of today their power, than the strength and virility of the Hermetic teachings, to which each and all of these systems of thought revert openly or otherwise for their authority. The doctrine of oneness with God or the essential unity of all things is fully expressed in the New Thought concept that God is all, God is good, and Christian Scientists treasure with the greatest reverence the cherished maxim of their late leader Mrs. Eddy, "God is my all." And right at this point it is well for the members of our Colleges to keep in mind constantly throughout the study of the Hermetic Sciences and Mysteries, the permanent mantra of the Hermetic Section, "In Him we Live, and Move, and have our Being." For on careful spiritual meditation it will be found to sum up the Hermetic philosophy in its entirety, and for that reason is given to the Colleges.[58]

---

57 Quimby, Phineas Parkhurst, "Defense Against an Accusation of Comparing Myself to Christ" (self-published pamphlet).
58 *Fr. K. X°*, **Hermes Mercurius Trismegistus: A Treatise Preliminary to the Study of the Hermetic Philosophy.**

THE KYBALION
AND PROSPERITY CONSCIOUSNESS

One of the most intriguing, and certainly the most Hermetic, of the New Thought books is a short treatise called *The Kybalion*. "Kybalion" does not correspond to any English or foreign word, and it's likely the invention of its credited author(s), the "Three Initiates."

The work itself claims to be part of a "secret" ancient Egyptian tradition, though no evidence of an actual ancient text by this name can be found. The book quotes this "ancient text" throughout, though the authors claim the original Kybalion was never a written text. This ancient tradition is described within *The Kybalion* thus:

> In the early days, there was a compilation of certain Basic Hermetic Doctrines, passed on from teacher to student, which was known as "The Kybalion," the exact significance and meaning of the term having been lost for several centuries. This teaching, however, is known to many to whom it has descended, from mouth to ear, on and on throughout the centuries. Its precepts have never been written down, or printed, so far as we know. It was merely a collection of maxims, axioms, and precepts, which were non-understandable to outsiders, but which were readily understood by students, after the axioms, maxims, and precepts had been explained and exemplified by the Hermetic Initiates to their Neophytes. These teachings really constituted the basic principles of "The Art of Hermetic Alchemy," which, contrary to the general belief, dealt in the mastery of Mental Forces, rather than Material Elements—the Transmutation of one kind of Mental Vibrations into others, instead of the changing of one kind of metal into another.

The authors' claim of an oral tradition makes it possible for them to infer that "Kybalion" is an errant spelling of "Kabbalah," which in Hebrew means "passed from ear to mouth."

The Kybalion was released by the Yogi Publication Society of Chicago in December, 1912. The company's publisher and main author was said to be Yogi Ramacharaka, a pseudonym for one of the most prolific and influential New Thought writers of all time, William Walker Atkinson.

Atkinson (1862–1932) dedicated his life to the cause of New Thought. His interest in the movement came when he discovered the New Thought teachings of Charles and Myrtle Fillmore after his work as a lawyer left him physically and mentally distressed. His first article, "A Mental Science Catechism," appeared in *Modern Thought*, one of the Fillmores' journals, in 1889.

Atkinson set up shop in Chicago, where he published the magazines *Suggestion* (1900–1901), *New Thought* (1901–1905) and *Advanced Thought* (1906). At the time, Chicago was a hub of New Thought activity, due to the prolific work of the Fillmores and Emma Curtis Hopkins. Among his many books published through the Yogi Publication Society was *Thought Vibration or the Law of Attraction in the Thought World* (1906), a title used extensively in Rhonda Byrne's *The Secret*, and excerpted later in this book. Atkinson also wrote several books on the powers of Mesmerism, which he is said to have practiced, a là Quimby. These include: *Practical Mental Influence: A Course of Lessons on Mental Vibrations, Psychic Influence, Personal Magnetism, Fascination, and Psychic Self-Protection.*

Atkinson was active in the study of all things occult, setting up his own exclusive psychic club and an organization called the "Atkinson School of Mental Science." He wrote extensively on all types of occult topics under various pseudonyms, including Magus Incognito, Theodore Sheldon, Theron Q. Dumont, Swami Pachandasi and Yogi Ramacharaka.

One of the best clues that Atkinson was one of the "Three Initiates" who wrote *The Kybalion* is that he had written *The Arcane Teachings*, a book outlining seven "Arcane Laws" that mirror the seven "Hermetic Laws" explained within *The Kybalion*. The differences between them are only syntactical.

The Yogi and the "Three Initiates"

In every country, you will find individuals of extraordinary mental or psychic powers, bordering on the miraculous. The ancients of India studied these powers systematically, and showed that they could be acquired by practice. They embodied their findings in a science called Raja Yoga. One of their conclusions was that the minds of individuals were parts of an external continuum which they called the Universal Mind. It was this that made seemingly miraculous phenomena like telepathy possible. They held that such phenomena were not supernatural but natural. (Today, we take for granted waves that enable us not only to see and hear, but also [to] burn, melt, cut, penetrate and carry information across space; we still do not know whether thought waves can do these or more!)

—Swami Vivekananda, "The Power of the Mind" lecture, 1900

Swami Vivekananda (1863–1902) is said to have been the first Indian swami to lecture and teach in America. He made his first appearance in 1893, at the World's Parliament of Religions, a division of the World's Fair in Chicago. It was here that Atkinson was first exposed to his ideas. Vivekananda was said to be a tremendous orator, dynamic and hypnotic, sparking the first yoga craze in America. At the time, he met with disapproval from Christian groups, due primarily to his heathen influence; many Americans began to seriously consider Hinduism, thanks to his teachings. Vivekananda was in the United States for only four years, but that was time enough for him to kick-start an Indian philosophy movement that swept the country.

Along with his public lectures and university tours, Vivekananda also taught privately. William Walker Atkinson is thought to have been one of his students. Vivekananda's theories were clearly resonant with Atkinson's New Thought ideas and the twenty books Atkinson published for Yogi Publication Society.

Yet beyond mental or intellectual power lies another distinct dimension that gives extraordinary power to Individuals to influence people. This can be simply stated as power of the personality . . . . This science calls for more application that any business can ever require . . . . It challenges comparison with any other science. There have been charlatans, there have been magicians, there have been cheats, more here than any other field. Why? For the same reason, that the more profitable the business, the greater the number of charlatans and cheats. But that is no reason why the business should not be good.

—Vivekananda, "The Power of the Mind"

But what about the other two Initiates credited in *The Kybalion*? Some people have suggested this could have included Vivekananda, but this is not likely, since *The Kybalion* was Hermetic rather than yogic. Most speculate that it was through Atkinson's Golden Dawn affiliations that he came upon the other two "Initiates" behind *The Kybalion*.

> There is a tradition within Builders of the Adytum (BOTA) that William Walker Atkinson (Yogi Ramacharaka, a former Golden Dawn chief) was the author of *The Kybalion*, and that Paul Foster Case (founder of BOTA) assisted him in the editing of the text. While in Chicago, Case read *The Secret Of Mental Magic* by Atkinson and wrote to the author. The two met and became well-acquainted. This eventually led to their collaboration on *The Kybalion*.
>
> —Rey De Lupos (OTO)

A likely "Initiate" was the occult personality **Paul Foster Case** (1884–1954), an author of several books and lessons, mainly on the tarot and Kabbalah. Case was gifted, having learned to read when he was only two years of age, and being an accomplished musician by his teenage years. Case was introduced to the tarot in 1900, and it consumed most of his life thereafter. (Both Aleister Crowley and Manly P. Hall believe that the tarot is a modern adaptation of the *Book of Thoth*; this is the title of Crowley's book on the subject.) Case often experienced vivid, lucid dreams, which spurred him to investigate the paranormal, especially after a brief correspondence he had about it with Rudyard Kipling.

When Case was studying Yoga and Pranayama[1], he made contact with Atkinson. Case had read Atkinson's work, *The Secret of Mental Magic*, that inspired his correspondence:

> Pioneers in the New Thought, like Helen Wilmans, William Walker Atkinson, Elizabeth Towns, Henry Wood and Judge Troward have all made valuable contributions. Manly Hall has awakened thousands from the dream of crass materialism. Dwight Goddard, from his retreat in Santa Barbara, spreads the wisdom of the Buddha throughout the English-speaking world. Alice Bailey has made the Arcane School a

---

1   Yogic breathing techniques.

powerful influence for good. The prodigious labors of Marc Edmund Jones have an effect that goes far beyond the limits of his circle of students. Despite differences of opinion and policy, all the Theosophical societies have done and are doing much to leaven Western thought with Eastern wisdom. The work of Rudolf Steiner and Max Heindel of the Unity School of Christianity, and of many others we lack space to mention, brings light and help to many persons whose mental bent does not dispose them to the special training offered by BOTA.[2]

Shortly after his corresponding with Atkinson, Case is said to have met a Master on the streets of Chicago who taught him of the innermost secrets of the mystery schools. He says the experience altered the course of his life forever. Case refers to this individual as "Dr. Fludd," a supposed Chicago physician, and sometimes as "Master R" (Ramacharaka?). Perhaps Atkinson was donning another secret identity. The secret master's name, Dr. Fludd, corresponds to Robert Fludd, a prominent figure in Hermetic history, who also inspired Franz Anton Mesmer. According to Case, this Dr. Fludd offered Case a choice: either he could continue with his successful musical career, or he could dedicate himself to humanity and thereby play a role in the coming age. Two years after this supposed encounter, *The Kybalion* was published.

Information regarding the third "Initiate" has been mired in obscurity, though most sources point to Michael Whitty.[3] Some claim that Whitty and Case first met in 1918, five years after the publication of *The Kybalion*, when Whitty initiated Case into the Thoth-Hermes temple of the Alpha et Omega group (succesor of the Hermetic Order of the Golden Dawn). But it is likely that the two had known one another for some time before Whitty would have invited him into such an exclusive order. Whitty was best known for the journal *Azoth*, which he published, edited, and occasionally wrote for.

Although the opinion may be disquieting to many, and rejected by most, we cannot believe, in the face of the evidence, that mankind as a whole has made any progress in the things that really matter. Materialism has, without a doubt, always existed, but the trouble with out present era is that the materialists, through the inadequacy and de-

---

2 Case, Paul Foster, *To Our Members*, The Wheel of Life, Autumn Equinox.
3 Greer, John Michael, *New Encyclopedia of the Occult.*

generacy of religious systems, have been so much in the majority over the idealists that they have dominated and controlled.[4]

After meeting Atkinson, Whitty launched a transformation that catapulted his occult career into the aether.

In 1914, Case was initiated into the Ordo Templi Orientis (OTO) after meeting Aleister Crowley. Was this a result of having written *The Kybalion*? Or was it through affiliations of Atkinson, a prominent Mason, Theosophist and former Golden Dawn high chief that this was arranged? It didn't take Case long, however, to develop a distaste for Crowley's ego, and he was known to have later stated, "We would not recommend Aleister Crowley as a guide in practical occultism. Yet his *Book 777* is the finest thing of its kind."[5]

Whitty was the Praemonstrator of the Thoth-Hermes temple of Alpha et Omega; Case was initiated into the order in 1918. Between 1919 and 1920, Case and Michael Whitty collaborated on the text which would later be published as *The Book of Tokens*. In 1920, Case rose in the ranks of the Rosicrucian order, becoming an Adeptus Minor. That same year, Michael Whitty died, and Case took his place as Praemonstrator.

No one is sure why Whitty passed on. According to Case,[6] Whitty expired due to his practices involving Enochian magic rituals. (One has to wonder if Case was present and/or participated in these rites.) Enochian magic is generally considered to be angelic, involving the invocation of angelic names in order to achieve certain goals. In the Golden Dawn tradition, Enochian magic was primarily based on the teachings of John Dee and Edward Kelley. After coming across Dee's notebooks, S.L. MacGregor Mathers, the founder of the Golden Dawn, reinvigorated this archaic system of magic which Dee claimed was given to him through conversations with angels. Sex magic is involved in these teachings, and Edward Kelley began having sex with John Dee's wife, stating the angels had ordered him to do so. Having studied with Crowley, Case would have been intimately familiar with these practices.

---

4   Whitty, Michael, Editorials. *Azoth*, May.
5   Case, Paul Foster, *To Our Members*. The Wheel of Life, Autumn Equinox.
6   As explained in his letters to Israel Regardie, another Golden Dawn member.

Case would write about these sex practices in several of his books and lessons. In *The Book of Tokens*, which he co-wrote with Whitty, Case comments on the sex function:

> You must wholly alter your conception of sex in order to comprehend the Ancient Wisdom . . . . It is the interior nervous organism, not the external organs, that is always meant in phallic symbolism, and the force that works through these interior centers is the Great Magical Agent, the divine serpent fire.

In his work, *The True and Invisible Rosicrucian Order and The Masonic Letter G*, Case wrote of practices involving the redirection of the sexual force to the higher centers of the brain where experience of supersensory states of consciousness become possible.[7]

It was due to the sexual nature of these teachings that Paul Foster Case was asked to leave his position at the Alpha et Omega. Moina Mathers, S.L. MacGregor Mathers' wife, asked Case to resign after she discovered his involvement with sex magic practices and some of the other members of the group, particularly one Lili Geise.[8]

When Case resigned, he wrote to Moina:

> I have no desire to be a "teacher and pioneer in this Purgatorial World." Guidance seems to have removed me from the high place to which I have never really aspired. The relief is great.

A couple of months after saying this, Case opened his own school, which offered courses in the ancient traditions of The Builders of the Adytum, which is still extant today. Case established its headquarters in Los Angeles in 1932, only two years before Manly P. Hall founded his Philosophical Research Society nearby.

From its start, the BOTA outlawed the practice of Enochian magic, and Case became a crusader to prevent other magical groups from practicing its rituals. After lecturing on the virtues of Enochian magic, Case became active in the unveiling of their

---

7   This can also be found described in Tantric yoga and Taoist and Siddha alchemical works.

8   Case later married Geise, who died several years after that. When approached by Moina about their relationship, Case replied: "The Hierophantria and I were observed to exchange significant glances over the altar during the Mystic Repast . . . . My conscience acquits me . . . . Our relation to each other we submit to no other Judge than that Lord of Love and Justice whom we all adore."

"volatile and dangerous" nature. In the *Wheel of Life* magazine, March 1937, Case described his views on Enochian material:

BOTA is a direct offshoot of the Golden Dawn, but its work has been purged of all the dangerous and dubious magic incorporated into the Golden Dawn's curriculum by the late S.L. MacGregor Mathers, who was responsible for the inclusion of the ceremonials based on the skrying of Sir Edward Kelly. There is much in these Golden Dawn rituals and ceremonies that is of the greatest value; but from the first grade to the last it is all vitiated by these dangerous elements taken from Dee and Kelly. Furthermore, in many places, the practical working is not provided with adequate safeguards, so that, to the present writer's personal knowledge, an operator working with the Golden Dawn rituals runs very grave risks of breaking down his physical organism, or of obsession by evil entities.

The Seven Hermetic Laws as Stated in *The Kybalion*

The Kybalion has had a cult following since its publication, and remains in print in various editions. The mysterious nature of the work probably adds to its attraction. Whether or not we can determine who wrote it, it presents well-researched Hermetic principles, though the language is archaic.

The Principles of Truth are Seven; he who knows these, understandingly, possesses the Magic Key before whose touch all the Doors of the Temple fly open.
— *The Kybalion*

The Seven Hermetic Principles, upon which the entire Hermetic Philosophy is based, are as follows:

I. THE PRINCIPLE OF MENTALISM
II. THE PRINCIPLE OF CORRESPONDENCE
III. THE PRINCIPLE OF VIBRATION
IV. THE PRINCIPLE OF POLARITY
V. THE PRINCIPLE OF RHYTHM
VI. THE PRINCIPLE OF CAUSE AND EFFECT
VII. THE PRINCIPLE OF GENDER

These seven Principles will be discussed and explained as we proceed with these lessons. A short explanation of each, however, should be given at this point.

I. The Principle of Mentalism

THE ALL is MIND; The Universe is Mental.

— *The Kybalion*

This principle embodies the truth that "All is Mind." It explains that THE ALL (which is the Substantial Reality underlying all the outward manifestations and appearances which we know under the terms of "The Material Universe," the "Phenomena of Life," "Matter," and "Energy"; and, in short, all that is apparent to our material senses) is SPIRIT, which in itself is UNKNOWABLE and UNDEFINABLE, but which may be considered and thought of as A UNIVERSAL, INFINITE, LIVING MIND. It also explains that all the phenomenal world or universe is simply a Mental Creation of THE ALL, subject to the Laws of Created Things, and that the universe, as a whole and in its parts or units, has its existence in the Mind of THE ALL, in which Mind we "live and move and have our being." This Principle, by establishing the Mental Nature of the Universe, easily explains all of the varied mental and psychic phenomena that occupy such a large portion of the public attention, and which, without such explanation, are non-understandable and defy scientific treatment. An understanding of this great Hermetic Principle of Mentalism enables the individual to readily grasp the laws of the Mental Universe, and to apply the same to his well-being and advancement. The Hermetic Student is enabled to apply Intelligently the great Mental Laws, instead of using them in a haphazard manner. With the Master Key in his possession, the student may unlock the many doors of the mental and psychic temple of knowledge, and enter the same freely and intelligently. This Principle explains the true nature of "Energy," "Power," and "Matter," and why and how all these are subordinate to the Mastery of Mind. One of the old Hermetic Masters wrote, long ages ago: "He who grasps the truth of the Mental Nature of the Universe is well advanced on The Path to Mastery." And these words are as true today as at the time they were first written. Without this Master Key, Mastery is impossible, and the student knocks in vain at the many doors of The Temple.

II. The Principle of Correspondence

As above, so below; as below, so above.
—*The Kybalion*

This Principle embodies the Truth that there is always a Correspondence between the laws and phenomena of the various planes of Being and Life. The old Hermetic axiom is "As above, so below; as below, so above." And the grasping of this Principle gives one the means of solving many a dark paradox and hidden secret of Nature. There are planes beyond our knowing, but when we apply the Principle of Correspondence to them, we are able to understand much that would otherwise be unknowable to us. This Principle is of universal application and manifestation, on the various planes of the material, mental, and spiritual universe—it is a Universal Law. The ancient Hermeticists considered this Principle as one of the most important mental instruments by which man was able to pry aside the obstacles which hid from view the Unknown. Its use even tore aside the Veil of Isis to the extent that a glimpse of the face of the goddess might be caught. Just as a knowledge of the Principles of Geometry enables man to measure distant suns and their movements, while seated in his observatory, so a knowledge of the Principle of Correspondence enables Man to reason intelligently from the Known to the Unknown. Studying the monad, he understands the archangel.

III. The Principle of Vibration

Nothing rests; everything moves; everything vibrates.
—*The Kybalion*

This Principle embodies the truth that everything is in motion, everything vibrates, and nothing is at rest; facts which Modern Science endorses, and which each new scientific discovery tends to verify. And yet this Hermetic Principle was enunciated thousands of years ago by the Masters of Ancient Egypt. This Principle explains that the differences between different manifestations of Matter, Energy, Mind, and even Spirit result largely from varying rates of Vibration. From THE ALL, which is Pure Spirit, down to the grossest form of Matter, all is in vibration, and the higher the vibration, the higher the position in the scale. The vibration of Spirit is at such an infinite rate of intensity and rapidity that it is practically at rest—just as a rapidly moving wheel seems to be motionless. And at the other end of the scale, there are gross forms of matter whose vibrations are so low as to seem at rest. Between these poles, there are millions upon millions of varying degrees of vibration. From corpuscle and electron, atom and molecule, to worlds and universes, everything is in vibratory motion. This is also true on the planes of energy and force (which are but varying degrees of vibration); and also on the mental planes (whose states depend upon vibrations); and even on to the spiritual planes. An understanding of this Principle, with the appropriate formulas, enables Hermetic students to control their own mental vibrations as well as those of others. The Masters also apply this Principle to the conquering of Natural phenomena, in various ways. "He who understands the Principle of Vibration has grasped the scepter of power," says one of the old writers.

IV. The Principle of Polarity

Everything is Dual; everything has poles; everything has its pair of opposites; like and unlike are the same; opposites are identical in nature, but different in degree; extremes meet; all truths are but half-truths; all paradoxes may be reconciled.
—The Kybalion

This Principle embodies the truth that "everything is dual," "everything has two poles," and "everything has its pair of opposites," all of which were old Hermetic axioms. It explains the old paradoxes that have perplexed so many, which have been stated as follows: Thesis and antithesis are identical in nature, but different in degree; opposites are the same, differing only in degree; the pairs of opposites may be reconciled; extremes meet; everything is and isn't, at the same time; all truths are but half-truths, every truth is half-false; there are two sides to everything, etc., etc., etc. It explains that in everything there are two poles, or opposite aspects, and that "opposites" are really only the two extremes of the same thing, with many varying degrees between them. To illustrate: heat and cold, although "opposites," are really the same thing, the differences consisting merely of degrees. (Look at your thermometer and see if you can discover where "heat" ends and "cold" begins.) There is no such thing as "absolute heat" or "absolute cold"—the terms "heat" and "cold" simply indicate varying degrees of the same thing, and that thing which manifests as "heat" and "cold" is merely a form, variety, and rate of Vibration. So "heat" and "cold" are simply the two poles of that which we call "heat"—and the phenomena attendant thereupon are manifestations of the Principle of Polarity. The same Principle manifests in the case of "light" and "darkness," which are again the same thing, the difference consisting of varying degrees between the two poles of the phenomena. Where does "darkness" leave off and "light" begin? What is the difference between "large" and "small"? Between "hard" and "soft"? Between "black" and "white"? Between "sharp" and "dull"? Between "noise" and "quiet"? Between "high" and "low"? Between "positive" and "negative"? The Principle of Polarity explains these paradoxes, and no other Principle can supersede it. The same Principle operates on the Mental Plane. Let us take a radical and extreme example—that of "love" and "hate," two mental states apparently totally different. And yet there are degrees of hate and degrees of love, and a middle point in which we use the terms "like" or "dislike," which shade into each other so gradually that sometimes we are at a loss to know whether we like or dislike—or neither. And all are simply degrees of the same thing. And, more than this (and considered of more importance by the Hermeticists), it is possible to change the vibrations of hate to the vibrations of love, in one's own mind, and in the minds of others. Many of you, who read these lines, have had personal experiences of the involuntary rapid transition from love to hate, and the reverse, in your own case and that of others. And you will therefore realize the possibility of this being accomplished by the use of the Will, by means of the Hermetic formulas. "Good" and "evil" are but the poles of the same thing, and the Hermeticist understands the art of transmuting evil into good, by means of an application of the Principle of Polarity. In short, the Art of Polarization becomes a phase of Mental Alchemy, known and practiced by the ancient and modern Hermetic Masters. An understanding of the Principle will enable one to change his own Polarity, as well as that of others, if he will devote the time and study necessary to master the art.

V. The Principle of Rhythm

Everything flows, out and in; everything has its tides; all things rise and fall; the pendulum-swing manifests in everything; the measure of the swing to the right is the measure of the swing to the left; rhythm compensates.

—*The Kybalion*

70

This Principle embodies the truth that in everything manifests a measured motion, to and fro; a flow and inflow; a swing backward and forward; a pendulum-like movement; a tide-like ebb and flow; a high-tide and low-tide between the two poles which exist in accordance with the Principle of Polarity described a moment ago. There is always an action and a reaction; an advance and a retreat; a rising and sinking. This is in the affairs of the Universe, suns, worlds, men, animals, mind, energy and matter. This law is manifest in the creation and destruction of worlds, in the rise and fall of nations, in the life of all things, and finally in the mental states of man (and it is with this latter that the Hermeticists find the understanding of the Principle most important). The Hermeticists have grasped this Principle, finding its universal application, and have also discovered certain means to overcome its effects in themselves by the use of the appropriate formulas and methods. They apply the Mental Law of Neutralization. They cannot annul the Principle, or cause it to cease its operation, but they have learned how to escape its effects upon themselves to a certain degree, depending upon the Mastery of the Principle. They have learned how to USE it, instead of being USED BY it. In this and similar methods consist the Art of the Hermeticists. The Master of Hermetics polarizes himself at the point at which he desires to rest, and then neutralizes the Rhythmic swing of the pendulum, which would tend to carry him to the other pole. All individuals who have attained any degree of Self-Mastery do this to a certain degree, more or less unconsciously, but the Master does this consciously, and by the use of his Will, and attains a degree of Poise and Mental Firmness almost impossible of belief on the part of the masses who are swung backward and forward like a pendulum. This Principle and that of Polarity have been closely studied by the Hermeticists, and the methods of counteracting, neutralizing, and USING them form an important part of the Hermetic Mental Alchemy.

VI. The Principle of Cause and Effect

Every Cause has its Effect; every Effect has its Cause; everything happens according to Law; Chance is but a name for Law not recognized; there are many planes of causation, but nothing escapes the Law.
—*The Kybalion*

This Principle embodies the fact that there is a Cause for every Effect; an Effect from every Cause. It explains that everything happens according to Law, that nothing ever "merely happens," that there is no such thing as Chance, that while there are various planes of Cause and Effect, the higher dominating the lower planes, still nothing ever entirely escapes the Law. The Hermeticists understand the art and methods of rising above the ordinary plane of Cause and Effect, to a certain degree, and by mentally rising to a higher plane, they become Causes instead of Effects. The masses are carried along, obedient to environment; the wills and desires of others stronger than themselves, heredity, suggestion, and other outward causes moving them about like pawns on the Chessboard of Life. But the Masters, rising to the plane above, dominate their moods, characters, qualities, and powers, as well as the environment surrounding them, and become movers instead of pawns. They help to PLAY THE GAME OF LIFE, instead of being played and moved about by other wills and environment. They USE the Principle instead of being its tool. The Masters obey the causation of the higher planes, but they help to RULE on their own plane. In this statement there is condensed a wealth of Hermetic knowledge—let him read who can.

VII. The Principle of Gender

Gender is in everything; everything has its Masculine and Feminine Principles; Gender manifests on all planes.
—*The Kybalion*

This Principle embodies the truth that there is GENDER manifested in everything—the Masculine and Feminine Principles ever at work. This is true not only of the Physical Plane, but of the Mental and even the Spiritual Planes. On the Physical Plane, the Principle manifests as SEX, on the higher planes it takes higher forms, but the Principle is ever the same. No creation, physical, mental or spiritual, is possible without this Principle. An understanding of its laws will throw light on many a subject that has perplexed the minds of men. The Principle of Gender works ever in the direction of generation, regeneration, and creation. Everything, and every person, contains the two Elements or Principles, or this great Principle, within it, him or her. Every Male thing has the Female Element also; every Female contains also the Male Principle. If you would understand the philosophy of Mental and Spiritual creation, generation, and regeneration, you must understand and study this Hermetic Principle. It contains the solution of many mysteries of Life. We caution you that this Principle has no reference to the many base, pernicious and degrading lustful theories, teachings and practices, which are taught under fanciful titles, and which are a prostitution of the great natural principle of Gender. Such base revivals of the ancient infamous forms of Phallicism tend to ruin mind, body and soul, and the Hermetic Philosophy has ever sounded the warning note against these degraded teachings which tend toward lust, licentiousness, and perversion of Nature's principles. If you seek such teachings, you must go elsewhere for them—Hermeticism contains nothing for you along these lines. To the pure, all things are pure; to the base, all things are base.

From Thought Vibration,
or The Law of Attraction in the Thought World
By William Walker Atkinson (1906)

Law, Not Chance

Some time ago I was talking to a man about the Attractive Power of Thought. He said that he did not believe that Thought could attract anything to him, and that it was all a matter of luck. He had found, he said, that ill luck relentlessly pursued him, and that everything he touched went wrong. It always had, and always would, and he had grown to expect it. When he undertook a new thing he knew beforehand that it would go wrong and that no good would come of it. Oh, no! There wasn't anything in the theory of Attractive Thought, so far as he could see; it was all a matter of luck!

This man failed to see that by his own confession he was giving a most convincing argument in favor of the Law of Attraction. He was testifying that he was always expecting things to go wrong, and that they always came about as he expected. He was a magnificent illustration of the Law of Attraction—but he didn't know it, and no argument seemed to make the matter clear to him. He was "up against it," and there was no way out of it—he always expected the ill luck, and every occurrence proved that he was right, and that the Mental Science position was all nonsense.

There are many people who seem to think that the only way in which the Law of Attraction operates is when one wishes hard, strong and steady. They do not seem to realize that a strong belief is as efficacious as a strong wish. The successful man believes in himself and his ultimate success, and, paying no attention to little setbacks, stumbles, tumbles and slips, presses on eagerly to the goal, believing all the time that he will get there. His views and aims may alter as he progresses, and he may change his plans or have them changed for him, but all the time he knows in his heart that he will eventually "get there." He is not steadily wishing he may get there—he simply feels and believes it, and thereby sets to operation the strongest forces known in the world of thought.

The man who just as steadily believes he is going to fail will invariably fail. How could he help it? There is no special miracle about it. Everything he does, thinks and says is tinctured with the thought of failure. Other people catch his spirit, and fail to trust him or his ability, which occurrences he in turn sets down as but other exhibitions of his ill luck, instead of ascribing them to his belief and expectation of failure. He is suggesting failure to himself all the time, and he invariably takes on the effect of the auto-suggestion. Then again, he by his negative thoughts shuts up that portion of his mind from which should come the ideas and plans conducive to success and which do come to the man who is expecting success because he believes in it. A state of discouragement is not the one in which bright ideas come to us. It is only when we are enthused and hopeful that our minds work out the bright ideas which we may turn to account.

Men instinctively feel the atmosphere of failure hovering around certain of their fellows, and on the other hand recognizes something about others which leads them to say, when they hear of a temporary mishap befalling such a one: "Oh, he'll come out all right somehow—you can't down him. It is the atmosphere caused by the prevailing Mental Attitude. Clear up your Mental Atmosphere!"

There is no such thing as chance. Law maintains everywhere, and all that happens happens because of the operation of Law. You cannot name the simplest thing that ever occurred by chance — try it, and then run the thing down to a final analysis, and you will see it as the result of law. It is as plain as mathematics. Plan and purpose; cause and effect. From the movements of worlds to the growth of the grain of mustard seed—all the result of Law. The fall of the stone down the mountain-side is not chance—forces which had been in operation for centuries caused it. And back of that cause were other causes, and so on until the Causeless Cause is reached.

And Life is not the result of chance—the Law is here, too. The Law is in full operation whether you know it or not—whether you believe in it or not. You may be the ignorant object upon which the Law operates, and bring yourself all sorts of trouble because of your ignorance of or opposition to the Law. Or you may fall in with the operations to the Law—get into its current, as it were—and Life will seem a far different thing to you. You cannot get outside of the Law, by refusing to have anything to do with it. You are at liberty to oppose it and produce all the friction you wish to—it doesn't hurt the Law, and you may keep it up until you learn your lesson.

The Law of Thought Attraction is one name for the law, or rather for one manifestation of it. Again I say, your thoughts are real things. They go forth from you in all directions, combining with thoughts of like kind—opposing thoughts of a different character—forming combinations—going where they are attracted—flying away from thought centers opposing them. And your mind attracts the thought of others, which have been sent out by them conscious or unconsciously. But it attracts only those thoughts which are in harmony with its own. Like attracts like, and opposites repel opposites, in the world of thought.

If you set your mind to the keynote of courage, confidence, strength and success, you attract to yourself thoughts of like nature; people of like nature; things that fit in the mental tune. Your prevailing thought or mood determines that which is to be drawn toward you—picks out your mental bedfellow. You are today setting into motion thought currents which will in time attract toward you thoughts, people and conditions in harmony with the predominant note of your thought. Your thought will mingle with that of others of like nature and mind, and you will be attracted toward each other, and will surely come together with a common purpose sooner or later, unless one or the other of you should change the current of his thoughts.

Fall in with the operations of the law. Make it a part of yourself. Get into its currents. Maintain your poise. Set your mind to the key-note of Courage, Confidence and Success. Get in touch with all the thoughts of that kind that are emanating every hour from hundreds of minds. Get the best that is to be had in the thought world. The best is there, so be satisfied with nothing less. Get into partnership with good minds. Get into the right vibrations. You must be tired of being tossed about by the operations of the Law—get into harmony with it.

The *Secret* Source of Prosperity Consciousness

Most of our obstacles would melt away if, instead of cowering before them, we should make up our minds to walk boldly through them.

—Orison Swett Marden

The Hermetic teachings—like all information—is a tool, and its usefulness depends upon how it's used. Often it is used for less-than-noble purposes. An infamous misuse of Hermetic knowledge came in the late Middle Ages when the sacred art of alchemy, or self-transformation, was widely used to transmute lead into gold. This was the base sort of alchemy that Zosimos and Enoch warned against: a lust for materialism rather than the advancement of the consciousness.

Alchemy and the Hermetic arts grew into disfavor after one too many con men claiming they had the ability to produce gold swindled their way into infamy. Alchemy became outlawed and punishable by death by the Catholic church, and has since been ridiculed in the annals of history as a medieval pseudoscience.

New Thought, the intimate movement that began with Phineas Quimby's Mesmer-inspired healings, was initially more interested in health than wealth, but within a decade it had shifted by large part to "Prosperity Consciousness," in which entrepreneurs employed the Law of Attraction to attract abundance, using the idea that riches will come if aspiring millionaires hypnotize themselves into the certainty of their wealth—before it physically arrives. Another necessary belief of Prosperity Consciousness is that our planet is an inexhaustible cornucopia constructed by God to fulfill everyone's material desires at the drop of a wish.

Some evangelical Christians (like Kenneth Hagin, Oral Roberts, and the strangely-but-appropriately-named Creflo Dollar) contend, despite contradictory evidence, that New Testament verse instructs us that poverty punishes non-believers, and that fully-committed believers in Jesus will be rewarded with Mercedes-rich prosperity.

The use of mystical ideas and odd interpretations of biblical quotes to justify and promote Prosperity Consciousness has been going on for well over a century. And it is the basis for the "revelations" contained within *The Secret*.

The Secret is the most famous manifestation of Prosperity Consciousness in recent decades, presenting the appealing idea that one's life can be easily transformed into a positive and rewarding experience, and that previous failures can be blamed on a concerted societal effort to bury the simple means of creating personal success.

Within a super-capitalist environment that repeatedly attacks the conscious mind with the idea that consumption is the only way to achieve satisfaction, it's easy to see why *The Secret* is brightening the often-dim bulbs of hope within our culture. One need only acquire a DVD or book to create a happier and financially remunerative state of mind! Thousands of testimonials on YouTube and blogs throughout the Internet speak gratefully of *The Secret* "working," that once fear and doubt and the expectation of failure was conquered, good things started happening.

Says teacher David Schirmer within *The Secret*:

When I first understood *The Secret*, every day I would get a bunch of bills in the mail. I thought, "How do I turn this around?" The law of attraction states that what you focus on you will get, so I got a bank statement. I whited out the total, and I put a new total in there. I put exactly how much I wanted to see in the bank. So I thought, "What if I just visualized checks coming in the mail?" So I just visualized a bunch of checks coming in the mail. Within just one month, things started to change. It is amazing: today I just get checks in the mail. I get a few bills, but I get more checks than bills."

Another thing Mr. Schirmer received in the mail was notification from the Australian Securities and Investments Commission in July, 2007, that he would be investigated for false promises made to investors who lost tens of thousands of dollars entrusted to a revered teacher from *The Secret*.

The Secret is certainly not the first bestselling success manual that plays to the reader's sense of hope and possibility. *Pushing to the Front* by Orison Swett Marden, published in 1895, heralded the genre of thick, gilded, expensive success manuals sold door-to-door by subscription book agents.

Pushing to the Front and other million-selling success manuals revealed the secrets of success to small-town nineteenth century Americans by quoting famous examples of the powerful and wealthy in human history. Marden's works suggest that success and prosperity is something that comes from having the appropriate mental state, that of boldness and confidence.

From Marden's *The Miracle of Right Thought*:

The Divinity of Desire

Believe with all of your heart that you will do what you were made to do. When the mind has once formed the habit of holding cheerful, happy, prosperous pictures, it will not be easy to form the opposite habit.

It does not matter how improbable or how far away this realization may seem, or how dark the prospects may be, if we visualize them as best we can, as vividly as possible, hold tenaciously to them and vigorously struggle to attain them, they will gradually become actualized, realized in the life. But a desire, a longing without endeavor, a yearning abandoned or held indifferently will vanish without realization.

It is only when desire crystallized into resolve, however, that it is effective.

Think and say only that which you wish to become true.

Faith is the substance of things hoped for, the outline of the image itself; the real substance, not merely a mental image. What we believe is coming to us is a tremendous creative motive. Your whole thought current must be set in the direction of your life purpose.

Whatever comes to us in life, we create first in our mentality.

Pushing to the Front, which is over a hundred years old, reveals its age in its suggestion that one must labor assiduously to reach a goal; likewise its mystical thoughts are meant to appeal to a primarily male audience who would respond well to the idea that the aggressive and persistent are the ones rewarded with success. Turn-of-the-century success manuals—like *Masters of the Situation, or Some Secrets of Success and Power* by William James Tilley

(1890), *The Royal Path of Life or Aids to Success and Happiness* by Thomas L. Haines and Levi W. Yaggy (1876) and *The Way to Win, Showing How to Succeed in Life* by John T. Dale (1890)—made it clear that good things happened to those who replicated the work habits of powerful, wealthy men.

The success manual turned more mystical and internal with the release of *The Science of Getting Rich* (1910) by Wallace D. Wattles (1860–1911), which inspired Rhonda Byrne to pen *The Secret* almost a century later. Wattles claimed to have been an object lesson for the principles discussed in his *Getting Rich* book, which is excerpted in this book on page xxx. Poor most of his life; only in his later years did Wattles become wealthy. The New Thought ideas are readily apparent in his work:

> By thought, the thing you want is brought to you. By action, you receive it.
>
> When you make a failure it is because you have not asked for enough. Keep on, and a larger thing than you were seeking will certainly come to you.
>
> The grateful mind is constantly fixed upon the best. Therefore it tends to become the best. It takes the form or character of the best, and will receive the best.
>
> The object of all life is development; and everything that lives has an inalienable right to all the development it is capable of attaining.

Charles F. Haanel (1866–1949) a businessman who was a Shriner, Rosicrucian, 32nd degree Mason and New Thought devotee, is extensively quoted throughout *The Secret*. Haanel is best known for his multi-volume prosperity manual, *The Master Key System* (1917). Napoleon Hill wrote to Haanel: "My present success and the success which has followed my work as President of the Napoleon Hill Institute is due largely to the principles laid down in *The Master Key System*."

The Prosperity Consciousness movement really took off in America during the Great Depression. New Thought offered personal power and, most importantly, a sliver lining in a very dark sky. Hundreds of public speakers and homespun authors promoted the positive vibe, with varying degrees of ability and success. Some consider the Prosperity Consciousness movement to be separate from the New Thought movement proper, and it can be said that the originators of New Thought were more concerned with health than wealth. Phineas Quimby offered his services to anyone, whether they could pay or not.

A second notable era of bestselling success manuals began in the midst of the Depression with Dale Carnegie's *How to Win Friends and Influence People* (1936). *Think and Grow Rich* by Napoleon Hill (1883–1970) was initially released in 1937, and has sold millions of copies in various editions, influencing people such Bob Proctor, the white shoe-wearing star of *The Secret* DVD, with his "thoughts are things" idea, in which the success-oriented attract like-minded people with whom they can accomplish anything.

Napoleon Hill grew up in a one-room log cabin in Wise County, Virginia. In his mid-twenties, Hill landed an interview with steel magnate Andrew Carnegie for an article about successful men. Carnegie recognized the young Hill's talent and challenged him to interview five hundred millionaires and write a book about their secrets of success. With Carnegie's help, Hill later published an eight-volume book titled *The Law of Success*. Examples of Hill's philosophies in their relation to New Thought can be seen in the following quotes from *Think and Grow Rich*:

Man, alone, has the power to transform his thoughts into physical reality; man, alone, can dream and make his dreams come true.

More gold has been mined from the thoughts of men than has been taken from the earth.

The battle is all over except the "shouting" when one knows what is wanted and has made up his mind to get it, whatever the price may be.

Think twice before you speak, because your words and influence will plant the seed of either success or failure in the mind of another. When your desires are strong enough you will appear to possess superhuman powers to achieve [them].

Your ability to use the principle of autosuggestion will depend, very largely, upon your capacity to concentrate upon a given desire until that desire becomes a burning obsession.

Dale Carnegie (1888–1955), coincidentally enough, was a distant cousin of Andrew Carnegie, so it can definitely be said that the steel magnate played a role in the Prosperity Consciousness movement. Born a poor farmer's boy, Dale Carnegie became a lard salesman for Armour & Company after getting an education at a state teacher's college in Missouri, and afterward developed the "Dale Carnegie Course" in public speaking. *How To Win Friends and Influence People* offered a variant of New Thought positivism intermixed with psychological hints to reveal that the best method to get ahead was to submerge the ego while sucking up to and praising others, and to hypnotizing oneself into conveying authentic interest and appreciation for even the homeliest aspects of other people.

Happiness doesn't depend on any external conditions, it is governed by our mental attitude.

It isn't what you have, or who you are, or where you are, or what you are doing that makes you happy or unhappy. It is what you think about.

Success is getting what you want. Happiness is wanting what you get.

The ideas I stand for are not mine. I borrowed them from Socrates. I swiped them from Chesterfield. I stole them from Jesus. And I put them in a book. If you don't like their rules, whose would you use?

When fate hands you a lemon, make lemonade.

When we hate our enemies, we are giving them power over us: power over our sleep, our appetites, our blood pressure, our health and our happiness. Our enemies would dance with joy if only they know how they were worrying us, lacerating us, and getting even with us! Our hate is not hurting them at all, but our hate is turning our days and nights into a hellish turmoil.

These extraordinarily popular Depression-era success manuals inspired a raft of imitative self-help manuals utilizing either the Law of Attraction or faux Jesus worship as their directives.

Ernest Holmes (1887–1960) founded Religious Mind, also known as Science of Mind, a New Thought movement adjunct that promoted the healing teachings of Phineas Quimby. Although Holmes' teachings did not emphasize getting rich, he integrated Prosperity Consciousness into his teachings. He stressed more that the Law of Attraction would bring like consequences. Here are excerpts from some of his works.

Destroy All Thoughts That We Do Not Wish to Experience.

We must resolutely set our faces to the rising consciousness of the Son of Truth; Seeing only the one power we must destroy the adversary and leave the field to God or good. All that is in any way negative must be wiped off the slate and we must daily come into the higher thought. To be washed clean of the dust and chaos of the objective life. In the silence of the soul's communion with the Great Cause of All Being, into the stillness of the Absolute, into the secret place of the most high, back of the din ceaseless roar of life, we shall find a resting place and a place of real spiritual power . . . . Daily practice the truth and daily die to all error-thought. Spend more time receiving and realizing the presence of the Most High and less time worrying . . . . Wonderful power will come to the one who believes and trusts in that power in which he has come to believe. In the last analysis, man is just what he thinks himself to be; he is big in capacity if he thinks big thoughts; he is small if he thinks small thoughts. He will attract to himself what he most thinks about. He can learn to govern his own destiny when he learns to control his thoughts. In order to do this he must first realize that everything in the manifest universe is the result of some inner activity of the mind. This Mind is God, producing a universe by the activity of his own divine thoughts; man is in this mind as a thinking center, and what he thinks governs his life, even as God's thought governs the Universe, by setting in motion all cosmic activities . . . . The seed that falls into the ground shall bear fruit of its own kind; and nothing shall hinder it.[9]

There is a power that responds to our consciousness exactly the way we think, like a mirror; and if I say—no matter what it looks like—"I am surrounded by love and by friendship; I am Love I am Friendship; I give and I receive and I believe it, and this is true now," the cause and effect is set in motion to make it come true and nothing can destroy it unless

---

9   Holmes, Ernest, *Creative Mind and Success.*

I do, myself . . . . All energy returns to its source. Einstein even has said that time, light, and space bend back upon themselves. Therefore our word tends to come back to us. "Whatsoever things are lovely and of good report—think on these things" the bible says. "As a man thinketh in his heart so is he." "Believe and it shall be done unto you."[10]

In the midst of the Korean War, commandeered by the Dale Carnegie lookalike Harry S. Truman, Protestant Minister Norman Vincent Peale released the enormously popular *The Power of Positive Thinking* (1952), which suggested to its millions of readers to implant positive affirmations into the unconscious mind: "Let them sink into your unconscious and they can help you overcome any difficulty. Say them over and over again. Say them until your mind accepts them, until you believe them—faith power works wonders." Peale's readers are instructed to pray ceaselessly, and to use his techniques repetitively and permanently. In an unattributed acknowledgement of New Thought movement ideas, Dr. Peale emphasized, "Thoughts are things," and "Change your thoughts and you change your world."

Another notable proponent of Prosperity Consciousness literature since the 1950s has been **Catherine Ponder**, the Palm Desert-based student of the works of Charles Fillmore, who was initiated into the New Thought movement Unity Church by Fillmore's son, Lowell. Ponder has published over a dozen Prosperity Consciousness tomes, most explaining how biblical characters like Moses, Isaac, Jacob, Joshua and Joseph became prosperous millionaires, and how it is our divine right to amass wealth. Ponder's mentor, Charles Fillmore, attempted to make a distinction between prosperity of the soul and prosperity of wealth:

Prosperity: The consciousness that [the] divine mind is [an] inexhaustible support and supply. The difference between spiritual prosperity and the material idea of prosperity is the spiritual prosperity is founded on understanding of the inexhaustible, omnipresent substance of Spirit as the source of supply; the material idea is that the possession of things constitutes prosperity. Man

10 Holmes, Ernest, *Ideas of Power*; Holmes papers, Vol. 3.

lays hold of the one substance with his mind, through understanding and faith. "Uncertainty of riches" indicates putting one's trust in the possession of things apart from the consciousness of the one substance as the source of all. Anxiety about supply can be overcome by a recognition of the omnipresence of Sprit substance and a centering of faith in it as the source of supply. The one substance is magnified and increased by thanksgiving and praise . . . . It is necessary to give as freely as we receive, because there is a law of giving and receiving. Giving opens the way to a greater inflow of substance. We should give cheerfully, freely, out of the consciousness that the supply is inexhaustible.[11]

Ponder's utilization of the bible to prove that people have an inherent right to wealth can be seen the passages of her writings:

___The Bible is a Prosperity Textbook. You can open your mind to prosperity when you realize that the Bible is the greatest prosperity textbook ever written, and begin studying it from that standpoint. The Bible is filled with stories about bread and fish. This is marvelous prosperity symbolism: The bread symbolizes the substance of the universe, which we mold and shape with our thoughts and words of prosperity. The fish symbolize ideas of increase.

The word "gold" appears more than four hundred times in the Bible. There are between three thousand and four thousand promises in the Bible, many of them literal prosperity promises.

Jesus' interest in prosperity is shown in the Lord's Prayer: "Give us this day our daily bread, and forgive us our debts, as we also have forgiven our debtors." Many of Jesus' miracles were prosperity miracles, and many of His parables were prosperity parables.

When Jesus said of the rich young ruler, "How hard it will be for those who trust in riches to enter the kingdom," it was because He knew that this rich man was possessed by his possessions rather than controlling them. A spiritual consciousness of prosperity gives you control over your possessions, rather than allowing your possessions to control you.

---

11 Fillmore, Charles, *Metaphysical Bible Dictionary.*

Prosperity, a Necessity for Your Growth

You can open your mind to prosperity when you realize that prosperity is a necessity for your spiritual growth, because prosperity gives you freedom to unfold spiritually.

Recently I sat next to a doctor of chiropractic at a banquet where we were both guest speakers. This man told me how much the mental and spiritual approaches to prosperity had meant to him over the years. He described how he had gone from being a struggling young doctor who had nothing, to being a happy, affluent one who now has his own clinic, a large practice, a nice home, a fine family, cars, investments, property—even a private plane. He said this: "I am a far better doctor, a far better husband and parent, a far better citizen today because I am prosperous. I now have time to study Truth, to unfold spiritually in a way I never had before. Everybody ought to be prosperous, because prosperity gives them freedom. Prosperity is a necessity for spiritual growth."

Hermetic philosophy taught that the adept could manifest whatever he aligned his mind to and it would protect and benefit him. But it should be noted that the Hermeticists were talking about aligning their mind to God, not to money:

The sole protection—and this we must have—is piety. For neither evil daimon; yea nor fate, can ever overcome or dominate a man who pious is, and pure, and holy. For God doth save the truly pious man from every ill.
—Hermes Trismegistus, Fragment XXIII from Cyril of Alexandria

The Human mind is God; if it be good, God then doth shower his benefits upon us.
—Fulgnetius the Mythographer, Hermetic Fragment XXVII

Here, too, we must keep in perspective that fact that the acquisition of wealth is not necessarily a "benefit," and it wouldn't solve one's deepest problems. In the ancient alchemical and Hermetic teachings, we are taught the opposite, not to go about getting everything we want, but rather, to frustrate our desires by not giving in to them. Carl Jung extrapolates on this Hermetic concept in his works on psychology and alchemy. It is precisely the frustration of desires that creates enough tension and heat to power the *calcinatio* stage of the alchemical operation itself.

> The necessary frustration of desirousness or concupiscence is the chief feature of the *calcinatio* stage. First the substance must be located; that is, the unconscious unacknowledged desire, demand, [or] expectation must be recognized and affirmed. The instinctual urge that says "I want" and "I am entitled to do this" must be fully accepted by the ego . . . . As a rule, life reality, if faced, provides plenty of occasions for the *calcinatio* of frustrated desirousness . . . when denied, it becomes enraged. This is the psychological homologue of the "Divine Wrath" that roasted Christ. Reality often generates fire by challenging or denying the demanding expectations of such desires. Denied justification, the frustrated desire becomes the fire of *calcinatio* . . . the fire of *calcinatio* purges these identifications and drives off the root.[12]

On a personal level, the expectation of easy riches combined with a sense of absolute entitlement indicates stunted psychological growth and a sense of failure if desires remain unfulfilled. And it should go without saying that the Prosperity Consciousness message, that everyone is entitled to fulfill all their consumerist desires without restriction, ignores the fact that our small planet has its physical limitations and is currently in the throes of potentially cataclysmic reactions against its six billion six hundred million human occupants, whether prosperous or not.

Though it goes against the Positive Thinking prescription for happiness to ever entertain a critical or negative concept, we embrace the Socratic view that the best ideas can easily withstand examination. As remarked by Carolyn Baker in her DailyScare.com blog:

> Only children and adolescents believe that they can, as *The Secret* insists, have anything they want. Rhonda Byrne of Prime Time Productions, one of the principal filmmakers and author of the book The Secret, says she was inspired by reading *The Science Of Getting Rich*,

---

12 Edinger, Edward F., *Anatomy of the Psyche: Alchemical Symbolism an Psychotherapy*

a 1910 book by Wallace D. Wattles, a New Thought transcendentalist, which proclaims that one's wealth or lack thereof is a product of one's thought and attitudes. Positive thinking attracts good things; negative thinking attracts lack. When I hear these concepts, I can only return to: How uniquely American! Can you imagine telling twelve-year-old girls in Chinese sweatshops—the ones who work sixteen hours a day for pennies, live in squalor, may get raped at any moment, and sometimes are found dead at the ripe old age of twenty at their sewing machines from working themselves to death—can you imagine telling them that their situation is the product of their thoughts? Examples of such ghastly human suffering are countless in a world where millions of human beings live on less than two dollars a day.[13]

The Right to be Rich
By Wallace D. Wattles (1910)

Whatever may be said in praise of poverty, the fact remains that it is not possible to live a really complete or successful life unless one is rich. No one can rise to his greatest possible height in talent or soul development unless he has plenty of money, for to unfold the soul and to develop talent he must have many things to use, and he cannot have these things unless he has money to buy them with.

A person develops in mind, soul, and body by making use of things, and society is so organized that man must have money in order to become the possessor of things. Therefore, the basis of all advancement must be the science of getting rich.

The object of all life is development, and everything that lives has an Inalienable right to all the development it is capable of attaining.

A person's right to life means his right to have the free and unrestricted use of all the things which may be necessary to his fullest mental, spiritual, and physical unfoldment; or, in other words, his right to be rich.

In this book, I shall not speak of riches in a figurative way. To be really rich does not mean to be satisfied or contented with a little. No one ought to be satisfied with a little if he is capable of using and enjoying more. The purpose of nature is the advancement and unfoldment of life, and everyone should have all that can contribute to the power, elegance, beauty, and richness of life. To be content with less is sinful.

The person who owns all he wants for the living of all the life he is

13 Baker, Carolyn, Apr 4, 2007, "The Secret": Creating a Culture of Cheerfulness as Rome Burns.

capable of living is rich, and no person who has not plenty of money can have all he wants. Life has advanced so far and become so complex that even the most ordinary man or woman requires a great amount of wealth in order to live in a manner that even approaches completeness.

Every person naturally wants to become all that they are capable of becoming. This desire to realize innate possibilities is inherent in human nature; we cannot help wanting to be all that we can be. Success in life is becoming what you want to be. You can become what you want to be only by making use of things, and you can have the free use of things only as you become rich enough to buy them. To understand the science of getting rich is therefore the most essential of all knowledge.

There is nothing wrong in wanting to get rich. The desire for riches is really the desire for a richer, fuller, and more abundant life—and that desire is praiseworthy. The person who does not desire to live more abundantly is abnormal, and so the person who does not desire to have money enough to buy all he wants is abnormal.

There are three motives for which we live: We live for the body, we live for the mind, we live for the soul. No one of these is better or holier than the other; all are alike desirable, and no one of the three—body, mind, or soul—can live fully if either of the others is cut short of full life and expression. It is not right or noble to live only for the soul and deny mind or body, and it is wrong to live for the intellect and deny body or soul.

We are all acquainted with the loathsome consequences of living for the body and denying both mind and soul, and we see that real life means the complete expression of all that a person can give forth through body, mind, and soul. Whatever he can say, no one can be really happy or satisfied unless his body is living fully in its every function, and unless the same is true of his mind and his soul. Wherever there is unexpressed possibility or function not performed, there is unsatisfied desire. Desire is possibility seeking expression or function seeking performance.

A person cannot live fully in body without good food, comfortable clothing, and warm shelter, and without freedom from excessive toil. Rest and recreation are also necessary to his physical life.

One cannot live fully in mind without books and time to study them, without opportunity for travel and observation, or without intellectual companionship.

To live fully in mind a person must have intellectual recreations, and must surround himself with all the objects of art and beauty he is capable of using and appreciating.

To live fully in soul, a person must have love, and love is denied fullest expression by poverty.

A person's highest happiness is found in the bestowal of benefits on those he loves; love finds its most natural and spontaneous expression in giving. The individual who has nothing to give cannot fill his place as a spouse or parent, as a citizen, or as a human being. It is in the use of material things that a person finds full life for his body, develops his mind, and unfolds his soul. It is therefore of supreme importance to each individual to be rich.

It is perfectly right that you should desire to be rich. If you are a normal man or woman you cannot help doing so. It is perfectly right that you should give your best attention to the science of getting rich, for it is the noblest and most necessary of all studies. If you neglect this study, you are derelict in your duty to yourself, to God and humanity, for you can render to God and humanity no greater service than to make the most of yourself.

There Is A Science of Getting Rich

There is a science of getting rich, and it is an exact science, like algebra or arithmetic. There are certain laws which govern the process of acquiring riches, and once these laws are learned and obeyed by anyone, that person will get rich with mathematical certainty.

The ownership of money and property comes as a result of doing things in a certain way, and those who do things in this certain way—whether on purpose or accidentally—get rich, while those who do not do things in this certain way—no matter how hard they work or how able they are—remain poor.

It is a natural law that like causes always produce like effects, and, therefore, any man or woman who learns to do things in this certain way will infallibly get rich.

That the above statement is true is shown by the following facts:

Getting rich is not a matter of environment, for if it were, all the people in certain neighborhoods would become wealthy. The people of one city would all be rich, while those of other towns would all be poor, or all the inhabitants of one state would roll in wealth, while those of an adjoining state would be in poverty.

But everywhere we see rich and poor living side by side, in the same environment, and often engaged in the same vocations. When two people are in the same locality and in the same business, and one gets rich while the other remains poor, it shows that getting rich is not primarily a matter of environment. Some environments may be more favorable than others, but when two people in the same business are in the same neighborhood and one gets rich while the other fails, it indicates that getting rich is the result of doing things in a certain way.

And further, the ability to do things in this certain way is not due solely to the possession of talent, for many people who have great talent remain poor, while others who have very little talent get rich.

Studying the people who have gotten rich, we find that they are an average lot in all respects, having no greater talents and abilities than other people have. It is evident that they do not get rich because they possess talents and abilities that others do not have, but because they happen to do things in a certain way.

Getting rich is not the result of saving, or thrift. Many very penurious people are poor, while free spenders often get rich.

Nor is getting rich due to doing things which others fail to do, for two people in the same business often do almost exactly the same things, and one gets rich while the other remains poor or becomes bankrupt.

From all these things, we must come to the conclusion that getting rich is the result of doing things in a certain way.

If getting rich is the result of doing things in a certain way, and if like causes always produce like effects, then any man or woman who can do things in that way can become rich, and the whole matter is brought within the domain of exact science.

The question arises here as to whether this certain way may not be so difficult that only a few may follow it. As we have seen, this cannot be true (as far as natural ability is concerned). Talented people get rich, and blockheads get rich; intellectually brilliant people get rich, and very stupid people get rich; physically strong people get rich, and weak and sickly people get rich.

Some degree of ability to think and understand is, of course, essential, but insofar as natural ability is concerned, any man or woman who has sense enough to read and understand these words can certainly get rich.

Also, we have seen that it is not a matter of environment. Yes, location counts for something. One would not go to the heart of the Sahara and expect to do successful business.

Getting rich involves the necessity of dealing with people and of being where there are people to deal with, and if these people are inclined to deal in the way you want to deal, so much the better. But that is about as far as environment goes. If anybody else in your town can get rich, so can you, and if anybody else in your state can get rich, so can you.

Again, it is not a matter of choosing some particular business or profession. People get rich in every business and in every profession, while their next-door neighbors in the very same vocation remain in poverty.

It is true that you will do best in a business which you like and which is congenial to you. And if you have certain talents which are well developed, you will do best in a business which calls for the exercise of those talents.

Also, you will do best in a business which is suited to your locality: An ice cream parlor would do better in a warm climate than in Greenland, and a salmon fishery will succeed better in the northwest than in Florida, where there are no salmon.

But, aside from these general limitations, getting rich is not dependent upon your engaging in some particular business, but upon your learning to do things in a certain way. If you are now in business and anybody else in your locality is getting rich in the same business, while you are not getting rich, it is simply because you are not doing things in the same way that the other person is doing them.

No one is prevented from getting rich by lack of capital. True, as you get capital the increase becomes more easy and rapid, but one who has capital is already rich and does not need to consider how to become so. No matter how poor you may be, if you begin to do things in the certain way you will begin to get rich and you will begin to have capital. The getting of capital is a part of the process of getting rich and it is a part of the result which invariably follows the doing of things in the certain way.

You may be the poorest person on the continent and be deeply in debt. You may have neither friends, influence, nor resources, but if you begin to do things in this way, you must infallibly begin to get rich, for like causes must produce like effects. If you have no capital, you can get capital. If you are in the wrong business, you can get into the right business. If you are in the wrong location, you can go to the right location.

And you can do so by beginning in your present business and in your present location to do things in the certain way which always causes success. You must begin to live in harmony with the laws governing the universe.

A Summary of The Science

There is a thinking stuff from which all things are made, and which, in its original state, permeates, penetrates, and fills the interspaces of the universe.

A thought in this substance produces the thing that is imaged by the thought.

A person can form things in his thought, and by impressing his thought upon formless substance can cause the thing he thinks about to be created.

In order to do this, a person must pass from the competitive to the creative mind. Otherwise he cannot be in harmony with formless intelligence, which is always creative and never competitive in spirit.

A person may come into full harmony with the formless substance by entertaining a lively and sincere gratitude for the blessings it bestows upon him. Gratitude unifies the mind of man with the intelligence of substance, so that man's thoughts are received by the formless. A person can remain upon the creative plane only by uniting himself with the formless intelligence through a deep and continuous feeling of gratitude.

A person must form a clear and definite mental image of the things he wishes to have, to do, or to become, and he must hold this mental image in his thoughts, while being deeply grateful to the supreme that all his desires are granted to him. The person who wishes to get rich must spend his leisure hours in contemplating his vision, and in earnest thanksgiving that the reality is being given to him. Too much stress cannot be laid on the importance of frequent contemplation of the mental image, coupled with unwavering faith and devout gratitude. This is the process by which the impression is given to the formless and the creative forces set in motion.

The creative energy works through the established channels of natural growth, and of the industrial and social order. All that is included in his mental image will surely be brought to the person who follows the instructions given above, and whose faith does not waver. What he wants will come to him through the ways of established trade and commerce.

In order to receive his own when it is ready to come to him, a person must be in action in a way that causes him to more than fill his present place. He must keep in mind the purpose to get rich through realization of his mental image. And he must do, every day, all that can be done that day, taking care to do each act in a successful manner. He must give to every person a use value in excess of the cash value he receives, so that each transaction makes for more life, and he must hold the advancing thought so that the impression of increase will be communicated to all with whom he comes into contact.

The men and women who practice the foregoing instructions will certainly get rich, and the riches they receive will be in exact proportion to the definiteness of their vision, the fixity of their purpose, the steadiness of their faith, and the depth of their gratitude.

{Section 3}

HERMES—WHO WAS HE?

What then is God? The Good that naught can change.
What man? The bad that can be changed.
—Hermes Trismegistus, *The Book of Tat,* from the *Corpus Hermeticum*

As we have seen, many philosophic systems have been inspired by the Hermetic Wisdom teachings. The Golden Dawn, Rosicrucians, Kabbalists and Sufis are all connected to the Hermetic mind. The fields of art, science, medicine, music, literature and architecture have all been touched by the Hermetic hand.

We have encountered the seven Hermetic Laws in the chapter devoted to the New Thought movement book, *"The Kybalion* and the Seven Hermetic Laws."

But where do the Hermetic ideals originate? Who invented them?

Hermeticism is defined as a set of philosophical and religious beliefs based on the writings attributed to a man named Hermes Trismegistus. But this being named Hermes may not have been a man at all. It's a name for a God, an angel, an avatar, and a man, depending upon the scholar or school of belief. Greek scholars, Arabic scholars and European scholars all butt heads regarding Hermetic identities.

The most acceptable idea seems to be that Hermes was in fact several people over time, perhaps even a direct line of sons who took over their fathers' teachings and kept them alive in the hearts of mankind. No two scholars seem to agree upon exactly what that lineage was and who was involved.

Some of the older sources include such figures as Zoroaster, Orpheus, Mithra and Alaophemus.[14] More traditional lineages usually state the following order: Poimandres, Thoth, Hermes, Asclepius, Tat.[15]

---

14 Marsilio, Ficino, *Theologia Platonica.*
15 Marsilio, Ficino, *De potestate et sepientia Dei.*

> The most classic genealogy . . . starts the Hermes series with Thoth . . . His son was Agathodemon, who himself begat the second Hermes, called Trismegistus, whose son was Tat. Apollonius Rhodius tells us that Hermes, through his son Aithalides, was a direct ancestor of Pythagoras, but nothing is more uncertain than divine genealogies [16]

The lineages are primarily derived from the *Corpus Hermeticum* and the Hermetic writings. The writings are almost always a dialogue between two individuals. One addresses the other in such a way that they are handing down the knowledge. Other scholars hold that some of the Hermes in the lineage were translators.

Some say that Hermes Trismegistus and Thoth are two separate individuals; other scholars say they are one and the same.

Here are the different versions of Hermes through time:

Thoth

Known as the God of wisdom, learning, and communication, Thoth was the first Magus and the first medical doctor. Some put Thoth as far back as the perhaps mythical time of Atlantis, around 10,000 BC, while others count him in the party of angels who fell to earth after the historic "war in heaven."[17]

Most Egyptian scholars say that Thoth lived in Egypt some time between 2000 and 1200 BC, but even this is highly debated. Thoth is also known as Djehuti (or Tehuti), Dhutii, and possibly Ptath.[18] Djehuti is one of his older Egyptian names and comes from the root word "Dhu" or "Tehu" which is translated as the old Egyptian words for ibis.[19] Thoth is affiliated with the ibis in Egyptian religion, and was usually depicted with the head of this sacred bird. The ibis was often mummified by ancient Egyptians as a symbol of the god Thoth, and was also invoked against incursions invasions of serpents, said Herodotus and Pliny the Elder. Thoth was also usually shown holding either a caduceus or a feather and a scroll. The caduceus was a symbol of his power, and the feather and scroll were to denote his role as the "scribe" of the gods. (Later the symbol was usurped by the medical community.)

---

16 Faivre, Antoine, *The Eternal Hermes*.
17 As listed in the *Book of Enoch*.
18 Some scholars separate these and others do not.
19 Mead, G.R.S., *Thrice Greatest Hermes*.

Even the description of Thoth's appearance has many variants. He is sometimes shown as a baboon or a dog, and was said to be capable of taking on any form he wished.

> He was notorious for his ability to keep changing his shape and appearing as this or that, or simply as the whole of creation [20]

Thoth is a self-begotten god in the Egyptian creation myths. According to the *Egyptian Book of the Dead*, Thoth has no mother and no father; he's a sourceless entity. In other versions of Egyptian cosmology, Thoth is an aspect of Ra. Thoth was said to have created the world by speaking it into being: "Thoth speaks forth the divine word which creates the world."[21]

This action is much like the Judeo-Christian God who creates the world with the Word, and the Vedic God Brahma who announces "*Nada Brahma*" (the world is sound). For this reason, Thoth was acknowledged to be the "tongue of Ra."[22]

Thoth was in charge of all forms of communication and language; he is said to have originated the hieroglyph. According to the oldest medical documents, the Ebers papyrus of 1550 BC:

> Thoth, who bestows on him the gifts of his speech, who makes the books, and illumines those who are learned therein, and the physicians who follow him, that they may work cures.[23]

He is described in the Egyptian creation mythologies as "Logos," meaning "word," a name that was later applied to Hermes Trismegistus, and also to Jesus Christ. Thoth was known as the interpreter or translator. His role was to translate the word of God into a language that man could understand. For this reason, he was also known as the messenger of the gods.

For the Egyptians and the Greeks, all medicine originated with Thoth, who was also a lord of the underworld, the god of the moon, and a psychopomp (one who helped guide souls to the world of the dead). In the *Egyptian Book of the Dead*, Thoth tells

---

20 Kingsley, Peter, *From Poimandres to Jacob Bohme*.
21 Mead, G.R.S., *Thrice Greatest Hermes*.
22 Ibid.
23 Ibid.

Isis the secret of immortality by breathing it into her ear so that she may resurrect Osiris. Through this parable, Thoth became affiliated with the knowledge of immortality and resurrection; both play large roles in Hermetic literature.

Egyptologist Gaston Maspero offers this about Thoth the Egyptian:

> Thoth represented an ibis or baboon, was essentially a moon god, who measured time, counted the days, numbered the months and recorded the years. Lunar divinities, as we know, are everywhere supposed to exercise the most varied powers: they command the mysterious forces of the universe; they know the sounds words and gestures by which these forces are put in motion, and, not content with using them for their own benefit, they also teach their worshippers the art of employing them. Thoth formed no exception to this rule. He was the lord of the voice, master of words and books, possessor and inventor of those magic writings which nothing in heaven, on earth or in Hades can withstand. He had discovered the incantations which evoke and control the gods; he had transcribed the texts and noted the melodies of these incantations; he recited them with that true intonation which renders them all powerful, and every one, whether god or man to whom he imparted them, and whose voice he made true became like himself the master of the universe. He had accomplished creation, not by a muscular effort to which the rest of the cosmogonical gods primarily owed their birth but by means of formulas or even of the voice alone, the first time when he awoke in the Nu. The articulate word and the voice were believed to be the most potent of the creative forces, not remaining immaterial on issuing from the lips, but condensing, so to speak, into tangible substances, into bodies which were themselves animated by creative life and energy.

Hermes Trismegistus

Was he one or many, merging
Name and fame in one,
Like a stream, to which, converging
Many streamlets run?
Who shall call his dreams fallacious?

Who has searched or sought
All the unexplored and spacious
Universe of though?

Who in his own skill confiding.
Shall with rule and line
Mark the border-land dividing
Human and divine?

Trismegistus! Thrice times greatest!
How thy name sublime
Has descended to this latest
Progeny of time!

—Henry Wadsworth Longfellow, "Hermes Trismegistus"

The name Hermes Trismegistus first appears to us in Hermopolis, the Greek name for the Egyptian city of Khemmenu. The name Hermes Trismegistus was found on a statue in the temple of Thoth at Hermopolis.

Evidence of the worship of Hermes Trismegistus in this city dates back to 2000 BC, around the same time some scholars place Thoth in Egypt, which contributes to the confusion of their identities. By the time the Greeks built temples in Hermopolis, the name Hermes Trismegistus was used instead of Thoth. Was Hermes a god-like Thoth, since he was worshipped in temples? Or was Thoth the god and Hermes the man? Clement of Alexandria says that Hermes once lived as a man amongst the Greeks and was later deified: "Of those too who once lived as men among the Egyptians, but who have been made Gods by human opinion, Hermes of Thebes and Asclepius of Memphis [are among them]."[24]

Hermes Trismegistus was also said to have translated the writings of Thoth into Greek. The Greek word for interpreter or translator is *hermeneus*, based on the name Hermes. The name "Trismegistus" means thrice great. The meaning of this title is debated; some take it to mean there were three of him over time,

---

24 Mead, G.R.S. *Thrice Greatest Hermes.*

98

others take it for what was exclaimed in the Hermetic temples at the time of sacrifice: "Great! Great! Great!" Others say the name Trismegistus denotes Hermes' teachings of the trinity of God with one Godhead.[25]

Hermes Trismegistus was also said to be the father of Agathodaemon, a Greek deity usually represented by a snake. (In Greek mythology, Agathos Daimon or Agathodaemon was the god of the vineyards and wine. In his honor, wine was poured into the dirt before a meal, a tradition which still exists today in many cultures. Agathodaemon was later deemed the daemon of good luck, particularly of food and drink.) Agathodaemon was in turn said to have fathered the second Hermes. In this case, the Hermetic teachings were passed along the bloodline of a patriarchy. Of the Hermetic texts to be found in the *Corpus Hermeticum*, most were said to have been authored by Hermes Trismegistus specifically.

Francis Barrett, born in the late eighteenth century and author of the occult classic *The Magus*, had this to say about Hermes Trismegistus:

He was called Ter Maximus, as having a perfect knowledge of all things contained in the world (as his Aureus, or Golden Tractate, and his Divine Pymander shews) which things he divided into three kingdoms, viz. animal, vegetable, and mineral; in the knowledge and comprehension of which three he excelled and transmitted to posterity, in enigmas and symbols, the profound secrets of nature; likewise a true description of the Philosopher's Quintessence, or Universal Elixir, which he made as the receptacle of all celestial and terrestrial virtues. The Great Secret of the philosophers he discoursed on, which was found engraven upon a Smaragdine table, in the valley of Ebron. There is no doubt but that he possessed the great secret of the philosophic work; and if God ever appeared in man, he appeared in him, as is evident both from his books and his Pymander; in which works he has communicated the sum of the abyss, and the divine knowledge to all posterity; by which he has demonstrated himself to have been not only an inspired divine, but also a deep philosopher, obtaining his wisdom from God and heavenly things, and not from man.[26]

---

25 Suidas, as quoted ibid.
26 Barrett, Francis, *The Magus*.

General Albert Pike, the Confederate General and Grand Commander of Scottish Rite Southern Jurisdiction Freemasonry, wrote about Hermes in his iconic book, *Morals and Dogma*:

> Hermes Trismegistus invented many things necessary for the uses of life, and gave them suitable names; he taught men how to write down their thoughts and arrange their speech; he instituted the ceremonies to be observed in the worship of each of the Gods; he observed the course of the stars; he invented music, the different bodily exercises, arithmetic, medicine, the art of working in metals, the lyre with three strings; he regulated the three tones of the voice, the sharp, taken from autumn, the grave from winter, and the middle from spring, there being then but three seasons. It was he who taught the Greeks the mode of interpreting terms and things, when they gave him the name of [Hermes], which signifies Interpreter. In Egypt he instituted hieroglyphics: he selected a certain number of persons whom he judged fitted to be the depositories of his secrets, of such only as were capable at attaining the throne and the first offices in the Mysteries, he united them in a body, created them Priests of the Living God, instructed them in the sciences and arts, and explained to them the symbols by which they were veiled.

There is also the Greek god Hermes. And later, the Romans syncretized this god and called him Mercury. Some say that this Hermes is a different figure than Hermes Trismegistus, and others say he is the same. According to the *Oxford English Dictionary*, Hermes was a deity and was worshipped as such. Countless cults were affiliated with Hermes throughout Greece and parts of Europe. Hermes was recognized by the Greeks as the god of science, commerce, language and writing. He is shown with a caduceus, just as Thoth was by the Egyptians. Hermes, like Thoth, also served as a psychopomp, an escort for the dead to help them find their way to the afterlife.

Hermes was the trickster god, like Thoth, and could also shift his shape.

> A faceless prophet, Hermes possesses no concrete or salient characteristics, differing in this regard from most of the major figures of the Bible and the Quran.[27]

---

27 Faivre, Antoine, *The Eternal Hermes*.

And like Thoth, Hermes is credited with founding of the art of Healing:

> While modern physicians accredit Hippocrates with being the father of medicine, the ancient Therapeutae ascribed to the immortal Hermes the distinction of being the founder of the art of healing.[28]

In Greek mythology, Zeus was Hermes' father, and Maia was his mother. (We owe our month of May to Maia's namesake.) There are some, like Augustus Le Plongeon, who made the connection between Egyptian deities of Egypt and those from the Christian faith. Le Plongeon wrote that Maia was later used by Christians to become their Mary who bore Christ from virgin birth.[29] An interesting idea when we consider that Hermes was born of God also, having been sired by Zeus when he lays with a mortal woman. Le Plongeon was not alone in noting this similarity, as Justin Martyr points out;

> But as to the son of God called Jesus, even though he were only a man born in the common way, yet because of his wisdom worthy to be called Son of God . . . and if we say that he was born in a special way, beyond his common birth, begotten of God as word of God, let us have this in common with you who call Hermes the word who brings tidings from God.[30]

Asclepius

Asclepius was a skilled physician who practiced in Greece around 1200 BC. He eventually became deified as the Greek god of medicine, and was written about in Homer's *Iliad*. He is traditionally depicted as a bearded man holding a staff with his sacred single serpent coiled around it, resembling the caducei of Thoth and Hermes. (From the early sixteenth century onwards, the staff of Asclepius and the caduceus of Hermes were widely used as printers' marks, especially as frontispieces to pharmacopoeias in the seventeenth and eighteenth centuries.)

According to Greek mythology, Asclepius is the son of Apollo and the nymph Coronis. While pregnant with Asclepius, Coronis secretly took a second, mortal lover. When Apollo found out, he sent

---

28 Hall, Manly P., *The Secret Teachings of All Ages.*
29 Le Plongeon, Augustus, *Origin of the Egyptians.*
30 Mead, G.R.S., *Thrice Greatest Hermes.*

Artemis to kill her. With Coronis burning on a funeral pyre, Apollo felt pity and rescued the unborn child from the corpse. Asclepius was taught about medicine and healing by the wise centaur, Chiron, and was so skilled that he brought back one of his patients from the dead. Feeling that the immortality of the Gods was threatened, Zeus killed the healer with a thunderbolt. At Apollo's request, Asclepius was placed among the stars as Ophiuchus, the serpent-bearer.

From the teachings of Asclepius, medical schools called Asclepions developed. In these schools, patients were cured by sleeping with harmless Ascclepian snakes after receiving a ritual from priests known as "The Asclepiadae." The worship of Asclepius spread to Rome and continued as late as the sixth century.

Asclepius is a direct receiver in the Hermetic tradition, as outlined in the "Asclepiad," sometimes called "Sermon to Asclepius," of the *Corpus Hermeticum*. This passage relates to Hermes conferring knowledge upon Asclepius.

Enoch and Metatron

The *Book of Enoch* has always been of great significance to Freemasons and . . . certain rituals dating back to [1730–1794] identified Enoch himself with Thoth, the Egyptian god of wisdom.

—Graham Hancock, *The Sign and the Seal*

According to Kenealy,[31] the Jews viewed Enoch and Hermes Trismegistus as one and the same. It is claimed that Enoch ascended to heaven without dying, where he was transformed into the highest-ranking angel of the hierarchies. According to the Jewish Targum; "He ascended to heaven and God called him by the name Metatron, the Great Scribe."[32] The name Metatron comes from the Greek *meta thronon*, "the one who sits on the throne."

Metatron is the nearest person to God, serving him; on the one hand his confidant and delegate, on the other hand the representative of Israel before God. . . . Metatron is also known as *Sar ha-Panîm*, "the Prince of the Countenance" or just as "the Prince," and he sits in God's innermost chamber (*penim*).

---

31 Kenealy, E.Y., The Book of Enoch.
32 Etheridge, J.W., *Targum Pseudo-Jonathan and Onkelos to the Pentateuco.*

Only two biblical characters got to see heaven without dying—Moses and Ezekiel—but they didn't get to stay there, and they definitely did not get too close to God, though Enoch was venerated by God as more special than all men.

> When Enoch, under the guidance of the angel Anpiel, was carried from earth to heaven, the holy beings, the ofanim, the seraphim, the cherubim, all those who move the throne of God, and the ministering spirits whose substance is of consuming fire, they all, at a distance of six hundred and fifty million and three hundred parasangs, noticed the presence of a human being, and they exclaimed: "Whence the odor of one born of woman? How comes he into the highest heaven of the fire-coruscating angels?" But God replied: "O My servants and hosts, ye, My cherubim, ofanim, and seraphim, let this not be an offense unto you, for all the children of men denied Me and My mighty dominion, and they paid homage to the idols, so that I transferred the Shekinah from earth to heaven. But this man Enoch is the elect of men. He has more faith, justice, and righteousness than all the rest, and he is the only reward I have derived from the terrestrial world.[33]

Enki

In Sumeria, we find evidence of a Hermes-type god, who was first known as Ea, and then given the title Enki, or Lord of the Earth. His symbol was one or two snakes wrapped around a pole, or the caduceus—the same one carried by Thoth, Hermes and Asclepius. Enki was the Sumerian high god of water and intellect, creation, wisdom and medicine, who could restore the dead to life. He was the source of all secret and magical knowledge of life and immortality. Enki possessed "The Secret," and was said to be the deciding factor in the evolution of the human species by the ancient Sumerians. Enki, like Thoth, was known to the Sumerians as the God of Knowledge, Bringer of Wisdom, and Messenger of the Gods. Enki is also the trickster in Sumerian mythology, like Thoth and Hermes. Enki is said to have held the Tablet upon which the rules of the universe were written, the description of which is similar to both the *Emerald Tablet* and the tablets of Moses.

---

33 Ginzberg, Louis., *Legends of the Jews.*

Pythagoras

Pythagoras was a Greek philosopher who specialized in esoteric knowledge of mathematics, astronomy and the theory of music. He founded the Pythagorean Brotherhood and formulated principles that influenced the thoughts of Plato and Aristotle.

The story of the life of Pythagoras is a difficult one to sort out, on account of the legends and myths built up around him. The approximate date of his birth was 575 BC, and his death was near 490 BC. According to legend, he was a huge man of impressive strength with a birthmark on his thigh that was said to be a mark of divine favor. Some say he was directly related to Hermes, and was held in great esteem by him.

> He was once born as Aethalides and was considered to be the son of Hermes. Hermes invited him to choose whatever he wanted, except immortality; so he asked that, alive and dead, he should remember what happened to him. Thus, in life he remembered everything, and when he died he retained the same memories . . . . He remembered everything—how he first had been Aethalides, then Euphorbus, then Hermotimus, then Pyrrhus, the Delian fisherman. When Pyrrhus died, he became Pythagoras.[34]

Many marvel at the similarities between the Hermetic and Pythagorean material. The Hermeticist Johannes Kepler said that he was certain the either Pythagoras was a Hermeticist or that Hermes was a Pythagorean.

Although Pythagoras traveled the world, studying with adepts from many nations, his initiation took place in Hermetic Egypt. Pythagoras is said to have ventured to Miletus and to have been taught there by the mathematician Thales and the pre-Socratic philosopher Anaximander. Thales, who had been the first person to actually predict a solar eclipse, was then too old to teach as he wished, but strongly advised the younger man to pursue his studies further in Egypt.

Pythagoras booked passage on a ship and to Egypt. The fellows who owned the ship planned to kidnap Pythagoras for a slave. But Pythagoras did not eat or sleep for the entire journey,

---

34 Diogenes Laertius, *Lives of Eminent Philosophers.*

he just sat at the bow of the boat and watched the sea steadily. Because of his severe nature and concentrative powers, he was recognized as a holy man, and escorted to the temple upon his arrival in Egypt. In Egypt, Pythagoras repeatedly tried to gain entry into the Mystery Schools of that country. Finally he was told that unless he went through a training of fasting and breathing, he would not be allowed to enter. He complied, and finally he underwent the Hermetic initiation process under the teacher Sonchis. During this time, he received the great Hermetic lineage.

Cambyses II, the king of Persia, invaded Egypt in 525 BC and made Pythagoras his prisoner, sending him to Babylon. This didn't stop Pythagoras from continuing to learn, however, and for the next twelve years he studied and was initiated into the Chaldean Mysteries. Leaving Babylon, he made his way through Persia to India, where he continued his education under the Brachmanes. Although Pythagoras went to India as a student, he left as a teacher. Even to this day he is known in that country as Yavanâchârya, the "Ionian Teacher."

He then returned to Samos, only to discover its temples and schools closed and its wise men fleeing from the persecution of the Persian conquerors. Instead of being welcomed by his countrymen, Pythagoras found them indifferent to the wisdom he was eager to impart. He left Samos and settled in Crotona, Italy. It was here that he opened his own school and taught what he had learned in his world travels, particularly the Hermetic philosophy. The Hermetic teachings of Pythagoras went on to inspire Plato himself.

The first English translator of Plato's texts, Thomas Taylor, believed that Plato was initiated into the Egyptian mystery schools at the age of forty-nine, in the Great Pyramid of Giza. Plato's writings were criticized by the Egyptians for revealing many of the Hermetic mysteries to those outside the mystery schools.[35] Said Pythagoras:

> By the assistance and cooperation of spiritual powers and the capacities inherent in man, as a result of his divine origin, he may become capable of a higher sphere of activity (other than generally known) within as well as without himself, which will give him dominion over his own and over surrounding nature.

35 Hall, Manly P., *The Secret Teachings of All Ages*.

Moses and Akhenaton

[Hermes Trismegistus] was reported to have been king of Egypt; without doubt he was an Egyptian; nay, if you believe the Jews, even their
Moses; and for the justification of this they urge, first, His being well
skilled in chemistry; nay, the first who communicated that art to the
sons of men; secondly, They urge the philosophic work, viz. of render-
ing gold medicinal, or, finally, of the art of making aurum potabile;
and, thirdly, of teaching the Cabala, which they say was shewn him by
God on Mount Sinai: for all this is confessed to be originally written in
Hebrew, which he would not have done had he not been an Hebrew,
but rather in his vernacular tongue. But whether he was Moses or not,
it is certain he was an Egyptian, even as Moses himself also was; and
therefore for the age he lived in, we shall not fall short of the time if
we conclude he flourished much about the time of Moses; and if he really was not the identical Moses, affirmed to be so by many.[36]

Were Moses and Hermes one and the same? The Jewish scholar
Artapanus says there is no doubt that Moses was one of the Her-
meses to be included in the Hermetic lineage. According to Stra-
bon, the Alexandrian scholar, the Egyptian priest, the prophet Moses of their Israeli neighbors, had been an Egyptian ruler who established a monotheistic belief system and built a solar city before
being forced into exile. If we examine the life of Moses, we find
many similarities to that of Hermes and the Hermetic tradition.
Moses lived in Egypt around 2000 BC, the same time as Hermes
and Thoth. Moses was also an interpreter to God. Moses brought
down the word of God in human writing on the tablets of the Torah. Moses, like Hermes and Thoth before him, also had a staff with
a snake (Numbers 21:18), and his staff could even turn into a snake.

Moses received his serpent staff after his revelation at the
burning bush (Exodus 4:4), a story that reads like Hermes' encounter in the Hermetic text *The Divine Pymander*. Known in
Judaism as "The Rod of Aaron," Moses' staff has a long biblical
history. According to the *Haggadah*, it is a branch from the Tree
of Life that was given to Adam by God. Adam then passed it to
Shem, who gavs it to Enoch, who gave it to Abraham, who gave it
to Isaac, who gave it to Jacob. From Jacob, the staff was stolen by

---

36 Barrett, Francis, *The Magus*.

Jethro, who planted it in a garden, and it was in the garden that Moses received it. From Moses it went to Joshua, then to Phineas, who buried it in Jerusalem. And later it was given to Jesus Christ by Joseph.[37]

According to several sources, Moses was a priest of one of the temples of Thoth, and in his time there, he translated some of the materials, just as Hermes is said to have done.

A variety of archaeological, historical and mythological evidence from Egypt suggests Moses was a priest of the moon god Thoth. Artpanus notes that Moses was adopted by the princess Meroe, who was barren, and that he was called *hermes*, interpreter [of the sacred texts]. This would precisely explain the birth of the teachings of Moses in the form of the Word of God—the logos.[38]

Moses was, at one time, king of Ethiopia. According to Josephus, at one point during this time, Moses' enemies surrounded his city with poisonous snakes. Moses sent out an army of ibises to attack the snakes. This is an interesting directive, considering that the ibis is the symbol for Thoth. It is also intriguing that the original name of Ethiopia was Aith Ophia, which means "fiery serpent."[39] The Greeks knew the Aithophians to be serpent worshippers who were Phonecian in origin, of whom Thoth, or "Athothon" was one of their main deities.[40] This is particularly important because the original inscription of the *Emerald Tablet*, ascribed to Thoth, was said to be written in Phoenician.

Another popular theory has it that the Pharaoh Akhenaton was actually Moses.

Sir Matthew Finders Petrie, James Henry Breasted and Arthur Weigall were all present at the discovery of the tomb of Tutankhamen. In his book *Dawn of Consciousness*, Breasted noted many similarities between the writings of Akhenaton and the Old Testament, particularly Psalm 104 and the Proverbs. Sigmund Freud's research into this area was published in *Moses and Monotheism*. In this work, Freud asserts that it was without a

---

37 Michas, Peter A., *The Rod of an Almond Tree in God's Master Plan.*
38 King, Chris, *Sexual Paradox.*
39 Jennings, Hargrave, *Ophiolatreia.*
40 Ibid.

doubt that Moses was in some way related to Akhenaton, if not the Pharaoh himself.

Akhenaton ruled with his mother Tiy, who was determined to be of Hebrew origin, due to inscriptions around her tomb. Akhenaton tried to change Egyptians' religion, attempting to make it monotheistic, to unify it under one single God. This was essentially what Moses did with the Jews. The Egyptian name of Moses was Amen-mose or Thut-mose, which was the name of a lot of pharaohs, more specifically a lineage of pharaohs who were related to Akhenaton. Akhenaton was driven out of Egypt (much like Moses in the Exodus), and his mummy was never found. The mummies of his wife and his mother were also never found. We also find an interesting coincidence in that the city with the most statues of Akhenaton was the same city devoted to Hermes Trismegistus, Hermopolis.

ENTER CHRISTIAN DOCTRINE AND THE BURNING OF THE BOOKS

> But when the pendulum swings once more towards the side of synthesis, as it must do in the coming epoch—for we are but repeating today in greater detail what happened in the early centuries—then scholarship will once more recognize the unity of religion under the diversity of creeds and return to the original doctrine of the Hermetic Mysteries.
>
> —G.R.S. Mead, *Commentary on the Pymander*

Most people are aware that the Christians destroyed the pagans in Egypt. But what most people are not aware of is that the pagans in Egypt were mostly Hermetic. The word "pagan" simply means civilian, or rustic villager. It was used by the Romans to describe people who weren't Christians, or more specifically to refer to Romans who lived outside the cities and clung to the old Roman religion. However, the Hermeticists weren't the only ones to be rooted out and destroyed. The Christians erased all traces of Hermeticism by murdering the priests, burning the texts and outlawing the language. The destruction began with Emperor Constantine around the year 312 AD and continued well into the sixth century.

> The Christian empire was fully implicated in these actions . . . Constantine and his successors did the same . . . After 312 [AD], first Constantine, then his devout son, Constantius II (337–361), and finally, Theodosius I (379–395) progressively forbade public [pagan] sacrifices, closed temples, and colluded in frequent acts of local violence by Christians against major cult sites—of which the destruction of the gigantic Serapeum of Alexandria, in around 392, was only the most spectacular.[41]

The language that Thoth had brought to man, that of the hieroglyph, was forbidden, and so fell into obscurity. A language said to have been brought to man by the messenger of God was struck from the tongues of all men, seemingly forever. In 384 AD, the Roman emperor Theodosius ratified a decree abolishing all writing and reading of the *Medwneter*,[42] the "divine words" of the sacred language of the Pharaohs. For just over 1,400 years, hieroglyphs were to remain a mystery as a result of this decree. Then, in 1822, Jean-Francois Champollion, a young linguist from Figeac, France, made an important discovery among the items Napoleon Bonaparte had plundered from Egypt twenty-three years earlier: a slab of black basalt with writing on it. This slab was to become known as the Rosetta Stone, and provided the key to unlocking the mysteries of the hieroglyphs, for upon it was a the same passage written in Hieroglyphics, Demotic script and Greek. Champollion worked feverishly to decode the message, and when he was through, the world again had access to the divine words of Thoth.

The hieroglyphic language wasn't the only thing that died with Theodosius' decree; so did tens of thousands of Hermeticists. From 315 through 500 AD, thousands of pagans were declared void of all rights and slain. Holding pagan services became punishable by death in 356 AD. Theodosius was so thorough in his genocidal pursuit that he had children executed because they had been playing with remains of pagan statues. The Christian priests Cyril of Heliopolis and Mark of Arethusa destroyed hundreds of Hermetic temples all across Egypt, leaving only the husks of ruined columns in their wake.

---

41 Brown, Peter, *The Rise of Western Christendom*, 2nd Ed..
42 *Medwneter* was the Egyptian word for their language, while the word hieroglyph came to us from the Greeks (hieros = holy, glyphs = carving).

During the reign of Christian Emperor Theodosius, bands of wandering monks attacked synagogues, pagan temples, heretics' meeting places, and the homes of wealthy non-believers in Mesopotamia, Syria, Egypt, Palestine, and North Africa. The bishop of Alexandria incited local vigilantes to destroy the Temple of Serapis [also known as the Serapeum], one of the largest and most beautiful buildings in the ancient world, that also housed a library . . . . Alexandrian Christians whipped up by Bishop Cyril rioted against the Jews in 415 [AD], and then murdered Hypatia, a wise and beloved Platonic philosopher.[43]

The Pyre of Ancient Wisdom

What happened to all of the sacred Hermetic texts is mired in scholarly debate. No one is quite sure who burned the libraries and when. All we know for sure is that there were two main strongholds of Hermetic literature that were completely eradicated: the Great Library of Alexandria and the library of the Alexandrian Serapeum.

The Great Library of Alexandria is said to have been built around 250 BC. Many stories exist about how the library acquired its material, not all of them admirable. (Some sources say that ships entering the harbor were forced to give up any manuscripts they had on board and take copies instead.[44]) According to Demetrius Phalereus, the papyrus rolls in the collection numbered at least 200,000. Later, many more scrolls are mentioned.

In the time of Callimachos 490,000 rolls are mentioned; later, Aulus Gellius and Ammianus Marcellinus speak of 700,000 rolls. Orosius, on the other hand, speaks only of 400,000, while Seneca says that 40,000 rolls were burnt (probably an error for 400,000).[45]

It was the Egyptian Greeks who translated and recorded the Hermetic teachings in a manner in which they would spread throughout the globe. Here, many of the ancient Egyptian works were translated by Greek scholars into the Greek language and later into Latin and European languages. Unfortunately, the works of the Hermeticists in Alexandria, which the Greeks had worked so hard on, were

---

43 Rubenstein, Richard E., *When Jesus Became God: The Epic Fight over Christ's Divinity in the Last Days of Rome.*
44 *The Catholic Encyclopedia*, Volume I.
45 Ibid.

mostly destroyed. Only a precious few remain. Iamblichus stated that Hermes wrote 20,000 works, of which forty-two were left in the library of Alexandria. And of these forty-two, only a handful remain, which are referred to collectively as the *Corpus Hermeticum*. There is quite a bit of debate as to the exact time period in which the *Corpus Hermeticum* was actually written. Most place it some time during the heyday of Alexandria, before it was destroyed by the Christians. Walter Scott puts it shortly after 200 AD, while Sir W. Flinders Petrie places it between 200 and 500 BC. Carbon dating of the texts has met with mixed results.

The library was damaged several times throughout history, and the Christians are not the only ones to blame. The culprits included one Roman (Julius Caesar), one Christian (Patriarch Theophilus) and one Moslem (Caliph Omar of Damascus).

As the story goes, in 47 BC, Caesar set fire to his fleet to escape an Egyptian onslaught. The fire then spread through the city and into the library, destroying nearly half of the collection. Some say these scrolls had been stolen from the library proper and were actually sent to Rome. [46]

The Christian destruction, generally ascribed to Theophilus, was likelier to have destroyed the smaller library, at the Serapeum. Before Theophilus wreaked his havoc, several others attacked the library. In 272 AD, Aurelian destroyed much of the city and the palace quarter. This was so close to the library that many of the texts were damaged.

Whatever was left of the library was destroyed by the Muslim invasion in 642 AD. Alexandria surrendered to general Amrou, who lead the armies of Omar, Caliph of Baghdad. It was written by Abulpharagius that, on the orders of Omar Caliph, the entire collection of books stored at the Library of Alexandria were burned as fuel to heat the city's public baths.

The Alexandrian Serapeum was one of the largest temples in all of Alexandria. Within the temple was a large Hermetic library of approximately 50,000 papyri scrolls. Bishop Theophilus of Alexandria was an active patriarch of the church when Emperor Theodosius forbade the practice of pagan rites and the temples were taken over and converted into churches. In Alex-

---

46 Orosius.

andria, Bishop Theophilus took over the temple of Dionysus. Secret caverns containing various sacred Hermetic texts were discovered beneath the temple. The Hermeticists attempted to recover the texts, but were attacked by Christians and forced to retreat into the Serapeum. According to Eunapius, the Neoplatonist, a Christian mob destroyed the temple, massacred the inhabitants and stole what was left.

We know that some Hermetic texts did survive destruction, thanks to those who ran away with them or buried them deep within the earth. The two most important discoveries of these buried treasures in recent times are the Library of Nag Hammadi and The Dead Sea Scrolls. Who knows what other texts remain underground awaiting discovery. Perhaps the *Emerald Tablet* itself will be unearthed some day.

Although the Christians seem like the villains in all of this, they also suffered at the hands of pagans, though this was primarily from the pagan Roman emperors, and not from Hermeticists.

The pagan Roman retaliation against the Christians began with Emperor Nero in 64 AD. Under Emperor Nero's rule, it was punishable by death to even profess Christian faith. An arrested Christian's only hope for freedom was to offer incense on a Roman altar, but most preferred to die rather than renounce their faith, and thus the martyr was born. Those who refused to bow before the Roman gods were imprisoned, tortured, and even thrown to the lions in the Coliseum.

The persecution of Christians by the Roman empire was put to an end in 306 AD, when Constantine fought the three other emperors to turn Rome into a Christian republic. All of the emperors consented to this except one, Maximinius, who continued his persecutions of the Egyptian Christians until confronted and defeated by one of the other emperors, Licinius. Constantine's order, which gave religious freedom to all under his rule, is known as the "Edict of Milan." After this edict, Christianity quickly spread all over the Roman empire, including Egypt, and started its persecution of pagans as vengeance.

After instating Christianity as the state religion, emperor Constantine assembled the Council of Nicea, who was responsible for the New Testament as we know it today. They edited out all of the Gnostic and apocryphal texts that did not suit the church, and decreed all non-canonical scripture heretical. This Council was the largest gathering of Christian bishops in the history of the Church, and its main purpose was to eradicate all Gnostic and Platonic scripture from the teachings of Christianity.

When the Christian faith became a secularized, sacerdotal autocracy supporting the depraved Roman emperor Constantine, the hierarchy of priests and potentates of the Church found it necessary to concoct a system of dogmas which would separate Christian theology from Platonism. Thus the councils of Nicea and others and the resulting doctrinal monstrosities.[47]

In 367 AD, after the council had decided which texts to use, a letter was issued to all Christian churches, known as the "Easter Letter from Athanasius." Within the pages of the letter were listed the twenty-seven canonical New Testament books, and a stern warning to the faithful to read no others.

The Hermetic Christ

Scholars speculate that the reason for the extreme persecution of the Hermeticists was the similarities in the mythos and personalities of Christ and Hermes. One of them had to be eradicated.

Jesus and Hermes were both part of a lineage of the same wisdom tradition: Hermes was the first (to our knowledge) of the long line of Messiahs or Avatars—which included Osiris, Zarathustra, Confucius, Buddha, Moses, Melchizedek, Enoch and Abraham, up to Jesus—and it is held by competent occultists and taught by many schools that all were the continued incarnation of one and the same Sun Spirit. If we shall know them by their works, then we should observe that in the *Book of the Dead*, the *Book of Light*, the *Golden Mean*, the *Song Celestial* and the *Sermon on the Mount*, identical forces are suffused through all these holy texts.[48]

It is said by some historians that Jesus spent time in Egypt, where as a youngster he learned more than a few Hermetic

---

47 Livergood, Norman D., *The Perennial Tradition.*
48 Fr. K. X°, *Hermes Mercurius Trismegistus: A Treatise Preliminary to the Study of the Hermetic Philosophy.*

tricks.[49] The Coptic church teaches many apocryphal scriptures that detail the stay of the holy family in Egypt, but these were left out of the New Testament by the Nicean council.

Jesus and Hermes share the same title, "The Shepherd of Man." Hermes was the first to be given this appellation. There existed an ancient Greek cult called "Kriophoros," which means, "the ram bearer." This cult worshipped Hermes as the bearer of the ram and named him "Hermes Kriophoros." This moniker is based on a legend in which Hermes saved the city of Tanagra from a plague by carrying a ram around the walls. Statues of Hermes in this manner date back to 500 BC, predating all Christian depictions.

Hermes Kriophoros

Some of the earliest depictions of Christ, where he is seen as the "Good Shepherd" carrying the lamb upon his shoulders, are identical to those of Hermes Kriophoros. It is generally agreed that the figure of Jesus carrying a lamb is taken directly from the statues of Hermes Kriophoros.[50]

The prototype of Christ as the Good Shepherd reaches much further back than Jesus. Statues of Hermes as the Kriophoros, or Hermes with a ram or lamb standing beside him, or in his arms, or on his shoulder, were one of the most favorite subjects for the chisel in ancient Greece. We have specimens dating to the most archaic periods of Greek art.[51]

The other place we find reference to the Shepherd of Man title within the Hermetic tradition is in one of the foremost texts of the *Corpus Hermeticum: The Divine Pymander*, or Poimandres. This name, Poimandres, directly links Thoth the Egyptian and Hermes Trismegistus with the Shepherd, to give the reader an idea of the antiquity of this phenomenon.

The Caducei of Hermes, Moses and Jesus

One of the main symbols associated with Thoth, Moses and Hermes

---

49 According to the Gospels of Matthew, Mary and Joseph, baby Jesus fled to Egypt to escape Herod's massacre of the innocents. In the non-canonical "Infancy Gospels," the child Jesus performed many miracles in Egypt before returning to Palestine.
50 Pausanias, iv. 33
51 Mead, G.R.S., *Commentary on the Divine Pymander*.

is the caduceus. As incredible as it sounds, Jesus Christ is also depicted holding a caduceus. More than that, the emblem of Jesus on the cross is itself the caduceus. Origen (Exodus Chapter vii) states: "This rod of Moses, with which he subdued the Egyptians, is the symbol of the cross of Jesus, who conquered the world."

There is also a legend of the staff of Moses that not only puts it directly in Jesus' possession, but also places it on the cross of his crucifixion:

> This legend of the rod is given by the Syrian Solomon in his *Book of the Bee* ("Anecdota Oxoniensia, Semitic Series," vol. i. part ii). According to it, the staff is a fragment of the Tree of Knowledge, and was successively in the possession of Shem, of the three Patriarchs, and of Judah, just as in the Jewish legend. From Judah it descended to Pharez, ancestor of David and of the Messiah. After Pharez's death an angel carried it to the mountains of Moab and buried it there, where the pious Jethro found it. When Moses, at Jethro's request, went in search of it, the rod was brought to him by an angel . . . . Joshua received it from Moses and made use of it in his wars (Josh. viii. 18); and Joshua, in turn, delivered it to Phinehas, who buried it in Jerusalem. There it remained hidden until the birth of Jesus, when the place of its concealment was revealed to Joseph, who took it with him on the journey to Egypt. Judas Iscariot stole it from James, brother of Jesus, who had received it from Joseph. At Jesus' crucifixion the Jews had no wood for the transverse beam of the cross, so Judas produced the staff for that purpose[52]

Other accounts of Jesus as caduceus exist throughout history.[53] A passage in the New Testament compares Jesus with the caduceus in the Gospel of John, third chapter:

> And just as Moses lifted up the serpent in the desert,[54] so must the Son of Man be lifted up, so that everyone who believes in him may have eternal life.

---

52 "Book of the Bee" citation given in *The Jewish Encyclopedia*.
53 For more examples of these, see *The Cross in Tradition, History and Art* by William W. Seymour.
54 Exodus 21:8: And the LORD said unto Moses, Make thee a fiery serpent, and set it upon a pole: and it shall come to pass, that every one that is bitten, when he looketh upon it, shall live.

This concept of Jesus on the cross and the serpent on the cross being symbolically identical was probably most celebrated by an ancient Christian cult called the Ophites.

The Ophites are thought to have been a Gnostic faction of Christianity dating to about 100 AD. "Oph" is an ancient Greek root word for serpent, as stated earlier when describing the ancient word for Ethiopia, "Aithophia" (land of the fiery serpent). The Ophites had several sub-sects, the Naasseners (from the Hebrew *naasch*, meaning snake), the Sethians, the Mandaeans, the Borborites and the Perates. Of these, the Naasseners and the Sethians can claim a pre-Christian origin, and they worshipped the snake as a source of wisdom even before Jesus came to be. The Sethians existed in Egyptian Hermetic circles, and they worshipped Seth the serpent as the bringer of knowledge to Thoth. Here we find another link directly to the Hermetic traditions from the Christian Gnostics: "Seth . . . is known in Islam, and usually assimilated to Agathodaimon[55], who is one of the great figures of Hermetic literature."[56]

In the fourth century AD, the Christian church obliterated all the Ophites' texts that they could get their hands on. What we know of the Ophites comes mostly from the writings of their enemies and, thankfully, some texts uncovered from various places underground, such as the Nag Hammadi Library.

To the Ophites, the serpent brought knowledge to Adam and Eve in the garden of Eden, just as the Seraphim Poimandres brings knowledge to Thoth in *The Divine Pymander*.[57] According to Philaster:

The Church placed the Ophites, the Cainites, and the Sethites at the head of all heresies, because they owed their origin to the serpent (the devil). The Ophites, Cainites, Sethites, Naasseni, etc., declared the serpent of paradise to be wisdom itself, since wisdom had come to the earth through the knowledge of good and evil which the serpent had brought. Hence they exalted Cain and Seth, who they held were endowed with this knowledge, as the heroes of the human race.[58]

---

55 The Snake Daimon.
56 Doresse, Jean, *The Secret Books of the Egyptian Gnostics*.
57 And the Nagas bring knowledge to Buddha and Nagarjuna, and Quetzalcoatl (a plumed serpent) brings knowledge to the Aztecs.
58 From JewishEncyclopedia.com

Equating Jesus with the serpent may not be so strange if we consider the fact that they are related in the Hebrew Gematria. In the Gematria, each letter of the Hebrew alphabet is assigned its corresponding number value, and words with the same numeric value are said to be spiritually connected. The words NChSh, (serpent) and MShICh, (Messiah) have the same exact value: 358.

Jesus is also affiliated with the serpent through the auspices of Apollonius of Tyana, who had no small amount of influence on the Christian church. Apollonius gathered his wisdom from the Naga sages of Kashmir.[59] According to Phillimore, Apollonius founded a church connected to a branch of the Essene known as the Therapeuts and Nazarenes. Indeed, there was a group known as the Apolloniei, adherents of Apollonius, who actually survived some centuries after his death. These constituted what became the Christian church after the Council of Nicaea, so Apollonius did indeed begin Christianity based upon serpentine myths and traditions of the oldest order.

> From this we can see clearly that the serpent was either a forerunner of man or a distant copy of the Anthropos, and how justified is the equation Naas [the serpent] = Nous = Logos = Christ = Higher Adam.
>
> —Carl Jung, Collected Works, Vol. 9.

Further Usurpation of Pagan Symbols

As well as *being* the caduceus, there are many symbolic references to Christ *holding* a caduceus. In addition to the above-mentioned passage where Jesus comes into possession of the Rod of Moses, we can find connections between the caduceus and Jesus' constant companion, the shepherd's crook. The shepherd's crook became interchangeable with the caduceus in several points of history as Hermes evolved into the Good Shepherd:

> As Arcadia has been from time immemorial the great pasture-ground of Greece, so probably the most primitive character in which Hermes appeared, and which he never abandoned, was the pastoral. He is the lord of the herds, *epimélios* and *kriophoros*, who leads them to the sweet waters, and bears the tired ram or lamb on his shoulders, and assists them with the shepherd's crook, the *kerykeion*.[60]

---

59 Serpent
60 Farnell, Lewis R., *The Cults of the Greek States.*

Kerykeion is the Greek word for caduceus, the latter of which being the Roman appelation for this symbol. In some cases, depictions of the Greek *kerykeion* can be a bit different from that of the traditional caduceus, and it ends up looking more like the top portion of the symbol for the planet Mercury.

The crook and flail were the symbols of divine authority carried by Egyptian Pharoahs in state ceremonies. The crook and flail are Shepherd's tools, taken from Thoth's association with the "Good Shepherd." These were adapted and mainly held to symbolize Osiris, however nearly any Pharoah's mummy can be found holding them. So too does Jesus usurp this symbol with the caduceus as its origin.

We can find blatant references to the Christian caduceus still being carried today by the most venerated members of its church. A crosier, or pastoral staff, is carried by high-ranking Roman Catholic, Eastern Orthodox, Angelican and Lutheran prelates. Traditionally, it is held by a Bishop or Cardinal, although it used to be that even the Pope himself carried it with him at al times. This was gradually phased out and replaced with a crucifix by the time of Pope Innocent III's papacy in the eleventh century. A Bishop bears the crosier to symbolize himself as "shepherd of the flock of God," and uses it during every sacrament. The Christian crosier takes one of several forms, a mimic of the Hebrew letter *tau* or two intertwined serpents meeting with a cross at the center being the most popular. The serpents on the cross reference Moses' staff , and their similarity to the caduceus is clear.

It is strange that Jesus and Hermes both have these major symbolic depictions in common with their characters. Strange enough to point to a hidden lineage of the same teachings expressed by both avatars.

Another name that Jesus and Hermes/Thoth share, in addition to the Good Shepherd, is that of Logos (word). In the Gospel of John, he states:

> In the beginning was the Word, and the Word was with God, and the Word was God . . . . And the Word was made flesh, and dwelt among us, (and we beheld his glory, the glory as of the only begotten of the Father) full of grace and truth.

We cannot help but be struck at how similar this passage is to the Egyptian creation myth:

> Light streamed from the body of this Divine Child, banishing darkness to the far reaches of the universe. Like a phoenix with flaming plumage He arose, uttering a cry that shattered the eternal silence. This was the first sound—the first Word—and that Word manifested as a living God. Thoth was His name: the Self-Created, the Logos, Wisdom.[61]

The referral to Jesus as the Logos, many say, comes from the Platonic influence on Christianity. Platonism was inspired by Pythagoras, who learned at the Hermetic temples in Egypt. Both Jesus and Thoth/Hermes are the physical manifestation of the word of God. Thoth brings the word of God to man as the messenger, and Jesus brings the word of God to man as the Messiah. There are those who call Christ only a messenger and not the Messiah, namely the Jews and the Muslims. There is at least one Christian scripture that refers to Jesus as a messenger. In "The Shepherd of Hermas," at one time considered authoritative scripture, Jesus is depicted as an archangel, a messenger of God.

The Blending of the Holy Texts

> Here, then, we have another element in the Hermes idea. In fact, nowhere do we find a pure line of tradition; in every religion there are blendings and have always been blendings. There was unconscious syncretism (and conscious also) long before the days of Alexandria, for unconscious syncretism is as old as our race-bindings. Even as all men are kin, so are popular cults related; and even as the religion of nobler souls is of one paternity, so are the theosophies of all religions from one source.
>
> —G.R.S. Mead, Commentary on the Pymander

If one were to sit down and read the Old or New Testaments (or the apocryphal writings or the Nag Hammadi) and the *Corpus Hermeticum* at the same time, one would be struck by an immense number of similarities. Ficino noticed some of the more

---

61 Leitch, Aaron, *The Egyptian Creation Epic.*

striking passages between the Poimandres, the most celebrated of the Hermetic documents, and the book of Genesis. When the Old Testament is reported to have been first written (1200 BC), Hermeticism was rampant.

The most blatantly Hermetic passages can be found in the texts from the Nag Hammadi library unearthed in Egypt in 1945. These documents had been concealed in the late fourth century, most likely by someone who was afraid the texts would be destroyed by heresy-hunting true believers. Perhaps one of the most famous texts from the Nag Hammadi treasure trove was the Gospel of Thomas. In the pages of the Gospel of Thomas we find the ever-famous words of the *Emerald Tablet*: "As above, so below."

> The Lord did everything in a mystery . . . . He said, "I came to make the things below like the things above, and the things outside like those inside. I came to unite them."
>
> Jesus saw infants being suckled. He said to his disciples, "These infants being suckled are like those who enter the kingdom." They said to him, "Shall we then, as children, enter the kingdom?" Jesus said to them, "When you make the two one, and when you make the inside like the outside and the outside like the inside, and the above like the below, and when you make the male and the female one and the same, so that the male not be male nor the female female; and when you fashion eyes in the place of an eye, and a hand in place of a hand, and a foot in place of a foot, and a likeness in place of a likeness; then will you enter the kingdom."

Compare this with the line from the *Emerald Tablet*:

> That which is above is from that which is below, and that which is below is from that which is above, working the miracles of one. As all things were from one.[62]

This declaration of "God is One" is a common theme in nearly all spiritual literature, including Hermetic, Judaic, Christian and Muslim. The Christians are commonly assumed to have stolen this from either the Jews or the Hermeticists.

---

62 From the Jabir ibn Hayyan translation.

> The acclamation "God is One," used by the earliest Christian com-
> munities . . . is derived from one employed in the service of Serapis
> ("One is Zeus-Sarapis" [Egypto-Hellenistic]), and this in turn comes
> from the early Egyptian theologians' form ("One is Amon," etc.).[63]

Another similarity is that both Jesus and Hermes perform the miracle of walking on water. We can read about Jesus doing this in the Gospels of John, Matthew and Mark. Dennis R. MacDonald, in his book *The Homeric Epics and the Gospel of Mark*, argues that Mark may have based his story in part on some of the elements in the tale of Hermes' flight to King Priam in Homer's *Iliad*. There are also interesting correlations between beginnings and endings to be found in both sets of literature:

> "I am the Alpha and the Omega," says the Lord God, "who is, and
> who was, and who is to come, the Almighty."
> —Book of Revelation, 1:8

> "I am the Universe, Past, Present and Future; no mortal made the
> acquittance of me."
> —Sanctuary of Neith in Sais (Plutarch and Proclos)

Ficino, Lactantius and Augustine all stated that the *Corpus Hermeticum* was simply a prophecy of the arrival of Christ in order to explain the unnerving similarities found within the writings. They used these texts in their minds to further validate Christian doctrines as truth. But it is impossible to ignore the remarkable similarities in the symbolism and metaphors which these two teachings attempt to convey.

Jesus' teachings concerning the necessity of spiritual rebirth unmistakably parallel the Hermetic and Platonic writings, as well as other embodiments of the Perennial Tradition such as alchemy and Sufism. Plato saw philosophy (the search for wisdom) as the actual achievement of a higher state of consciousness, gained through self-discipline and mystical contemplation. According to Plato, *philosophia* is the actual practice of learning to leave the body and live in the soul, the spiritual body.

---

63 Morenz, Seigfreid, *Egyptian Religion.*

Hermetic Influence on Christian Scripture

There are logical explanations as to why these two doctrines of theology could have so much in common. Namely, Christianity and its gospels developed for the most part in the Hermetic hub, Alexandria, where Christians, Jews, Arabs, Hermeticists and other pagans studied side by side. In the early church, Alexandria was considered the international center of the highest learning and scholarship. By the fourth century, Alexandria became the biggest seat of Christian learning in the world. Greek-speaking Christians constituted the greater part of the early Church, and since Greeks were already prominent scholars in North Africa as well as the Mediterranean, it is not difficult to see how they influenced the rapid spread of Christianity once they converted. Greeks and Romans made the rise of Christianity as a world religion possible.

The influence of Alexandria and the Hermeticists began even before the New Testament, with the first translation of the Hebrew Old Testament into Greek:

> The Greek translation of the Old Testament [was] made at Alexandria and known as the *Septuagint* (third to second century BCE) on account of the seventy translators employed on it. This eventually became almost a kind of holy writ for Christians. It can be demonstrated that the place of translation left its mark on many passages . . . it is in Septuagint that we find an invocation unknown to Israelite or Judaic theology: *"Lord, lord, king of the gods."*[64] This may be explained without difficulty if one assumes that the translators had in mind a designation of God which combined two proper names with the title "king of the gods." (*Kudios* also renders the proper name of Yahveh.) This is precisely the case with Amon-Rasonther, i.e. "Amon-Re, king of the gods," who at that time was still important..[65]

This translation was commissioned specifically for its inclusion in the library of Alexandria, to be used by scholars of all faiths. The version of the *Septuagint* most used by Christians today was prepared by Origen, a Christian scholar in Alexandria around

---

64 "I prayed therefore unto the Lord, and said, O Lord, lord, king of the gods, destroy not thy people and thine inheritance . . . —Deuteronomy 9:25 (*Septuagint*)
65 Morenz, Seigfried, *Egyptian Religion.*

235 AD. This version is commonly referred to as the "Hexapla." Origen made several changes to the originals, inserting various Platonic ideals, and it is not know to what extent they differ from the originals. Plato was the famous pupil of Socrates and, like Socrates, an initiate of the Pythagorean and Orphic tradition, which was Hermetic in origin. Many of the early church Fathers, such as Clement of Alexandria, Marcion, Valentinus, and Origen, were profoundly influenced by Plato's teachings. Because of this, early Christianity was inherently infused with Platonic (and therefore Hermetic) ideology.

Origen was one of the most distinguished early fathers of the Christian Church. His name is Graeco-Egyptian in origin and means "Horus-born" (Horus being one of the primary dieties in the Egyptian religion), an ironic name for a Christian scholar. Origen was an ardent Platonic idealist, and felt that the material world should be forsaken. He was so zealous in his beliefs that he is rumored to have self-castrated, eliminating any possibility that physical desires should hinder him. Origen studied the Gnostic scriptures intensely, but made sure to temper these ideas with Christianity, so as not to lose favor with the church. His references to the similarites between Hermeticism and Christianity are thinly veiled, and J.M. Roberts' work, *Origen Stating Christianity and Paganism are Identical* makes this quite plain.

In 250 AD, Origen was included among those who suffered for having any trace of Hermeticism in their work. Although his works were destroyed in some areas, this did not prevent him from becoming a major influence in the church, and his works were critically acclaimed and venerated.

Two other early church fathers who helped bring Hermetic ideology into the Church were Justin Martyr and Augustine. Justin Martyr (105–165) wrote *First Apology*, which incorporated Greek Hellenistic ideals into Christian Theology. He essentially used Greek philosophy as the stepping-stone to Christian philosophy. His Greek influences included Pythagoras, Plato, Plotinus, Aristotle and Stoicism. Augustine (354–430), the medieval mystic, wrote *De Trinitate, Confessions*. Augustine brought Platonism and Christianity together, emphasizing that the soul's search for God was made possible by the illumination of the mind of God.

Horny Angelic Beings

(Opposite Page Top) The Horned Moses
(Opposite Page Bottom) Adam Kadmon, The Hermetic Hermamphodite
(This Page) Moses Serpent

THE STAFF OF HERMES

(This Page clockwise from top left)
The Staf Of Hermes, King Solomon, Hermes Angel

Emerald Tablet

REJUVENATION

Vol. III　　　DECEMBER, 1922　　　No. III

SPECIAL ARTICLES

ETHEL STAAL

Rejuvenation Magazine, 1922

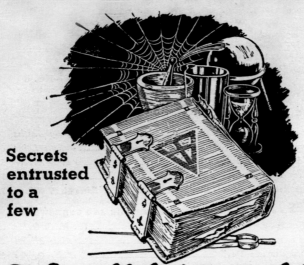

Secrets entrusted to a few

The Unpublished Facts of Life

THERE are some things that cannot be generally told—*things you ought to know.* Great truths are dangerous to some—but factors for *personal power* and *accomplishment* in the hands of those who understand them. Behind the tales of the miracles and mysteries of the ancients, lie centuries of their secret probing into nature's laws—their amazing discoveries of *the hidden processes of man's mind,* and *the mastery of life's problems.* Once shrouded in mystery to avoid their destruction by mass fear and ignorance, these facts remain a useful heritage for the thousands of men and women who privately use them in their homes today.

THIS FREE BOOK

The Rosicrucians (not a religious organization) an age-old brotherhood of learning, have preserved this secret wisdom in their archives for centuries. *They now invite you to share the practical helpfulness of their teachings.* Write today for a free copy of the book, "The Mastery of Life." Within its pages may lie a new life of opportunity for you. Address: Scribe B.M.M.

```
┌---- SEND THIS COUPON ----┐
│ Scribe B.M.M.                           │
│ The ROSICRUCIANS (AMORC)                │
│ San Jose, California                    │
│ Please send me the free book, The Mastery│
│ of Life, which explains how I may learn to│
│ use my faculties and powers of mind.    │
│ Name.................................   │
│ Address..............................   │
│ City.................................   │
└-----------------------------------------┘
```

The Rosicrucians (AMORC)   SAN JOSE, CALIFORNIA, U.S.A.

3

Vivekananda

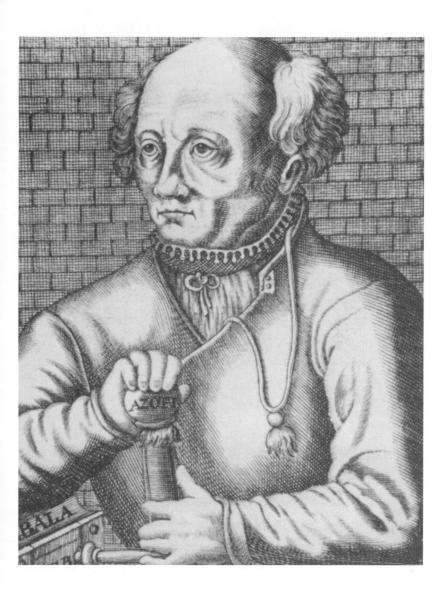

Paracelsus

(This Page clockwise from top)
Mesmer, Animal Magnetism, Svengali and Trilby

Stop Forgetting ad

SUCCESS
MAGAZINE
AUGUST 1908

SUCCESS UNLIMITED

THE MAGAZINE WITH ~~VE~~ MENTAL ATTITUDE

60¢
SEPT.
1972
47366

YOGA:
THE 4,000 YEAR-OLD
SUCCESS SECRET

FIVE
ROADBLOCKS
TO YOUR
PROMOTION

A 6,000 WORD
BOOK CLASSIC
HOW TO MAKE
OTHERS LISTEN
PLUS
HOW TO DRESS
FOR SUCCESS
THIS FALL

Success Magazine; 1908 (left), and 1972

Cabala

Robert Fludd illustrating the connection of mind and body to god

THOUGHT CHART

WHAT STREAM OF THOUGHT ARE YOU TUNED INTO AT THE

MOMENT?

Universal Thought Chart  Copyright 1950 Haydn Cooks

HEALTH - UNDERSTANDING GRACE - WISDOM SPIRITUAL POWER - SERENITY — Complete Reliance on God

			Sense of
UNSHAKABLE CONFIDENCE	THE MIGHT OF RIGHT	RESISTLESS GOOD	Sense of God Power
SENSE OF STRENGTH	ACTIVE SENSE OF UNITY	ASSURANCE	Awareness of the indwelling Christ
PRAISE / PRAYERFUL	WILLING COOPERATION	GENEROSITY	Sense of GRATITUDE
GENTLENESS - HUMILITY FIDELITY - WARMTH	PATIENCE APPRECIATION		LOVE
CONCRETE HELPFULNESS	MATERIAL & MENTAL	HELP BEYOND DUTY	Sense of SERVICE
SPIRITUAL VISION JOYOUS EXPECTANCY	EVIDENCE OF GOOD THINGS NOT SEEN	DAWNING SENSE OF GOD POWER	FAITH
TRUTHFULNESS		SCRUPULOUS EXACTNESS	Sense of JUSTICE
UNFAIR USE OF POWER	GET AS MUCH AS YOU CAN	UNFAIR COMPETITION	Spiritual Indifference
EXPECTING DISHONESTY	GIVE AS LITTLE AS YOU CAN	TRUTHFUL WHEN CONVENIENT	Every Man for Himself

DANGER

TIME IS NOT RIPE	NO OPPORTUNITIES	I SUFFER FOR OTHERS MISTAKES	SENSE OF PERSECUTION	SELF PITY
SELF CONDEMNATION	LOST OPPORTUNITIES	AFRAID TO TRY		FEAR
DESIRE TO DESTROY	STUPID & UNTRUE CONCLUSIONS	DANGEROUS DECISIONS		ANGER
DISTORTS EVERYTHING	IT IS ANGER and SELF PITY GONE STALE	DEFACES BEAUTY		Bitterness
SELFISHNESS	BRUTALITY	CONTEMPT FOR RIGHT or JUSTICE		REVENGE
MENTAL·PHYSICAL·SOCIAL, FINANCIAL CRASHES · PLOTS · LYING · POISONING THOUGHTS				HATRED
DISASTER DEATH	NARCOTICS HOPELESSNESS	CRIME RECKLESSNESS		Abandonment

LOVE · TRUTH · PEACE SECURITY · SUCCESS — SEX Masculine and Feminine Quality of Thought — Complete Reliance on God

Sense of				
Sense of God Power	HEALING	ACCOMPLISHMENT	UNFAILING SUPPORT	ETERNAL SUPPLY
Awareness of the indwelling Christ	SENSE OF ALIVENESS	SENSE OF ETERNAL COMPANIONSHIP		LIGHT
Sense of GRATITUDE	THANKFULNESS FOR ALL	SEES MULTIPLIED BLESSINGS EVERYWHERE		HAPPY TO BE ALIVE
LOVE	JOYOUS CONTEMPLATION OF LIFE	GRACE TENDERNESS DEVOTION		HOPETH ALL THINGS
Sense of SERVICE	TOLERATION	COOPERATION SYMPATHY	GIVING FOR THE JOY OF GIVING - NO OTHER REWARD	
FAITH	HOPE FOR EXPRESSION BEYOND OUR NORMAL CAPACITY		SUSTAINING BELIEF IN GOD - POWER	
Sense of JUSTICE	FAIRNESS · HONESTY	SENSE OF RESPONSIBILITY		RELIABILITY
Honest but Selfish	INORDINATE LOVE OF MONEY	Unpleasantly Aggressive Business Methods	SQUEEZE THE LITTLE MAN	
Always Critical				CURSE THE BIG MAN

ZONE

SELF PITY	INACTION WEAKNESS	ALWAYS SOMEONE ELSE TO BLAME FOR MY DISCOMFORTS OR FAILURES			LAZINESS
FEAR	INSECURITY FAILURE	LACK OF BELIEF IN ONES OWN CAPACITY	SICKNESS		SUSPICION
ANGER	BIASED JUDGEMENT	HASTY ACTION	LACK OF CONTROL		RUTHLESSNESS
Bitterness	TAINTS AND DISCOLORS EVERY DEPARTMENT OF ONES LIFE				
REVENGE	MENTAL STOPPAGE	FUTILITY			LACK OF MENTAL RESOURCE
HATRED	STUPIDITY BLIND FURY	MENTAL ABSCESS	MISERY	CRUELTY	MURDER
Abandonment	FAMILY NEGLECT	BUSINESS NEGLECT	CONFUSION DRINK		SEX

Thought Chart

THOUGHT VIBRATION

OR

THE LAW OF ATTRACTION IN THE THOUGHT WORLD

BY

WILLIAM WALKER ATKINSON

PREFACE BY FRANKLIN L. BERRY

"The Law of Attraction is a real thing, and many are using it consciously or unconsciously, some having learned to make use of it by observation and reason, while others have stumbled on it or have had it unfolded from the depths of the sub-conscious or super-conscious.

"I BELIEVE that the mind of Man contains the greatest of all forces, that Thought is one of the greatest manifestations of energy.

"I BELIEVE that the man who understands this law, can make of himself practically what he will.

"I BELIEVE that not only is one's BODY subject to the control of the mind, but that, also one may change environment, 'luck,' circumstances.

"When we think, we set into motion vibrations of a very high degree, but just as real as the vibrations of light, heat, sound, electricity, etc. And when we understand the law governing the production and transmission of these vibrations, we will be able to use them in our daily life just as we do the better known forms of energy."

WHAT IS IT ABOUT?

IT'S about the "mighty law that draws to us the things we desire or fear, that makes or mars our lives"; about "positive" and "negative" thought, and how to "rise to the upper chamber of your mental dwelling"; about Active and Passive Mentation, and "the attraction of THE ABSOLUTE"; about mind-building and the conquest of the lesser self by the Real Self; about Will Power; about Fearthought and how the man who fears, calls into operation the wonderful Law of Attraction to his own disaster; about Worry, the offshoot of Fear, and how to transmute it into golden metal; about asserting the Life Force, and the laws of Mental Control; about our Subconscious Mentality and how to set it to work; about Emotions and what to do with them; about eradicating undesirable states of feeling and how to develop new brain cells that will manifest along desirable lines; about Desire, that "Manifestation of the Universal Life Love"; about Energy and Invincible Determination, the two qualities "which sweep away mighty barriers and surmount the greatest obstacles"; about the great people of the world and why they ARE great; about the Law of Attraction and how it "takes you in earnest"; about the difference between the Slave of Circumstances and the Master of Circumstances; about Failure and how to bring it to you, IF YOU WANT IT; about Chance—which never was—and Law, which ever is; about The Causeless Cause, which is back of all Law; and about the Create and the Uncreate.

IS THAT ENOUGH?

The book assembles the most forceful work from Mr. Atkinson's pen since the memorable year of 1902. It is clear, vigorous, free from technicalities or affectation, intensely practical and written in Mr. Atkinson's inimitable, sparkling, intimate style. He is not speaking in dignified tones to "the public"; but in the language of a friend, to YOU. If we haven't received an order from you for this vital book, "DO IT NOW!"

PRICE $1.00, POSTPAID

Twenty-four hours' examination permitted, and "*money back if you don't like it.*" PERFECTLY SAFE PROPOSITION FOR US. Address,

Louise Radford Wells, Manager, THE LIBRARY SHELF, 1299 Farwell Ave., Chicago

William Walker Atkinson ad

{Section Four}

THE SOURCE OF THE SOURCE: HOLY KNOWLEDGE OR DEMONIC INSURRECTION?

Now that we have explored written history regarding Hermes and Thoth, the question remains: where did their information originate?

A serpent, a giant fiery serpent with wings.

In *The Divine Pymander*, one of the main texts from of the *Corpus Hermeticum*, Thoth is given the Hermetic information by Poimandres, a huge, fiery, winged serpent.[66]

> Hermes, while wandering in a rocky and desolate place, gave himself over to meditation and prayer. Following the secret instructions of the Temple, he gradually freed his higher consciousness from the bondage of his bodily senses; and, thus released, his divine nature revealed to him the mysteries of the transcendental spheres. He beheld a figure, terrible and awe-inspiring. It was the Great Dragon, with wings stretching across the sky and light streaming in all directions from its body. [The Mysteries taught that the Universal Life was personified as a dragon.] The Great Dragon called Hermes by name, and asked him why he thus meditated upon the World Mystery. Terrified by the spectacle, Hermes prostrated himself before the Dragon, beseeching it to reveal its identity. The great creature answered that It was *Poimandres*, the Mind of the Universe, the Creative Intelligence, and the Absolute Emperor of all.[67]

The teacher of Thoth, then, is a gigantic serpent, who is also considered the mind of the world. The notion that knowledge originates from serpents is certainly not a novelty; holy books of nearly every religion refer to knowledge gained from some kind of serpent.

---

66 Some scholars actually identify Thoth and Poimandres as being one and the same.
67 Hall, Manly P., *The Secret Teachings of All Ages*.

> Ophiolatreia, the worship of the serpent . . . is one of the most re-
> markable . . . forms of religion the world has ever known. There is
> hardly a country of the ancient world where it can not be traced,
> pervading every known system of mythology . . . Babylon, Persia,
> Hinduostan, Ceylon, China, Japan, Burmah, Java, Arabia, Syria, Asia
> Minor, Egypt, Ethiopia, Greece, Italy, Northern and Western Europe,
> Mexico, Peru and America.[68]

The ancient Rishis in India were said to gain knowledge from the Nagas, which are huge serpents. Buddha himself was taught and protected by a Naga. Quetzalcoatl, a winged serpent, imparted knowledge to the ancient Aztecs. Egypt especially is flooded with depictions of winged serpents. In the Hieroglyphic language, the symbol for Thoth and Hermes takes the form of a staff, a caduceus, made up of two intertwined serpents.

In Egypt, the serpent permeated nearly all facets of divinity:

> The Serpent entered into the Egyptian religion under all his charac-
> ters—of an emblem of divinity, a charm or oracle and a God . . . . The
> Divine spirit dominated Kneph and described him as the original,
> eternal spirit, pervading all creation, whose symbol was a serpent.[69]

Why place faith in a serpent, and one with wings? Why should such an entity find itself the object of such veneration all over the globe? Is this being essentially a dragon, a creature that permeates mythologies of all races?

There comes a point where a schism erupts when trying to determine the source and nature of the Hermetic wisdom. Depending upon which scholar you are studying, and from what religious background, the angels that bring the teachings of Hermes to mankind may be either good or evil. In Alexandria, the Hermetic teachings are shared with the Christians, the Jews and the Muslims. These three religions ascribe the source of the Hermetic teachings to angelic deities, but the nature and intent of these deities is not always beneficial to mankind. And within the Christian religion, we have on one hand the Catholic church pronouncing

---

68 Jennings, Hargrave, *Ophiolatreia*.
69 Ibid

the teachings Satanic, while on the other hand, some of the most adroit Christian mystics (like Thomas Aquinas) swear by them.

Interesting passages of winged serpents come to us in the Old Testament in Isaiah, Deuteronomy and Numbers.[70] The Hebrew word used specifically for fiery flying serpents is Seraphim, which also refers to a group of angels. The Seraphim are the highest order of angels in the hierarchy, as they are the angels of love, light and fire, and are in direct communication with God at all times. They are His messengers, His translators, His interpreters, and are often described as being serpentine in form.[71]

It is said that whoever laid eyes on a Seraph would be incinerated because of its brightness, so they may not be viewed directly. Consider that Poimandres changes from a giant serpent into a pillar of blinding light in front of Thoth. Could it be that Thoth and Hermes received their information directly from an angel?

Hermes the Angel

> For Lactanius, then, Hermes was very ancient; moreover, he was one who descended from heaven and had returned thither.
>
> —G.R.S. Mead, *Thrice Greatest Hermes*

Is it possible that Hermes himself was an angel? The oldest words for angels all translate to mean "Messenger of God."[72] This is exactly the role of both Thoth and Hermes Trismegistus. Angels are messengers, bringing and translating God's message to mankind. The Seraphim are the translators of God's word, just like Thoth and Hermes.

Raphael was the third angel to be referred to by name, and his name means "God has healed." In images, he can often be seen holding the caduceus, or the serpent on the cross.

Each of seven Archangels is said to rule one of the seven main planetary bodies. Raphael rules over the planet Mercury,[73]

---

70 In Numbers, Chapter 21, we read that the wandering Israelites continued to complain about their living conditions until the Lord sent "fiery serpents among the people, and they bit the people; and much people of Israel died."
71 [from what part of the Bible is this?] Acknowledging their sinfulness to Moses they asked the prophet to pray that the Lord "take away the serpents from us." The Lord told Moses to make a fiery serpent and set it on a pole, "and it shall come to pass, that every one that is bitten, when he looketh upon it, shall live." Following the Lord's directive, Moses made a "serpent of brass, and put in on a pole" and those who "beheld the serpent of brass" lived.
72 The Hebrew word for angel is *malakh*, and means messenger as well
73 Also, Mercury is the planet closest to the sun, as Hermes is closest to God.

which has the Roman name of Hermes. Raphael, like Hermes, is affiliated with language, intelligence, writing and communication, and is an Archangel of the east, mentioned by name in the Book of Tobit and the Book of Enoch.

Hermes and Raphael's role from the beginning was to help man to sort out the cryptic nature of God's wishes, thus aiding man to come into better relation with the universe:

> That Hermes is, in our hymn, called the redeemer is because it is through the Understanding of divine things that man is alone able to achieve his redemption. The name, which signifies both rock and interpreter, implies that the rock on which the true Church is built is neither a person nor a spirit of credulity, however devout, but the Understanding. Like the Hebrew Raphael, to whom he corresponds, Hermes is called also the physician of souls, in token that a right understanding of divine things is indispensable to the soul's health and welfare.[74]

Adam, the Hermaphrodite Angel

A mystery unfolds when we examine the Old Testament's first man, Adam, and his kabbalistic origins. Scholars have noted the similarities of Thoth and Adam, so the history of Adam becomes pertinent to our attempt to identify the Hermetic source. Both Thoth and Adam receive knowledge via a serpent.

Thoth is responsible for the naming of things, and according to the Old Testament, so is Adam:

> And out of the ground the LORD God formed every beast of the field, and every fowl of the air; and brought them unto Adam to see what he would call them: and whatsoever Adam called every living creature, that was the name thereof. And Adam gave names to all cattle, and to the fowl of the air, and to every beast of the field.
>
> —Genesis 2:19–2:20

In another striking similarity, both Adam and Thoth are hermaphrodites, containing both the male and the female sex or-

---

74 Maitland, Edward, *The Bible's own Account of Itself.*

gans. This feature also happens to be shared by all of the angels in heaven. The word hermaphrodite itself has Hermetic origins, as it combines the names Hermes and Aphrodite, both of whom were portrayed as androgynous in their temples. In the *Corpus Hermeticum*, it is written that an androgyne created the first man:

> An androgynous *Nous* sends forth a demiurge *Nous* . . . . Then the first *Nous* produces his favorite son, the first man, like to itself, that is, bisexual . . . .Physis embraces him passionately and gives to the world seven androgynous beings corresponding to the seven planets. These men become the leaders of the peoples, whose gods are the lords of the planets and of destiny. When the time was accomplished, the *Nous* decided to divide the double beings into male and female, whom he ordered to unite and multiply."[75]

In Hermetic philosophy, the hermaphrodite conjoins two opposing universal forces—yin and yang, male and female, hot and cold—to symbolize the original cohesive form of matter and the return to unity with the creator. When the Great Work, the alchemical Hermetic operation, is completed, the individual would return to the form of the first man, Adam, and unite all opposing forces of the universe into one harmonious state of being. This principle of unifying the sexes extended not only into Jewish Kabbalistic traditions, but, surprisingly, can also be found in Christian dogma, particularly in the works of Clement of Alexandria. "When the two shall be one, the outside like the inside, the male with the female neither male nor female."[76]

> This is the unity of primal creation, before the making of Eve, when man was neither male nor female. According to the Gospel of Philip, the division of the sexes—the creation of Eve taken from the body of Adam—was the principle of death. "Christ came to re-establish what was thus [divided] in the beginning and to reunite the two. Those who died because they were in separation he will restore to life by re-uniting them![77]

75 Delcourt, Marie, *Hermaphrodite*.
76 Clement of Alexandria, *Second Epistle of Clement*.
77 Eliade, Mircea, *The Two and the One*.

Jacob Böhme wrote that, thanks to Christ, man would again become an androgyne, like the angels.

In Jewish tradition, Adam is like a freakish superhero, gigantic and strange:

> Like all creatures formed on the six days of creation, Adam came from the hands of the creator fully and completely developed. He was not like a child but a man of twenty years of age. The dimensions of his body were gigantic, reaching from heaven to earth, or what amounts to the same from east to west. Among later generations of men there were but few who in a measure resembled Adam in his extraordinary size . . . . Eve was but an ape compared with Adam. His person was so handsome that the very sole of his foot obscured the splendor of the sun.[78]

Along with his superhuman size, Adam also had the superhuman capacity of a unified sexuality. According to *midrash*, Adam Kadmon is androgynous, incorporating all the aspects of both male and female. The Talmud and the Zohar also have such references.[79] Rabbi Samuel ben Nachman said, "When the Holy One, blessed be He, created the first man, he created him as a hermaphrodite." This statement was also echoed by Rabbi Levi: "When man was created, he was created with two body fronts, and He sawed him in two, so that the two bodies resulted, one for the male and one for the female."[80]

The original Adam Kadmon was made to look like an angel:

> For in the resurrection they neither marry, nor are given in marriage, but are as the angels of God in Heaven—Mt. 22:30—Clearly, the messiah is telling them that the angels are sexless, which means they are male and female with themselves, or Hermaphrodites. The male and female principle exists separately only in the earth plane. Remember, when Elohim formed Adam he created him in his image, male and female within himself.[81]

---

78 Ginzberg, Louis, *The Legends of the Jews*.
79 Judy Weinberg, "All You Ever Wanted to Know About Lilith," *Lilith* magazine, 1976.
80 According to many Jewish writings, a female equal to Adam Kadmon was created as the same time. She was named Lilith, but was Adam's adversary and used Adam's wet dreams to populate the world with demons. For more information on this, see Gershom Scholem, *On the Kabbalah and its Symbolism*.
81 Warren, Dr. Lee, *Angels*.

This likeness was not favored by the angels, and many revolted at the thought of such a creature. Though God incinerated many angels due to this disregard for Adam, whenever he did anything wrong, the angels were quick to remind God of his folly. Said Rabbi Hiyya:

When the Holy One created man to dwell upon the earth, he formed him after the likeness of Adam Kadmon, the heavenly man. When the angels gazed upon [Adam Kadmon], they exclaimed: "You have made him almost equal to God and crowned him with glory and honor." After the transgression and fall of Adam, it is said the Holy One was grieved at heart because it gave occasion for repeating what they had said at his creation, "What is man that You should be mindful of him, or the son of man that You should visit him?"

Horny Angelic Beings

Perhaps if Hermes wasn't originally an angel, he was transformed into one after a serpentine visit. The Jewish version of Hermes, Moses—like Enoch—is partially transformed into a seraphim when his face turns into flame after receiving the word of God:[82]

Hereupon God commanded Metatron, the Angel of the Face, to conduct Moses to the celestial regions amid the sound of music and song, and He commanded him furthermore to summon thirty thousand angels, to serve as his bodyguard, fifteen thousand to right of him and fifteen thousand to left of him. In abject terror Moses asked Metatron, "Who art thou?" and the angel replied, "I am Enoch, the son of Jared, thy ancestor, and God has charged me to accompany thee to His throne." But Moses demurred, saying, "I am but flesh and blood, and I cannot look upon the countenance of an angel," whereupon Metatron changed Moses' flesh into torches of fire, his eyes into Merkabah wheels, his strength into an angel's, and his tongue into a flame, and he took him to heaven with a retinue of thirty thousand angels, one half moving to right of them and one half to left of them.[83]

---

82 Moses is in effect transformed into a messenger of God.
83 Ginzberg, Louis, *The Legends of the Jews*.

Manly P. Hall believed that Hermes Trismegistus was a man named Thoth who was raised to the status of a god.[84] But was it more than just his status? Was his body and soul elevated as well?

> From this Enochic account we learn that the vision of the Divine face had dramatic consequences for Enoch's appearance. His body endures radical changes as it becomes covered with the divine light. The important detail here is that the luminous transformation of Enoch takes place in front of the radiant "face" of the Lord . . . . The text describes the actions of Michael, who anoints Enoch with delightful oil and clothes him . . . the oil emanates the rays of the glittering sun "greater than the greatest light."

Let's examine the implications used in the description of shining, radiant face of Moses. The Hebrew word *qaran* (not to be confused with the Muslim holy text) is chosen to describe this event, which has two separate meanings: "radiant light" or "to grow horns." The Torah scholar, Rashi, states that "Moses' face shown as if it were horned," combining both meanings of *qaran*. Moses is sometimes depicted as having horns when he descends Mount Sinai with the Torah.

In Greek mythology, Pan, son of Hermes, was the god of shepherds and their flocks,[85] hunters, forests, wildlife, and fertility—or the god of nature. From his name we get the word *pantheism*: Pan, the god of all religions. The pantheistic idea suggests that God-consciousness is everywhere in the natural world, a concept inherent in Hermetic literature. Is it a mere coincidence that horns appear both on the head of Moses (a variant of Hermes) and Hermes' son, Pan?

The Egyptian precedent for Pan comes from their God, Kneph:

> The Wind, or Air, or Breath of our bodies, [he] was supposed to be the god of Animal and Spiritual Life. He has the head and horns of a ram.[86]

According to Philo of Biblos, Kneph is also associated with Agathodaimon, the serpent god of the vineyards[87] Agathodaimon is also seen as the father of Hermes and the son of Thoth. It seems

---

84 Hall, Manly, P., *The Hermetic Marriage*.
85 Hermes was also worshiped as a god of shepherds.
86 Samuel Sharpe, *Egyptian Mythology and Egyptian Christianity*.
87 Turcan, Robert, *The Cults of the Roman Empire*.

the horns are conferred upon those who are enlightened by God, thus altering their nature as human beings and changing their very form. Metatron is also depicted with horns at times.

Alexander the Great had perhaps the largest influence in spreading Hermetic teachings, by establishing Alexandria. Alexander was said to have been initiated into the Hermetic mysteries, and that he even discovered the *Emerald Tablet* of Hermes. Alexander portrayed himself with the horns of a ram after learning from a seer that Zeus was his true father, who visited his mother in the form of a snake. According to Plutarch:

> Once, moreover, a serpent was found lying by Olympias as she slept, which more than anything else, it is said, abated Philip's passion for her; and whether he feared her as an enchantress, or thought she had commerce with some god, and so looked on himself as excluded, he was ever after less fond of her conversation.

Alexander referred to the god Zeus-Ammon as his real father, and was thereafter portrayed with horns on top of head.

Zeus-Ammon was the syncretized name merging the Greek god Zeus with its Egyptian prototype, Ammon. Ammon was believed to be the Breath of Life, and most scholars place him as identical with Kneph. St. Jerome made a reference that the horns of Alexander were identical with the horns of Moses.

Fallen Angels and the Daimons

The appearance of horns on angels and deities plays an important role in the early Christian moral teachings that attempted to submerge Hermetic thought (that it did not assimilate) into obscurity and taboo.

Though Lucifer was depicted as a pagan goat-god, he was not always disfavored by God. Before his fall, Lucifer was the prince of the Seraphim, and Metatron later assumed his position.[88] In the apocryphal literature, and most extensively in the Book of Enoch, a war is described in heaven in which the Seraphim are divided, and Lucifer and his followers fall from heaven, finding themselves part of the earthly realm.

88 Davidson, Gustav, *A Dictionary of Angels.*

The fallen Seraphim are also affiliated with serpents; the main form Lucifer takes after the fall is, of course, the snake, in which he delivers the tree of knowledge to mankind (much like Poimandres gives Thoth his knowledge).

> For in his days the angels of the Lord descended upon earth—those who are named The Watchers—that they should instruct the children of men, that they should do judgment and uprightness upon earth.[89]

According to Zosimos, who lived in Alexandria, with full access to its library, alchemy[90] came to man from fallen angels, as discussed in the book of Enoch. In *Isis the Prophetess to Her Son Horus*, based on an earlier Egypto-Hebraic source known as Isis the Prophetess, Zosimos explains that alchemy comes from the Nephilim, or the Fallen Angels, who taught it to Isis in exchange for sexual intercourse.

> That the sons of God saw the daughters of men that they were fair; and they took them wives of all that they chose.

In the Book of Enoch, fallen angels came to earth and conveyed knowledge such as language, medicine, agriculture, mathematics and more to humans:

> And [the angel] Azazel taught men to make swords, and knives, and shields, and breastplates, and made known to them the metals of the earth and the art of working them, and bracelets, and ornaments, and the use of antimony, and the beautifying of the eyelids, and all kinds of costly stones, and all the coloring tinctures. (Enoch 8:1)

And then fiery angels come to earth and created a half-breed known as the Nephilim, sometimes referred to as the Annunaki, and also referred to as the Ellu, or "Shining Ones." These "Shining Ones" are often depicted with horns on their heads (like Pan and Moses):

The Watchers were a specific race of divine beings known in Hebrew as "*nun resh ayin irin*," meaning "those who watch" or "those who are awake," which is translated into Greek as *egregoris* or *grigori*, meaning "watchers." These Watchers feature within the main pag-

89 *The Book of Jubilees*
90 Alchemy is derived directly from the Hermetic teachings.

es of pseudepigraphal and apocryphal works of Jewish origin, such as the Book of Enoch and the Book of Jubilees. Their progeny, according to Hebrew tradition, are named as *nephilim*, a Hebrew word meaning "those who have fallen" or "the fallen ones," translated into Greek as γιγαντες, *gigantes*, or "giants"—a monstrous race featured in the Theogony of the Hellenic writer Hesiod (c. 907 BC).[91]

Thus was created an entire lineage, a half-angelic race who gave humans special knowledge.

> It is stated in the holy scriptures or books . . . that there exists a race of daimons who have commerce with women. Hermes made mention of them in his *Physika*; in fact almost the entire work, openly and secretly, alludes to them. It is related in the ancient and divine scriptures that certain angels lusted for women, and descending from the heavens, they taught them all the arts of nature. On account of this, says the scripture, they offended God, and now live outside heaven—because they taught to men all the evil arts which are of no advantage to the soul.[92]

The view here of the daimon as an evil entity is really a matter of perspective. In pre-Christian times, the terms angel and daimon were used interchangeably.[93] As Plutarch tells us, daimons are intermediate beings, but their divine nature is joined with a body capable of pleasure and pain. Like humans, daimons are subject to carnal desire, and good and evil. The definition of daimon originated in Greek, meaning "divine spirit" or "divine entity"; and according to Greek mythology, the daimons have as important a role here on earth as the angels do in heaven. As above, so below:

> These are the men who, having learned from Hermes that the atmosphere is full of daimons, inscribed it on *stelae* . . . they became initiators of men in arts and sciences and all pursuits, as well as lawgivers. These men, having learned from Hermes that things below are ordered sympathetically by the Demiurge to those above, instituted the sacred procedures (*hieropoiias*) on earth which are vertically aligned (*proskathetous*) to the heavenly mysteries.[94]

---

91 Collins, Andrew, *From the Ashes of Angels—The Forbidden Legacy of a Fallen Race.*
92 Zosimos, as quoted in George Synkellos, *Ecloga Chronographica.*
93 Davidson, Gustav, *A Dictionary of Angels; Including the Fallen Angels.*
94 *Corpus Hermeticum*, vol. IV.

According to Zosimos, the being who the Hebrews called Adam and the Egyptians called Thoth was tricked by the daimons into clothing himself as a corporeal Adam. As a result, the light of the spiritual Adam became trapped and divided in matter. In two of his works, *On the Letter Omega* and *The Final Quittance*, Zosimos said that there are two kinds of alchemy: one that further enslaves us to the material world and one that frees us from it.

If one were to agree with Zosimos and the Gnostics teachings, the angels or daimons—whatever you want to call them—are responsible for dividing man from God and bringing him to earth. They then interbreed with man, and in turn, give man the Hermetic knowledge to reunite with God, rectifying a disunion caused by man's descent into the material world.

> Hermes is a generic name like Manu and Buddha. It designates a man, a caste and a god at the same time. As a man, Hermes is the first great initiator of Egypt; as a caste, Hermes is the priesthood, the depository of esoteric traditions; as a god, Hermes is the planet Mercury, including in its sphere a category of spirits and divine initiators . . . . In the spiritual economy of the world all these things are bound together by secret affinities as by an invisible thread. The name Hermes is a talisman which sums them up, a magic sound which calls them forth.[95]

95 Schure, Edouard, *The Great Initiates: A Study of the Secret History of Religions.*

{Section Five}

HOLY HERMETIC WRITINGS

During their heyday, you had to be an initiated priest fluent in several languages to get your hands on Hermetic teachings. The teachings were first written down on papyrus in the language of Thoth, the hieroglyph, by the Egyptians. They were also carved into the stone exteriors of ancient temples.

Just before the Great Flood, Thoth preserved the ancient wisdom by inscribing two great pillars and hiding sacred objects and scrolls inside them. Egyptian holy books refer to these sacred pillars, one located in Heliopolis and the other in Thebes, as the "Pillars of the Gods of the Dawning Light." They were moved to a third temple where they later became known as the two "Pillars of Hermes." These splendorous columns are mentioned by numerous credible sources down through history. The Greek legislator, Solon, saw them and noted that they memorialized the destruction of Atlantis. The pillars were what the historian Herodotus described in the temple of an unidentified Egyptian god he visited. "One pillar was of pure gold," he wrote, "and the other was as of emerald, which glowed at night with great brilliancy." In *Iamblichus: On the Mysteries*, Thomas Taylor quotes an ancient author who says the Pillars of Hermes dated to before the Great Flood and were found in caverns not far from Thebes. The mysterious pillars are also described by Achilles Tatius, Dio Chrysostom, Laertius, and other Roman and Greek historians.[96]

The Book of Thoth

The *Book of Thoth* was one of the most secret and desired objects of the Hermetic wisdom teachings. It contained spells that were said to be capable of manipulating the very fabric of our world. According to Manly P. Hall, it contains within its pages the key to immortality. And it is possible that it still exists.

According to legend, the *Book of Thoth* was kept in a golden box in the inner sanctuary of the temple. There was but one key and this

---

96 Hall, Manly P., *The Secret Teachings of All Ages*.

was in the possession of the "Master of the Mysteries," the highest initiate of the Hermetic Arcanum. He alone knew what was written in the secret book. The *Book of Thoth* was lost to the ancient world with the decay of the Mysteries, but its faithful initiates carried it sealed in the sacred casket into another land. The book is still in existence and continues to lead the disciples of this age into the presence of the Immortals. No other information can be given to the world concerning it now, but the apostolic succession from the first hierophant initiated by Hermes himself remains unbroken to this day, and those who are peculiarly fitted to serve the Immortals may discover this priceless document if they will search sincerely and tirelessly for it. It has been asserted that the *Book of Thoth* is, in reality, the mysterious Tarot of the Bohemians—a strange emblematic book of seventy-eight leaves which has been in possession of the gypsies since the time then they were driven from their ancient temple, the Serapeum.[97]

A more recent claim about the discovery of the Book of Thoth was made by the scholars Richard Jasnow and Karl Zauzich. The men found a papyrus of fifteen columns written in Demotic script in the Berlin museum. (The Demotic script was used by priests in the Ptolemaic Alexandrian period mainly for translating Egyptian into Greek. Very few people can decipher the script today, and as a result, many ancient papyri lie about in museums untranslated.) Since the announcement of the discovery in 1995, Hermetic scholars have been poring over its contents. Jasnow and Zauzich wrote a book titled *Ancient Egyptian Book of Thoth: A Demotic Discourse on Knowledge and Pendant to the Classical Hermetica in Two Volumes*, which consists of a translation and avid commentary of the papyri, along with some Hermetic history. The text is mainly a dialogue between Thoth (who is named in the text as "Thoth the thrice great," a handle also applied to Hermes Trismegistus) and a student described as "The one who loves knowledge." Scribal craft, sacred geography, the underworld, wisdom, prophecy, animal knowledge, and temple ritual are all discussed.

The *Book of Thoth* shows why the Hermetic teachings were kept so secret. Advanced spells of all sorts were contained within the sacred texts:

---

97 Hall, Manly P., *The Secret Teachings of All Ages.*

The so-called Hermetic literature . . . is a series of papyri describing various induction procedures . . . . In one of them, there is a dialogue called the Asclepius (after the Greek God of healing) that describes the art of imprisoning the souls of demons or of an angel in statues with the help of herbs, gems and odors, such that the statue could speak and prophesy. In other papyri, there are still other recipes for constructing such images and animating them, such as when images are to be hollow so as to enclose a magic name inscribed on gold leaf.[98]

The *Emerald Tablet*

The Emerald Tablet, also known as *The Smaragdine Table* or *Tabula Smaragdina,* is a mysterious piece of writing said to be a primary source of Hermetic wisdom. It is also seen in the DVD and used in an initial quote for *The Secret. The Emerald Tablet* is said to have been engraved by Thoth himself into a huge example of the precious stone. The word "emerald" comes from the Greek *smaragdos,* which simply means "green stone." The *Emerald Tablet* is considered the primary text of Western alchemists, though no scholar has actually seen it.

The *Emerald Tablet* is said to have been forged by Thoth himself, but no written form of the Tablet appeared until 650 AD. Though it is considered by scholars to belong to Hermetica, its first appearance comes much later than most of the *Corpus Hermeticum* proper.

After the Christians destroyed the Library of Alexandria and the Moslems took over Egypt, many of the existing manuscripts ended up in Arabia . The post-Alexandrian period saw a flourishing of alchemy in the Arab world, due largely to the arrival of these manuscripts.

After extensive and painstaking research into the history of the *Emerald Tablet,* I discovered that a revised Greek translation of the original text was issued around 300 BC. This translation was performed by three groups of Alexandrian alchemists, who were attempting to use the mysterious tablet to unify conflicting Jewish,

---

98 James, Julian, *The Origin of Consciousness in the Breakdown of the Bicameral Mind.*

Greek, and Egyptian versions of alchemy. The mixing of cultures in Alexandria caused a shattering clash of dogmas that shook alchemy to its roots. But because these ideas were treated with such secrecy among the ruling classes, the masses (and history) took little note of the potentially catastrophic nature of the conflict. Even today, it is hard for us to imagine the shattering impact this crisis of interpretation had on the world. Alchemy was considered a gift direct from God and was the hidden foundation upon which the world's religions and sciences were built. The truths of alchemy were a nation's highest secrets and were revealed only to a small group of worthy priests and philosophers.[99]

It wasn't long before the *Emerald Tablet* made its way back to Europe. The popularity of the *Emerald Tablet* in European Alchemy circles was epidemic. Translations into many other languages, including Sanskrit, Chinese and Russian, followed. An English translation from the original Arabic version reads:

Balinas mentions the engraving on the table in the hand of Hermes, which says:

Truth! Certainty! That in which there is no doubt!

That which is above is from that which is below, and that which is below is from that which is above, working the miracles of one.

As all things were from one.

Its father is the Sun and its mother the Moon.

The Earth carried it in her belly, and the Wind nourished it in her belly, as Earth which shall become Fire.

Feed the Earth from that which is subtle, with the greatest power.

It ascends from the earth to the heaven and becomes ruler over that which is above and that which is below.

And I have already explained the meaning of the whole of this in two of these books of mine.[100]

Later, the *Emerald Tablet* was translated by Dr. John Everard and published in the 1600s. This copy of his translation includes his original commentary on the text:

99 Latz, Gottfried, Dr., *The Secret of the Emerald Tablet*, Translated by Dennis William Hauck from *Die Alchemie*.
100 Holmyard, E. J., *Alchemy*.

Tabula Smaragdina
or
The Tablet of Emerald
said to be found
in the Sepulchre of Hermes
by John Everard, Doctor of Divinity

1. It is true without any lying, certain and most true, that which is inferior, or below, is as that which is superior or above, there being one Universal matter and form of all things, differenced only by accident, and particularly by that great mystery of Rarefaction and Condensation, and that which is superior as that which is inferior, to work and accomplish the Miracles of one thing, and to show the great variety and diversity of operations wrought by that Spirit that worketh all things in all things.

2. And as all things were from ONE, by the Mediation of one, God having created all things in the beginning, which is the beginning of all things, and the wisdom of his Father, so all things spring and took their original from this one thing by adaptation or fitting itself accordingly in number weight and measure, for Wisdom builds her own house.

3. The Father of this one thing, or that which he useth instead of an Agent, in all the Operations thereof, is the Sun, and the mother thereof or which supplies the place of a female and Patient is the Moon; the Nurse thereof receiving in her lap all the influences of heat and moisture, the Sulphur and Mercury of Nature (for the Spirit of GOD moveth not but upon the Face of the water) is the Earth. The Wind or Air carried in its Belly as one of the links in the chain, that link superior things to them that are below.

4. This is the Father original and fountain of all perfection, and all the secret and miraculous things done in the world; whose force is then perfect and complete to perform those Miracles, and many more when it is turned into Earth; that is from a volatile and unfixed thing as it was both before and in the preparation, to a most fixed Earth, but quintessential, wherein all the virtues are both concentred and doubled, nay infinitely increased. To which purpose Thou shalt separate the Earth from the Fire, for they being united, and the subject being but one thing (like Adam and Eve before their separation, or Plato's Hermaphrodite, a man and a

woman joined together back to back) could not generate or beget, till all parts be separated, and purged; and the subtle or fine aethereal from the thick or gross, sweetly and with much leisure all haste being from Hell, and with a greate deal of wit, judgment and discretion: for to every thing there is an appointed time, and for the production of all animals, vegetables and minerals, the measure of the Igne [fire] is measured, 2. Edras 4, 37. And therefore is requisite both patience to persevere and expect the appointed time, and wit or judgment to find, and order the fire. It ascendeth from Earth to Heaven, and descendeth from Heaven to Earth, even as the rain, which in like manner is often cohobated upon the earth; and one part of it is by the appointment of wisdom fixed into earth, whilst another part of earth is attenuated and dissolved; this being the perpetual motion of wisdom itself; and by this means it acquireth the virtue and power of all things above, the subtlety, purity, penetrative activity of fire, light, heaven and things below, the fluidness, fixedness and capableness of all influences, which the lower elements of Earth and Water have. So shalt thou have the glory of the whole world which consisteth in long life, health, youth, riches, wisdom and virtue, Therefore shall all obscurity fly from thee the obscurity and darkness of the body, its distemper and sickness; of the Soul and Mind, that which ariseth from these ignorances which is cured not in the branch only but in the root, when we have put our light in a clear glass. This is the most strong strength of all strength, the mightiest expression of all the power strength and efficacy of nature which can be in sublunary things, for it will overcome any subtle thing, as metals in Mercury, and the spirit of the bodies; which though they be thin it will be congealed, and though they be volatile, it will fix: and likewise in living weight, there is no disease so spiritual but it will root it out: and every hard thing it will pierce as well in compact metals with whom it will join inseparably, as in diseases that affect the solidest part of bodies. Thus was the World created: Therefore do the philosophers call their Stone, the little world made of the same Chaos, and after the same manner that the great one was. From whence will be wonderful adaptations, or fittings of Agents and Patients, and by that means strange productions in all the kingdoms of Nature, animal, vegetable and mineral : and the manner of them is this, which is showed and set down before, and the method of operation the same: Therefore am I called Hermes Trismegistus or the thrice greatest Mercury, having the three parts of the philosophy of the whole world, and endowed with the knowledge of the Body, Soul and Spirit, whereof all things consist, and of all things that are in the three

142

kingdoms of Nature. Thus endeth that which I have spoken of the operation of the Sun: for whatsoever is made or done in all sublunary matters, is done only by the power of the Sun, of whom the Psalmist saith the Almighty hath placed his Tabernacle, it being the Fountain of all natural heat or Nature itself in the Creatures, which is nothing but the finger or ordinate power of the Almighty; And the finger or power of God, is God himself, to whom is due all that, and infinitely more, than the creatures can possibly ascribe unto him.

One of the most intriguing stories of the *Emerald Tablet's* origin states that Hermes received the *Emerald Tablet* from Lucifer himself, because it came off of his crown as he fell from grace. An intriguing allegory, when one considers that Hermes received his knowledge from a giant serpentine Seraphim, as well as the serpent of Genesis conferring knowledge on Adam and Eve.

In Christianity, we see the legend perpetuated in the form of The Holy Grail, the earliest discussion of which is in *Parzival* by Wolfram von Eschenbach, near 1200 AD. Within these pages, Eschenbach relates the story of The Holy Grail's origin, namely that it was a green stone that fell from the crown of Lucifer as he descended to earth. In this, and subsequently in Wagner's opera *Parsifal*, the Grail is known as *Lapis Exillis*, which could translate to mean "exiled stone" or "worthless stone."

Although later mentions of the Grail claim that it only possesses the powers of immortality after it has been infused with the blood of Christ, in earlier legends, it had this power before Christ ever touched it. In Hermetic teachings, the thing that confers immortality is commonly known as the Philosopher's Stone.

The Grail castle recalls the pagan otherworld, where there is no aging and no disease, and where the immortals feast on whatever they like best. But the Grail is now a stone which resembles the Philosopher's Stone of the alchemists. It too surpassed all earthly perfection, cured disease, and kept its possessor forever young.[101]

The Philosopher's Stone is an object that is reputed to have the power to turn any substance into gold, heal any sickness and prolong any life indefinitely. It is the object all alchemists seek as a goal in the "Great Work."

101 Cavendish, Richard, *Man, Myth & Magic: An Illustrated Encyclopedia of the Supernatural.*

There are a couple of Hermetic explanations for the Christian Grail legend: Either it have combines the Philosopher's Stone with the *Emerald Tablet* to form one entity, or the *Emerald Tablet* could be considered a form of the Philosopher's Stone. Although the Holy Grail is commonly depicted as a golden, jewel-encrusted cup, there were earlier descriptions of a much plainer item, and the gem-bedecked versions came much later.

Another theory is that the Holy Grail was a green cup, based on another mysterious object present at Jesus' Last Supper. There was an enigmatic bowl that Jesus used, known as the *Sacro Catino*, or sacred washbowl. If his bowl was green, might not his cup have been, also? Or perhaps the cup and bowl are one and the same?

This bowl found its place in front of Jesus by way of none other than the Queen of Sheba.[102] Sheba was the Queen of Ethiopia (Aith Ophia), and was married to King Solomon. According to the Bible, when King Solomon passed away, he left the Queen of Sheba with a very valuable item; the Ark of the Covenant.

The Ark of the Covenant is a fancy box that contains the stone tablets of the Torah that Moses received from Heaven with the word of God written upon them. It also contained the "rod that budded": Moses' serpent staff, the caduceus.

Remember, Hermes received the *Emerald Tablet*, which contained the word of God, from a fiery flying serpent. Moses received the Torah from God and a host of Seraphim, after ascending to Heaven. Could it be possible that the *Emerald Tablet* of Hermes is one and the same as the Torah, and, furthermore, that this tablet made its way to Jesus, eventually becoming known as the Holy Grail?

The Torah, the Emerald Tablet and the Holy Grail

What is called the Grail is a celestial stone that fell on our earth, when Lucifer's crown burst into a thousand pieces in the war of Heaven. Only if we succeed to put together the dispersed pieces, Lucifer will be atoned for. Because he is the Morning Star, the star of Elella, the guard of our Love.

—Miguel Serrano,

---

102 Steele, R. and Singer, D.W., *"The Emerald Table,"* [Table ok?] Proceedings of the Royal Society of Medicine, Vol 21.

Could this stone that fell from the sky actually be one of the most important items in religious history? Could the same stone be the tablets of Moses, the Holy Grail, *and* the most important piece of Hermetic literature? Or is there some sort of cyclical lineage, where different individuals receive these tablets from heaven over time?

First, consider that the tablets of Moses are described as "Emeralds of Paradise" in Arabic tradition:

> It is told that the tablets were made of emerald from paradise, and as attributed to the prince of believers he said that they were of green emerald and God commanded him (Moses) to take them with power and heart, and take it with its best virtues like patience for good and keeping away from the wrong-doing and patience for adversities and forgiveness and purity and be satisfied with whatever God did destine for them . . . so when the days of Moses were over [the forty days] God inspired to him to keep them in a mountain called Zainah and they were made of paradise's emerald, so when Moses went to the mountain, it did split into two and then he kept the tablets inside it and they were covered, so when put them there the mountain did get back to its normal state and they remained there until the prophecy of Muhammad when God revealed Gabriel down to him so he told him about it so then he got them out looked at them and read them and they were in Hebrew and then he called the prince of believers and said to him: keep those for they have the knowledgement of the first and the last and they are the tablets of Moses and God ordered me to give them to you, until he said: so `Ali passed one day and he knew everything in it by God's teaching, so then the prophet ordered him to copy it and so he did on a piece of skin and it is the Cipher that had all the knowledgement of the first and last nations, and Al-Sâdiq said: and they are with us, and the tablets are with us and the staff of Moses is with us and we inherited all the prophets.[103]

In Islamic tradition, Mohammed gained custody of the Ark of the Covenant, and thus the stone tablets of the Torah. Mohammed was another figure who received the word of God from a Seraphim,

---

103 Abdul-Sâhib Al-Hasani Al-'âmili, THE PROPHETS, THEIR LIVES AND THEIR STORIES.

Gabriel, around 610 AD. This is important because the first written version of the *Emerald Tablet* was in Arabic, by way of the Muslims in 650 AD, which means that the Arabic translation of the *Emerald Tablet* could possibly have been taken from the stone tablets of the Torah that Mohammed had. This first translation of the *Emerald Tablet* came to us only twenty years after the death of Mohammed, and forty years after he claimed to receive the word of God from a fiery serpent, Gabriel (just as Moses and Hermes did).

Apart from the Moses' tablets being referred to as emeralds from Paradise, they are also sometimes called "divine sapphire."

> While upon the heights of Mount Sinai, Moses received from Jehovah two tablets bearing the characters of the Decalogue traced by the very finger of Israel's God. These tables were fashioned from the divine sapphire, *Schethiyâ*, which the Most High, after removing from His own throne, had cast into the Abyss to become the foundation and generator of the worlds. This sacred stone, formed of heavenly dew, was sundered by the breath of God, and upon the two parts were drawn in black fire the figures of the Law. These precious inscriptions, aglow with celestial splendor, were delivered by the Lord on the Sabbath day into the hands of Moses, who was able to read the illumined letters from the reverse side because of the transparency of the great jewel.[104]

According to the story, these sapphire tablets were too brilliant for the Israelites, and Moses destroyed them, replacing them with the more mundane stone version of the tablets. Some rabbinical accounts, however, state that Moses used sapphire to write the second set of tablets, which he presented to his followers.

> Moses had in his tent a block of sapphire, created for the very purpose, from which he hewed the second set of tables . . . . This sapphire was of a nature that admitted of the tables being rolled up (Ex. R. viii.; Cant. R. v. 14). Moses having thrown away the first set, it was only fair that he should provide the second (Deut. R. iii.). The sapphire from which Moses hewed the tables had been quarried from the solar disk.[105]

104 Hall, Manly P., *The Secret Teachings of All Ages.*
105 Emi G. Hirsch, Wilhelm Bacher 2002. *Tables of the Law* from The Jewish Encyclopedia.com

Moses destroyed the first set of tablets because he came down to discover that the Israelites were worshiping the golden calf, and deemed them unworthy to receive the information. Some renderings of the tale say he smashed them, while others say the original tablets simply flew back up to heaven.

According to another version, the letters supported themselves as well as the stone in which they were encased; but, learning of Israel's lapse from grace, they flew back to heaven, and thus Moses was left, too feeble to carry the heavy burden. Again, the account is varied to introduce a struggle between God and Moses, or between Moses and the letters, Moses doing his utmost to save the tablets from falling (Yer. Ta'an. iv.). The tables were not of earthly but of celestial origin. The stone had been in existence from the very beginning of time, and the writing, too, had been extant equally long (ib.). The letters *mem* (final) and *samek* were miraculously supported in the stone, indicating Metatron and Sandalfon[106]

It is interesting here to note the reference to Metatron, for we are taken back to Enoch, another Thoth prototype who received tablets from Heaven. When Enoch ascended to heaven, he was given tablets of law by the angel Uriel, who, it should be mentioned, is also a Seraphim. Enoch wrote the contents of these heavenly tablets onto stone, and then passes them to Noah's father, Methuselah.

In the Book of Enoch it was the archangel Uriel ("God is my light") who showed Enoch the secrets of the Sun (solstices and equinoxes, 'six portals' in all) and the 'laws of the Moon' (including intercalation), and the twelve constellations of the stars, 'all the workings of heaven.' And in the end of the schooling, Uriel gave Enoch—as Shamash and Adad had given Enmeduranki—'heavenly tablets,' instructing him to study them carefully and note 'every individual fact' therein. Returning to Earth, Enoch passed this knowledge to his old son, Methuselah.[107]

But even before these biblical patriarchs, there was the original prototype of this story told through Adam Kadmon, the first man, who also received tablets from an angel. There is a Jewish religious

---

106 Ibid
107 Sitchin, Zecharia, *When Time Began.*

text known as the *Sefer Raziel HaMalakh*, which translates to "Book of Raziel the Angel." According to Jewish tradition, this book was given to Adam from the Angel Raziel. The name Raziel translates to mean "Secrets of God." The account of this story appears in the *Zohar*, the book of Enoch, and in the *Targum*. The book of Raziel, much like the Torah, was reportedly written on sapphire. The story of Adam receiving the text from Raziel is related beautifully by Louis Ginzberg:

On the third day [Adam] had offered up this prayer, while he was sitting on the banks of the river that flows forth out of paradise, there appeared to him, in the heat of the day, the angel Raziel, bearing a book in his hand. The angel addressed Adam thus: "O Adam, why art thouh so fainthearted? Why art thou distressed and anxious? Thy words were heard the moment when thouh didst utter thy supplication and entreaties, and I have received the charge to teach thee pure words and deep understanding, to make thee wise . . .and now Adam come and give heed unto what I shall tell thee regarding the manner of this book and its holiness." Raziel the angel then read from the book, and when Adam heard the words of the holy volume as they issued from the mouth of the angel, he fell down affrightened. But the angel encouraged him . . . . In the moment when Adam took the book, a flame of fire shot up from the river, and the angel rose heavenward with it. Then Adam knew that he had spoken to him was an angel of God, and it was from the holy King Himself that the book had come, and he used it in holiness and purity. It is the book out of which all things worth knowing can be learnt and all mysteries, and it teaches also how to call upon the angels and make them appear before men, and answer all their questions. But not all alike can use the book, only he who is wise and God-fearing, and resorts to it in holiness. Such a one is secure against all wicked counsels, his life is serene, and when death takes him from this world, he finds repose in a place where there are neither demons nor evil spirits, and out of the hands of the wicked he is quickly rescued.[108]

Very much like Thoth, the angel Raziel teaches Adam the power of speech. Raziel discloses the alphabet to Adam and shows him

108 Louis Ginzberg, *The Legends of the Jews*, the Jewish Publication Society of America: Philidelphia

how to combine the letters to form names. The Angel Raziel also taught Adam the power of speech, the power of thoughts and the power of a person's soul within the confines of the physical body and this physical world. Raziel essentially imparted all the knowledge with which one can harmonize physical and spiritual existence in this physical world. There is also a special kind of writing within the book, magical writing which, according to the Zohar (I 55a), contains the 1,500 keys to the mysteries of the world, which were withheld even from the angels themselves. The Jewish Encyclopedia has this to say on the subject:

The Book of Raziel:

An ancient cabalistic book composed of various parts. It was claimed to have been given to Adam after the fall, in order to save him from sin and from the power of Samael, the evil one. Adam aqcuired so much wisdom from the book that the angels became envious, stole it and cast it into the sea, and it was only at the command of God that the sea restored it to Adam. After the latter's death, the book dissapeared, but it was revealed to Enoch and later to Noah, who built the ark from its specifications. It was then transmitted successively through Shem, Abraham, Jacob, Levi, Moses and Joshua to Solomon. The book contains mystic lore on the letters of the alphabet, an extensive account of heaven and the angels, and various magic receipts and amulets. Zunz ascribed the nucleus of the book to Eliezer Ben Judah of Worms but Adolf Jellnek disputed this.[109]

The Book of Raziel was also written on sapphire, and in the Kabbalistic work The Sefer Noah (vol III pg 119) it is written that the sapphire on which the book was engraved gave the light necessary for the inamates of the Ark. Some Jewish scholars ascribe the first written version of this book and story to an ancient Rabbi named Isaac Ben Eliezer Halevi (1002–1070), who was also known as Eliezer of Worms. Eliezer was the teacher of the revered rabbi and teacher Rashi. The next account of this work did not appear until the Zohar was published, compiled mostly by Moses de Leon sometime in the thirteenth century.

---

109 Landman, Isaac, *The Universal Jewish Encyclopedia* Volume 9

The main purpose for copies of this work in present day seem to be for protection against evil. As the text contains many talismans, there are Jews who believe that simply keeping a copy on your person is enough, even if you don't know how to read Hebrew.

The similar theme all of these stories share is that stone tablets containing the word of God are given to certain men by Seraphim, and the *Emerald Tablet* was one of these. Now, either this happened several times, or this is just the retelling of the same story over and over again. Either way, one thing is clear: the *Emerald Tablet's* origins are much older than what was written down in 650 AD!

Discovering Hermes' *Emerald Tablet*

The most prevalent story has Alexander the Great prying the tablet out of Hermes' cold hands at his tomb in Egypt. Alexander was an avid student of the mysteries, and his boyhood tutor was Aristotle.

Alexandria was founded in Egyptin 334 BC as Αλεξαν–δρια. Alexander left only a few short months later for the East, and never returned. His death is mired in mystery, and though it was said that he was buried in Egypt, there whereabouts of his tomb remain unknown. According to some legends, Alexander was buried with the *Emerald Tablet*, which is where Apollonius is said to have discovered it.

Balinas / Apolloinius of Tyana

The earliest surviving translation of the Emerald Tablet is in an Arabic book known as The Book of Balinas the Wise on Causes, written around 650 AD. Balinas was another name for Apollonius of Tyana, who, some say, was an inspiration for the entire story of Jesus.

> Apollonius was a contemporary of Christ, and early Christians felt he was much too like their own Son of God. By 400 AD, every one of the scores of books Apollonius wrote in Alexandria and all of the dozens of temples dedicated to him, were destroyed by Christian zealots. But Apollonius still stands as the third Hermes in our hyper-history, because he did more than any other person in the modern era to assure that the *Emerald Tablet* and its principles survived.[110]

---

110 Hauck, Dennis William, *The Emerald Tablet: Alchemy of Personal Transformation.*

Apollonius traveled extensively, including journeys through China and India, learning the mystery traditions. At the age of sixteen, Apollonius became a disciple of Pythagoras, forsaking sex, meat and shoes. His hair and beard grew long and he essentially became a "Nazarene," as the Pythagoreans were commonly called. Apollonius eventually settled in Alexandria, where he made the discovery of the *Emerald Tablet*. According to legend, Apollonius came upon the hidden tomb of Alexander the Great (which has not been discovered to this day by archeologists). In the tomb, Apollonius did the same thing to Alexander that he had done to Hermes centuries before: he pried the tablet away from the corpse.

Here is what the priest Sagijus of Nabulus has dictated concerning the entrance of Balinas into the hidden chamber:

> After my entrance into the chamber, where the talisman was set up, I came up to an old man sitting on a golden throne, who was holding an emerald tablet in one hand. And behold the following—in Syriac, the primordial language—was written thereon:
>
> 1) Here [is] a true explanation, concerning which there can be no doubt.
> 2) It attests: The above from the below, and the below from the above—the work of the miracle of the One.
> 3) And things have been from this primal substance through a single act. How wonderful is this work! It is the main [principle] of the world and is its maintainer.
> 4) Its father is the sun and its mother the moon;
> 5) The wind has borne it in its body, and the earth has nourished it;
> 6) The father of talisman and the protector of miracles
> 6a) whose powers are perfect, and whose lights are confirmed,
> 7) A fire that becomes earth.
> 7a) Separate the earth from the fire, so you will attain the subtle as more inherent than the gross, with care and sagacity.
> 8) It rises from earth to heaven, so as to draw the lights of the heights to itself, and descends to the earth; thus within it are the forces of the above and the below;
> 9) Because the light of lights within it, thus does the darkness flee before it.
> 10) The force of forces, which overcomes every subtle thing and penetrates into everything gross.

11) The structure of the microcosm is in accordance with the structure of the macrocosm.

12) And accordingly proceed the knowledgeable.

13) And to this aspired Hermes, who was threefold graced with wisdom.

14) And this is his last book, which he concealed in the chamber.[111]

Another legend has it that Sarah, wife of Abraham, stumbled upon the *Emerald Tablet* in a cave near Hebron and, like Alexander and Apollonius, pried it loose from the stiff fingers of a mummified corpse. Another story has Adam himself giving the tablet to Hermes. Sarah and Abraham lived in Egypt around 2000 BC, which would make them contemporaries of Hermes and Thoth. The *Emerald Tablet* story is nearly the same as the Torah Moses brought down from his revelation on Mt. Sinai.

Attraction of the Sexes

In a volume concerning the law of attraction it seems only too fitting to include a chapter upon its relation to the attraction and repulsion of eroticism and sexuality. When we say erotic we mean not only that of a carnal nature, but in its true sense of the driving force that guides all opposing forces to and away from each other.

The mysterious force of animal magnetism, which Mesmer drew from, certainly applies equally as forcefully between the sexes and our reproductive nature.

To use our thoughts to attract things to us is probably no where as powerfully utilized than in the phantasms of our sexual fantasies. There have been no small amount of individuals who have striven to contain that force and use it for manipulative purposes as well as those whose attempts to harness the erotic law of attraction for the reason of divine love and transcendence from earthly vices.

When we consider sway and the power of influence there are perhaps few places it is more powerful than in the realm of the sex magician, be they male or female. The persuasive nature of charm and affinities of an enchantress make up many stories in the myths of all cultures.

While the rogue hypnotists and Svengalis certainly can be said to have used the attraction of the sexes for their own devices,

---

111 Another Arabic Version (from the German of Julius Ruska)

there is also the more fully formed and structured sex magician whose knowledge of the occult and esoteric hermetic material is put to use during the physical act of creation itself to produce a desired outcome, through magnetizing the mind to attract a phenomenon during copulation.

Magic, in general, operates through influence. The will affects the world through sway. There is an idea of being overtaken by an all permeating enclosure of energy that can drive decisions when influence comes into play. The intimation of the removal of our free will and the slavery to a zombie master is not a foreign concept in magical circles. This more insidious implication of magic is interesting, when we look deeper into the roots of what it is to influence something outside of ourselves. The word influence itself speaks not of an unavoidable enslavement, but rather of an energetic flow or destined pathway, and even of destiny from the stars:

Influence:
An astrological term, "streaming ethereal power from the stars acting upon character or destiny of men," from O.Fr. influence "emanation from the stars that acts upon one's character and destiny" (13c.), also "a flow of water," from M.L. influentia "a flowing in" (also used in the astrological sense), from L. influentem (nom. influens), prp. of influere "to flow into," from in- "in" + fluere "to flow"[112]

This influence is made up of two main forces, attraction and repulsion, ebb and flow. These forces in turn are contained within a larger force; the Erotic. The driving singular mechanism for all magic is Eros. In fact, one could argue, the Erotic is the driving force for the material universe. A lot of people think the concept of Eros is purely sexual, arriving from our loins and taking us over in a hot flash of stimulating ecstasy reaching levels beyond our control. But Eros is more than simply sexual attraction, it is all forms of attraction and repulsion combined in an intricate, intimate dance that extends past our nether-regions to deep inside our bodies. So deep in fact, that it is at the core of each of our atoms. Every proton and electron within our flesh are involved in

112   http://www.etymonline.com/index.php?term=influence

an erotic dance between positive and negative, male and female, held together into the elements that compose our inner universe. As the alchemists point out, this same relationship extends outwards and upwards into the heavens in a mirror, as above so below. The same erotic thrill compelling the particles, drives the planets together to organize into swirling shows of affection. The gravitational attraction and repulsion keeps them bound to each other, unavoidably, mythically into their repetitive cycles, driven together and apart through the stories of their orbits.

The Magician is the individual, who is aware of these forces, within, without, inside and outside the flesh. Awareness and attention to the pull of these forces are the Magician's main tools for manipulation of influence on all things, from creating rain to instigating feelings of love or hatred. In fact, there are some who have stated that Eros itself IS magic:

> "The connection between Eros and magic is so close that the difference between them is a matter of degree."[113]

The main operators in magic are Sympathy, (as in the Shaman pretending to BE the thing he is trying to affect) Attraction, (magnetizing your thoughts to a thing to make it come to you) and Contagion (as in voodoo). All three of these operators are erotic in nature.

But what exactly is Eros? What does that word mean? If it is more than mere sexuality, what are we speaking about? When we investigate the origins of the word itself we are brought back to one undeniable location, Love:

Eros

God of love, late 14c., from Gk. eros (pl. erates), lit. "love," related to eran "to love," erasthai "to love, desire," of uncertain origin. Freudian sense of "urge to self-preservation and sexual pleasure" is from 1922."[114]

---

113 Culianu, Ioan P. 1987. *Eros and Magic in the Renaissance University Of Chicago Press 271 ppgs.*
114 http://www.etymonline.com/index.php?term=Eros

This entangles the concept of the Erotic inextricably with Love and Desire. It is complicating enough to keep these concepts straight in our own affairs with each other, much less attempt to understand these mechanistic forces in terms of planets. How can we hope to understand the desires of the planet Jupiter when we cannot grasp our own? The Magician understands that their own desires are not so far from those of the outermost planets and stars, and in fact originate therein.

> **desire (v.)**
> early 13c., from O.Fr. desirrer (12c.) "wish, desire, long for," from L. desiderare "long for, wish for; demand, expect," original sense perhaps "await what the stars will bring," from the phrase de sidere "from the stars," from sidus (gen. sideris) "heavenly body, star, constellation" (but see consider). Related: Desired; desiring. The noun is attested from c.1300, from O.Fr. desir, from desirer; sense of "lust" is first recorded mid-14c."[115]

To "wish upon a star" is to align with the source of your desire. This flow from the stars harkens right back to where we started, influence. It is no small matter of consequence that Magicians study astrology and the nature of the stars in order to ascertain influence over matter. Some of the world's most infamous magicians throughout history look first to the stars before the cauldron for concoction.

Many religions count desire as a downfall, a destructive influence. But the further back one travels through the annals of time, desire was viewed as a gift conferred from the stars into the hearts of man. It is important to see desire not just as a harbinger of debauchery, but also as an inspiring force and truly what leads to all creations, including the creation of our own bodies. Erotic desire confers form and matter into existence. Forms that range from an oil painting, to a sculpture, to a human infant.

This also may begin to put the ramifications of our wanton desires into perspective. Our desires have nothing less than universal ramifications in this sense. These desires connect us with all things, from outer space to the most infinitesimal here on earth.

---

115 http://www.etymonline.com/index.php?search=desire&searchmode=none

"Everything is linked to the seven wandering heavenly bodies by invisible bonds. The magician has in the first place expert knowledge of these bonds, he is able to classify every object by these bonds."

Every plant, every blade of grass, every type of stone, every animal, fish insect and human will have a particular formula of planetary, or star affiliations. Influence and inspiration of desire operate through finding a sympathetic note within the formula of the object the magician wishes to manipulate.

This is where the darker side of the ability to hold sway can come into the foreground. As anyone involved in a penetrating love affair can attest, its grip can be suffocating.

The manipulator, the Svengali is the abuser of this force. How can it be that Love can cause sickness? That this gift of desire from the stars may shift to malefic form? Love should set you free and yet under its shackles and bonds we all may twist and whither. Amazingly enough, when we peer into the source of the word "free" Love lives there also.

free (adj.)
O.E. *freo* "free, exempt from, not in bondage," also "noble; joyful," from PIE *prijos* "dear, beloved," from base *pri-* "to love" (cf. Skt. *priyah* "own, dear, beloved," *priyate* "loves;"

The primary sense seems to have been "beloved, friend, to love;" which in some languages (notably Germanic and Celtic) developed also a sense of "free," perhaps from the terms "beloved" or "friend" being applied to the free members of one's clan (as opposed to slaves, cf. L. *liberi*, meaning both "free" and "children"). Cf. Goth. *frijon* "to love;" O.E. *freod* "affection, friendship," *friga* "love," *friðu* "peace;" O.N. *friðr*, Ger. *Friede* "peace;" O.E. *freo* "wife;" O.N. *Frigg* "wife of Odin," lit. "beloved" or "loving;" M.L.G. *vrien* "to take to wife, Du. *vrijen*, Ger. *freien* "to woo."[116]

This seems so contrary for a force equitable with freedom to be so severely able to enslave. Opposition though, is a driving force

116 http://www.etymonline.com/index.php?term=free

of attraction, so what frees can enslave, what cures may poison and that this line between love and hate becomes all too apparent. Thus we are lead to the morbidity of fascination. The danger of erotic attraction comes through fascination, something that consumes us, something we are unable to turn away from. As with the flickering star in the center of the darkness of the night.

The word Fascinate originally means to bewitch or enchant, but it is literally a flickering light. Something shining that you can't stop looking at. The best example of this can be seen in the relationship of the moth to the flame. The moth becomes so enraptured with the light of the flame all other thoughts are eclipsed and the very essence of its life is sacrificed in order to merge with this luminosity. Love ruins in this way, this trick of the light that lures in through the eyes and makes all else in life evaporate before it.

This Erotic, Attractive Love, forms a force more powerful than the will to live. It becomes more simple to sympathize with the terror of the magician. If one has ever felt the full brunt of a light extinguished in the heart, the thought of being compelled to dive to the flame as the moth is rather unbearable.

It is important to remember, however, that there are many different kinds of sex magicians. There are those who seek to manipulate, it is true, however, there are also those who seek divine union and empowerment through the use of the power of attractive erotic force. Perhaps the most famous sex magician who had a huge hand in bringing sex magic into popular culture was Paschal Beverly Randolph. Randolph was a black man who bought himself out of slavery in the 1800's. Randolph was a medical doctor, well educated and belonged to several occult groups, including the Rosicrucians. Randolph made it his life's work to publish books on the mysteries, and placed special importance on educating the masses about the mysteries of the power of sex.

The type of sex magic Randolph advocated was to utilize the powerful force of the orgasm when shared between two people in order to make a type of wish, or prayer, focused intensely on love for the other person, and love of God. In this way, the practitioner could become divine by focusing on divinity in that moment of creative power. This used the power of attractive force to attract divine love into the body of the two people who were practicing sex magic. He was very verbal about expressing the inadvisable trap for using this power for anything other than the intention to focus on love and spoke very plainly about the risks involved for using it as a means to power.

His penultimate work on these philosophies was *Eulis; Affectional Alchemy*[117]:

Love in very deed lies at the foot of all, and its mystic and ideal meaning outweighs the material and popular ones by as many degrees as the pure soul of that baby-girl outweighs the corrupt body of the low-lived debauchee. We may be hugged, embraced, kissed into heavenly states, or into their exact opposites! Hence, aside from common relational lip-contacts, they are worse than unwise who touch lips unless love be the underlying prompter; for if the kissed or kisser be bad, just so much of that specific evil is sure to flow from the magnetic poles of either pair of lips to the soul of him or her upon whose mouth they are laid.

XXV.

Unquestionably while we occupy flesh and blood bodies, and probably after we wear our electric or ethereal ones subsequent to death, Love, other than amicive and filial, will depend upon the magnetic congeniality existing between the two concerned; although even the most perfect state of magnetic fusion and reciprocation is liable to be disturbed by any one of quite a numerous list of causes.

We are all of us, more or less, counterparts and embodiments of nature; and nature has her ups and downs, fogs and sleets, storms and heats, ice and fire, volcanoes and wintry blasts; and so do, so 7nust we, just as long as the earth and nature are as at present; when they change, so will we, and very likely not much before. If between a couple there be a full and mutual play of magnetism, if neither draws from the other, except to replace with his or her own, there is a good chance of general harmony, joy and content for them. If not, then not. If one party overflows with magnetism, and the

117   Paschal Beverly Randolph, M.D. 1896. *Eulis; Affectional Alchemy: The History of Love; Its Wonderous Magic, chemistry, Rules, Laws, Modes, Moods &Rationale, Being the Third Revelation of Soul and Sex.* 3rd edition. Randolph Publishing Company. Toledo Ohio

other has but a scanty supply, strong love may exist between them, all other things being equal; and the weak one will depend almost for life itself upon the strong; and the strong be firmly drawn toward the weak. But there must be an assimilation between, and blending *of*, the two magnetisms, else they will assuredly antagonize and repel each other! One party may be very glowing and loving and magnetic, say, for instance, on plane A, — a solid, physical, muscular, heedless, jolly, deyil-me-care-sort of individual — say a man; such an one could make a perfect heaven — on *his* plane — with a woman of the same grade; but how would it be were he conjoined with a joyous, rich-souled, healthy, magnificent, intellectual, refined, delicate and spiritual woman, — equally magnetic as himself, but the grade of whose magnetism was as satin compared to his own — tow-cloth? Now just such couples, or those as naturally and organically incompatible, somehow or other, manage to get together, and the consequence is a life removed from happiness by a great, yawning, impassable gulf, whose black and sullen waters cannot be bridged....

XVIII.

Love, I have stated, is magnetic, and subject to magnetic law. It is a *force* also, capable, as all know, of exerting very strange effects both upon human souls and bodies. But how? that's the question! Tell us that! I will, listen: —

Matter and mind, in some mysterious way, are not only both alike and unlike, and conjoin to form the thing called man, but they act together directly and indirectly, fully or partially, and yet are not of the same nature, albeit they act and react upon each other in myriad ways, a fact which every one's experience demonstrates beyond cavil. One thing is absolutely certain; that the mind resides in the brain; that in it inheres what constitutes us human; and that the conscious point resides in the centre of the encephalon, at that spot where all three brains meet, viz., cerebrum, cerebellum and medulla, or spinal marrow, which is an elongated brain, is a clear fact, the proof of which can be found by consulting any good anatomical and physiological atlas. In this central point, as through and around the corpus callosum, there is, in death, a nervous and spheral waste; in life a brilliantSun varying in size from that of a large pea to a perfectly gorgeous sun-shining diamond three inches in diameter. — A ball of dazzling White Fire ! — and this is the Soul—the being par excellence, the tremendous human mystery. It has a double consciousness; one facing time and its accidents and incidents; the other gazing square and straight right into eternity. For its hither use it fashions material eyes; for its *thither* use every one of a myriad rays darting from it is an eye whose powers laugh Rosse's Telescope to scorn! But there arises a fog from the body which mainly so envelops this central point that the Eyes are veiled; sometimes in magnetic or other sleep the clouds shift, and then one or more eyes glance over infinite fields, and momentarily glimpse the actualities of space, time, possibility and eternity. [Were I, at this point to reveal what I know of soul, its destiny, nature, and the realities of the ultimate spaces, this world would stand agape! but I resist the temptation, and go on with this book.]

This central ball draws its supplies from space, air, ether, and being mystic and divine, directly from the Lord of the universe, — the Imperial Mystery, — Infinite and Eternal God. [About which mystery the *Savans* are as greatly at fault as they are concerning the facts of Growth.] It breathes; has its tides, its diastole, systole, flux and ebbs; and, being compelled to gaze on the outer world through opaque glasses, diseased bodies, it takes but distorted views of things, and scarce ever can rely upon the absolute truth of what the Senses tell it; from which results mistakes, confusion, misapprehensions, crime, and whatever else of evil betides its fortunes here. The breath of the body is atmospheric air, which air is more or less penetrated with the ether of space, the breath of God, and the magnetism of the heavens surrounding the entire material universe. On these it subsists; *and* when it *means* a thing it discharges a portion of its own sphere, its divine nerval life toward the object of its desire and attention; and the vehicle is magnetism, and magnetism is that specific *vif* or fluid life manufactured by the sexual apparatus of either gender, as said before. The thing conveyed by it is the purpose of a soul; the result, a certain yielding of any other...

Many people of both sexes often experience a *terrible* attraction toward another, that resembles, but is *not*, love. On the contrary, it is a fearful, monstrous passion, and they almost vainly struggle to escape it. Such persons are vampyrized; and a vampyre is a person born *love-hungry*, who have *none* themselves, who arc empty of it, but who fascinate and literally suck others dry who *do* have love in their natures. Detect it thus: the vampyre is selfish, is never content but in handling, fondling its object, which process leaves the victim utterly exhausted, and they don't know why. Break off *at once*. Baffle it by steady refusal; allow not even hands to touch, and remember that the vampyre seeks to prolong his or her own existence, life and pleasure, at the expense of your own. Women when thus assailed should treat the assailant with perfect coldness and horror. Thus they can baffle this pestiferous thing — which is more common than people even suspect; in fact, an *everyday affair*. *Many a man and wife have parted, many still live unhappily together, some aware, but many unconscious, that the prime* cause of all their bickerings and discontent is vampyrism on the part of one or the other. It causes fretfulness, moodiness, irritability; a feeling of repugnance arises toward the one who should be most dear; and eventually positive dislike takes the place of that tender affection which should ever grow more and more endearing between those who have given themselves to each other. This dislike becomes in many cases so strong that the parties cannot endure each other's presence; and separation becomes inevitable, neither, perhaps, conscious of the true cause. This is sometimes owing to an inferior development of amativeness, sometimes to debility, lack of vitality, the consequence of a feeble or shattered nervous system; and in either case the cure is to be found in less frequent contact, separate rooms, health, and mutual endeavor to correct the fault....

LVIII.

When teaching those who were desirous of mastering the principles pervading the books, and constituting the soul of the system evoked and elaborated by him whose pen scores these lines, it was the custom for him to address them in these following words, or their equivalents: First, the mystery of Life, and Power, Seership, — in its loftier, not merely its lesser meanings, — forecast, endurance, insight, farsight, longevity, silent energy, mental force, magnetic presence, and impressive capacity, lie in, flow out of, pertain to, and accord with, the SHE or mother-side of Deity, the love-principle of human-kind, and the sexive natures of the complicate homos. Outside of its sphere of operations all is cold and deathful; within its mystic and magic circle dwells all there is of fire, latent and active, actual and metaphysical; all there is of energy, procreant power, physical, mental, spiritual, and all other; and it — Love — is the master-key unlocking every barred door in the realms that are. Remember, O Neophyte (and reader of this book), that I am not dealing in mere philosophical formula?, "recipes," or trashy " directions," but in, and with fundamental principles, underlying all being. Fix this first principle firmly in your memory, and roll it under the tongue of your clearest understanding; take it in the stomach of your spirit; digest it well, and assimilate its quintessence to, and with, your own soul. That principle is formulated thus: LOVE LIETH AT THE FOUNDATION (of all that is); and Love is convertibly passion; enthusiasm; affection; heat; fire; SOUL; God. Master that. Second, the nuptive moment, the instant wherein the germs of a possible new being are lodged, or a portion of man's essential self is planted within the matrix, is the most solemn, serious, powerful, and energetic moment he can ever know on earth; and only to be excelled by correspondent instants after he shall have ascended to realms beyond the starry spaces.

LIX.

If a man actualizes that moment while under the dominion of animal instinct, or human lust alone, then the effect is losing, unmanning, degrading, to both himself and her; murderous toward the recipient, and suicidal to himself. It means hatred, disease, and magnetic ruin to both; its influence for evil spreads over a wide area on earth; feeds and sustains barbarism; nourishes the monstrous Larva? of the middle kingdoms of the *cered* habitats of disembodied beings, even when no progeny results. But if there *hall*, then he and she generate misery, crime, and possible murder as the heritage of that child. If, on the other hand, love be the prompting angel at the hearthnuptial, then strength, goodness, truth, harmony and sweet melodies of life ensue to the twain, and are insured to the offspring God shall give them. Third, at the very instant his seminal glands contract to expel their treasures, at such instant his interior nostrils open, and minute ducts, which are sealed at all other times, then expand, and as the lightning from his soul darts from the brain, rushes down the spinal-cord, leaps the solar plexus, plunges along the nerval filaments to the prostate gland to immortalize the germal human being; and while the vivific pulse is leaping to the dark chamber wherein soul is clothed in flesh _iid blood, at that instant he breathes in through the inner nostrils one of two atmospheres underlying, inter-penetrating—as the spirit does the body—the outer air which sentient things inhale. One of these auras is deeply charged with, because it is the effluvium of, the unpleasant sphere of the border spaces, where is congregated the quintessence of evil from every inhabited human world in the entire congeries of soul-bearing galaxies of the broad universe; else he draws in the pellucid aroma of divinity from the far-off multiple heavens. It follows that as are the people at *that moment* so will be that which enters into them from the regions above, beneath, and round about; wherefore, whatsoever male or female shall truly will for, hopefully pray for, and earnestly yearn for, when love, pure and holy, is in the nuptive ascendant, in form, passional, affectional, divine and volitional, that prayer will be granted, and the boon be given. *But the prayer must precede.*

Discord reigns in marriage-land to-day, and one principal cause is, that while the magnetic tide is at its height, and before the soul withdraws its power from the pelvis back to the brain-seat, they part company, and the spiritual auras and vital air escapes into the external world, instead of being stored up and absorbed by the woman's spirit and soul.

XC.

There cannot be a doubt but that the " Philosopher's Stone" of ancient and mediaeval lore, and the "Elixir Vita? " Water of Life and Perpetual Youth, so vaguely hinted at by old writers, and which constitutes the burden of the celebrated book "Hermipus Redivivus" OR THE SAGE'S TRIUMPHOVER DECREPITUDE AND DEATH, means this identical triple mystery, which scarce any one practically knows, but which all should learn, and which every physician and divine in the land ought to be *compelled* to teach their subjects under heavy penalties of neglect, because it is the secret of sustained youth, grace and beauty; it is the gate of power, and the crown and signet of ineffable human glory; it unveils the throne of Will, and taps the fountains of excessive joy; it is the Jemschidgenie of Persian story; and he or she who knows, appreciates diviner and celestial bearings of life and its meanings, becoming indeed a child of the Infinite, and no longer a stranger to the Father's face; and they alone who have it, are able to reach that magnificent sweep of clairvoyant vision, which, leaping from earth at a bound, scans the unutterable glories of space, and beholds the rain of starry systems as we view a gentle summer shower.

XCI.

The great source of crime, illness, wretchedness, and suffering has been traced to its one single source, and that is, the abuse, improper use, and mismatching of people in their loves, conjugal relations, and sexual incompatibilities.

It is proven that these bad conditions are frequently the result of organization, and sometimes spring from incompatible, electric, magnetic and chemical relations between couples. That absolute separation is the only cure for some who are wretched in theii married state, or inter-relationship; while attention to health, and a fair amount of Try is a certain cure for other cases.

XCII.

The body of man is a mere conglomerate of earths ana metals, gases and fluids wholly material, but penetrated and permeated in every atom by imponderable elements essentially electric in their nature. Thus beneath, and lining our eyes are ethereal organs corresponding thereto; beneath our limbs, heart, lungs, brain, in short, all our parts are corresponding electric organs, and the totality of these constitutes the ethereal, spiritual, death-proof man or woman, and when dissolution occurs this inner man or woman *oozes* out of the material structure, becomes self-conscious again, and takes its place among the countless armies of the departed, but neither lost or dead; and this internal, ethereal man, woman or child, can be contadted by us in the flesh, by conforming to the laws governing such contact, and the observance of a few simple rules.

XCIII. A passionless man or woman is a human nonentity. It is only when we are wholly man or woman in the higher, holier, and also physical sense, that we can reach the loftier and more significant heights of any sort of power whatever; therefore, those who would cultivate those loftier instincts, and gain mental wings wherewith to scale the heavens, should at once attend to the business of regaining perfect health, mental, physical, emotional and passional. Presentiy great-hearted love and blessed compassion will nestle in all our hearts, and in this glad, prophetic hope we may all be happy yet. We are none of us ever wise except when merciful. Let us all be so, for only then can we be perfectly human — only then 'become vessels for the influence and effect of God-ness. Never yet did man come to the absolute conviction of Soul and Immortality, but he also came to that of God and Prayer; for, say what you will, both are and ever will be positive realities in the universe.

In Love alone lies the boon of IMMORTALITY! INJUSTICE reigns to-day. Sad are the times when wedded wives decay,

And brothels flourish, and Cyprians bear the sway;
These are the times! their scarlet banner waves,
And honest wives, neglected, fill up a million graves! "When woman's
eye grows dull, And her cheek paleth,
When fades the beautiful, Then man's love faileth;
He sits not beside her chair, Clasps not her fingers,
Twines not the damp hair That o'er her brow lingers."He comes but
a moment in,
Though her eye lightens, Though her check, pale and thin,
Feverishly brightens. He stays but a moment near, When that flush fadeth,
Though true affection's tear Her soft eyelid shadeth."He goes from
her chamber straightInto life's jostle;
He meets at the very gate Business and bustle;
He thinks not of her within, Silently sighing;
He forgets, in that noisy din, That she is dying."And when her heart
is still,What though he mourneth,
Soon from his sorrow chill Wearied he turneth.
Soon o'er her buried head Memory's lights setteth,
And the true-hearted dead Thus man forgetteth. "

But it won't be so when both sides have found out, as a rule and law,
that no happiness is diredt, although joy may be — but always reflect-
ed; in other words, that to be happy, and loved, we must first love and
render happy some other soul. This is the eternal law of Love's equa-
tion, and is as absolute, rigid, and unalterable, as are the laws of number, refle&ion and gravitation.

We all need, at times, a little, and occasionally a good deal of, coax-
ing. We are a perverse set, and oftentimes refuse to do the very identical thing others want, and we ourselves are aching, dying, to do, simply
because some witling has not sense enough to coax us; and many a
good man, and better woman, has been suffered to gallop straight into
the jaws of death, right into the mouth of hell, for want of a little, gentle persuasion, even of the blarney sort; especially is this true of men,
even quite as much as of the other sections of the human being.

Let me restate the law in clearer terms: ist. The joys of Love are con-
sequent upon the rush of nervous fluid along the nerval fibrils, filamen-
tal cords, or wires of the system, centring in the vital ganglia of either
sex. When it flows alone it is electric. When it contacts on both sides
it is magnetic. 2d. The fulness of Love-joy depends upon the plethora

of vital life and nerve-aura stored up in the ganglia of the system, but especially upon the greater or less stock magazined within the mystic cripts appointed of Nature for that purpose. 3d. The conditions essential to the maintenance of any special power of either soul or body, especially of Love and its offices, which involves both, are: Regular remission, voluntary cessation of its activities for a period more or less protracted, and whose term depends upon, ist, the amount of force expended in other directions; and, 2d, upon the recuperative energies of the individual. 4th. In order to reach the highest possible affectional life, there must be lengthened terms of inaction, during which period the forces accumulate; the nervous magazines expand; the filaments grow stronger, more conductive, and sensitive at the same time; while morbid inflammations cease and normal appetite succeeds to insane physico-passional burnings, — which latter are unnatural, while the former is healthful. 5th. The intimate relations between soul and body render each at times the tormented victim of, and martyr to, the other; hence Love-offices are never in order save when each mind and each boay agrees with the other, and the four combine and unite to one common purpose. Otherwise disastrous results inevitably follow; for loveless union is like a money-lender, — it serves yeu in the present tense, lends you in the conditional mood; keeps you in the subjedtive; rules you in the future, and puts a period to you in the end; whereas Loving union wafts you up to Godness; ripens you; increases the bulk of soul and adds immeasurable joys to the sum total of life. ThereFore TAKE CARE YOUR LOVE DON'T PERISH IN THE USING OF IT!

6th.
Remember that the human soul is a musical instrument played

7th.
Life without love is perpetual death! To be truly human and purely good, we must love. To be strong, something must lean upon us; and they who live apart, isolated lives, are dwelling in the midst of viewless horrors, ready at any moment to take form and lash their souls to frenzy. We were born to love; to beget our kind; to bear children to the world and God; and failing therein, we defeat the very purposes for which Deity launched us into being.

Love's Alchemy—The Marrow; Res Gestae; Summing Up.

166

CVIII.

Human *marriage*, being triplicate,—material, mental, emotional, — has three offices, clear and distinct. ist. Its functions are humanizing and perpetuating; 2d. They are refining, elevating, a means of soul-growth; and, 3d. The purpose it serves is a mystic one, for beyond all doubt the ultimate of the human is deific — a fusion mingling, interblending—at-one-ment with the Omnipotent God; what came from, must return to, the centre; and he who would be nearer God is he who loves the purest.

CIX.

The test of all Love is its self-sacrificing unselfishness; and all amative love is false, unclean, abnormal, unless it be based upon the «0«-physical; it must be builded of respect, affection, that which is mental and spiritual; else *it lasts not.*

CX.

Woman loves easier than man, and it is easier broken, unless its roots are grounded in her very soul; then it is next to death to give it up. When a man loves in right down earnest, and from the feminine side of his soul, it, all other things being equal, evermasses, overweighs, any love modern women — Society people, I mean — are capable of. But take the two and probably the loves will balance each other, with this eternal fact in woman's favor; she is self-sacrificing, and her love, when it *is* love, is untainted with earth; is never external, never merely sensual.

CXI.

Woman can conceal, dissemble, pretend love,— not a spark of which she really feels, — to perfection; and hoodwink any man she chooses to play upon; but a woman with her eyes open cannot be served the same way by a man; for love, if it be real, tells its own story. More men love their wives than wives their husbands! He cannot make believe half as well as she; for the lady can coolly kiss a man with the intent of playing upon him at the very first chance; embrace him, with a load of deceit in her heart. But when a man loves he loves all over. Blast it, and you destroy him. But in these days love as true and solid as that is exceedingly rare indeed!

167

The undetected and unconvicted adulterers exceed the uncaught ones five hundred to one. This result from the non-understanding of the real and radical differences existing between true soul-love and its mere passional and magnetic counterfeits — which are fifty times more abundant than the other.

CXII.

No wicked person can truly love and remain wicked. That is the redemptive, salvatory and alchemical power of the divine principle! True-heartedness is the corrective agency of the great human world and human soul. Without it we are ships on the stormy deep, with a wild rush of angry waters threatening to submerge us at any instant! With it, we are life-boated into fair havens and secure anchorage! With it, we arise into bliss and blessedness; without it, misery is our lot; for it is the telegraphic System wherewith God engirdles the worlds! From Him it goes; to Him it returns, bringing up from the deeps the poor forlorn ones it finds there, and stringing them like beads to hang round the neck of the ineffable and viewless Lord of infinite and superlative glory!

CXIII.

At first Lpve springs up and surges in our souls, a newborn and strange power, which rules us with a rod of iron. At the start it is vague, general, diffusive; and we are glad without knowing the reasons why, like unto the babe quickened *en utero;* and we are irresistibly urged to centre it on some one, some reciprocating soul; and unless we do, wretched are we! If we fail so to do, but expend its forces here, there, everywhere, anywhere, we speedily cease to be truly human; but sink till we are the bond slaves of pernicious, debasing, demoralizing habit, from which there may be deliverance, but a very troublous one. We must love *one;* for unless we do the measure of our life on earth is unfilled.

CXIV.

The new soul descends to man; by him is bequeathed and entrusted to the dear mother's care, during those mysterious forty weeks. By her it is robed in flesh and blood, and during the wonderful and thrice holy process she needs all the vital life that he can spare; and it is his bounden duty to impart it in every possible form, from the gentle caress to the kind word and act of tender gallantry. *She* knows when she requires magnetism, and *she* is to be *sole* and supreme judge of *when,* and *where* and *how* that vital power shall be imparted! Do not forget this.

An hour's rest on his loving shoulder at the eventide, just as they sit by the open casement, is sometimes of more value to an unwell woman, than untold gold and diamonds would be at another time, and under different conditions.

Moreover, I have no patience with the puerile jargon of the "Physiologists," to the end that the great climax of *connubiality* ought always to cease from the conceptive moment till after lactation ;—that non-intercourse should be the rule, and rigidly enforced, all of which I regard as stupid nonsense — prefixed with a dash and two d's, — because we are human beings, not mere animals; and both the mother and babe require that magnetic life and *vif* which only the father and husband can supply.

There is a very curious thing right here: Instances are numerous of a wife descending, subsequent to conception, to other than the father of her child. In such case, the second man determines the shape, quality and calibre of the unborn infant's soul! The woman has no right to wrong any man in that style; for she ranks but as a cyprian, and the child is essentially an illegitimate; because, whereas, the husband has given body to his offspring, the other supplies it with the elements of spirit, and the babe will be *more* like *him* than its *own* father! because spiritual laws are of stronger force than physical! Don't forget this!

But the husband has no more rights in this respect than his wife; because wherever he goes he is sure to bring back a non-assimilable, foreign, magneto-vital influence, which neither his wife nor child can appropriate and absorb ; and thus he warps the babe's soul, if not its body, and infuses an aura into the very marrow of the being of both his dependents, which is injurious to all, and may crop out in physical disease or mental ailment, in after years, by the hair-graying conduct of his angular child!

When babes and children have trouble, they cry themselves to sleep; when men and women have trouble, slumber flies their weary eyes. Now when men are careless concerning the substance of this paragraph, they indicate a bad state of puerility; for of all human duties, the grandest is that of fathering those who shall be superior to ourselves. "But how? Suppose an inferior woman to be already pregnant, how shall I, her husband, correct the faults of haste, imperfect organization, — in a word, suppose the child to be has been launched into existence under very unfavorable conditions; how shall I correct the bad bias; and what shall I do that it may come to the world a far better and nobler being than if things ended just as they began? Tell me this, O man of Eulis, and I — I will thank you on bended knee!"

XV.

Love, and love only, can secure the devotion and heartfidelity of a woman, and any other sort is not worth having. When a woman loves, even if unreturned, she is a heroine; but if returned, she is happy, which is a great deal better than heroism!

CXVI.

Married people rain their homes, even though loving ones, by unwise and untimely association. It should never be a matter of course, but ever and always a dual inspiration; otherwise it is defective.

CXVII. Woman and man are not equals. They are diverse compatibles ; each contrasts and opposites the other, — offsetting in all ways. The two, together, constitute the being called man. Either alone is but an incompleteness, — a halfness. Neither owns the other, but are joint interestants in the social compact. The idea of ownership is what has made marriage as it is to-day, — a jangle, wrangle, tangle, — anything, everything, but what it should be. It were well if we would each of us constantly bear in mind that we conquer oftenest when we stoop to do so; and that more is to be gained by graceful sacrifice than stubborn reliance upon reserved rights.

CXVIII.

The second purpose of marriage is the peopling of the Spaces; its essence is spiritual. In true marriage there is a mutual infiltration of soul, whence it happens that nature, in slowly moulding each to resemble the other, proclaims that marriage real and true; but not all the ceremonies on earth could fuse a couple of natural antagonists.

170

If these likenesses are not observed, it is a pretty sure sign that there is but little love coursing round that homeside, and still less flowing through the channel of theii lives.

We do not want to find ourselves growing away from each other ', but in fusing natures and blending spirits, to coalesce with our opposites, effecting a chemical union, admitting no separation, and the only solvent of which is the grand Alcahest — Death : — And if the marriage be perfect, even death is unable to change it.

Reader: don't be a fool! don't lavish your love on one who talks, but never acts it. I, the author of this book, tell you that if your heart is overflowing with affection, you are in all the greater danger of first filling some empty, bladder-like being, with your own soul's sphere, then falling desperately in love with *it,* only to waken from the dreadful sleep to find him or her a diabolic sham, and yourself wrecked, ruined, prostrate, helpless, broken-hearted, deserted, and wretched beyond description. Prove all things, especially proffered Love, and when you find it *real,* give rein to your soul: — But not till then!!

CXIX.

When a couple are alike, equally choleric, mental, physical, frigid or the reverse; passive, positive, magnetic, electric, tall, slender, fat, active, indolent; then such are constitutionally, temperamentally, and in most other respects, non-adapted to each other; and if they are not careful, there will be more down than up, discord than its opposite, in that family. *But,* where such persons have already cast the die of what passes current in these days as marriage, there's wisdom in seeking to create or build up an artificial harmony, which care and time will render habitual, natural andpermanent; because Habit becomes even stronger tnan nature, as witness the use of narcotics, which all are disgusted with at first. If people will but attempt in thus making a second nature, the barrenness, usual in such cases, will be obviated, as well as the premature senility and impotence resultant; for that both these effects are often owing to such causes is as clearly established as any other medical fact, albeit the sufferers are not always aware of the reason.

CXX.

In all males of the human species the personal, physical charms of woman, based upon desire, is the central attractive point, round which all desires cluster. His better, nobler, higher love comes afterward. Reverse the case for woman. Her love *never* has that rise. She takes to the better side first — his social, mental, moral, spiritual manhood; and only after the lapse of time, frequently a whole year, does she awaken to the realization of the purely sensuous or passional; and uncounted thousands there are who never awaken thereto at all from the altar to the grave. In all such cases he is an unwise man who does not by careful and assiduous attention, by every delicate and tender means, seek to establish the natural equilibrium; by all true human methods arouse the dormant power in the breast of her who shares his lot and life.

CXXI.

Prior to the *actual marriage* the husband loves deepest, most intensely and devotedly. But after that, his ardor cools, and a revulsion of feeling, amounting to dislike, is almost sure to follow; in which he is the exact opposite of woman; for it is then only that she begins to cling to him with a depth and fervor surprising to him, astonishing to herself. Wise is he who then gives her reason to make that love permanent, solid, lasting, even to the brink of the grave.

Men, all males in fact, love fiercest before *marriage ,'* all females, subsequent thereto. It is the Law. But a man must so comport himself at these primal interviews as not to wound her sensitive spirit, or cloud her life with gloom, dread, fear, suspicion. First impressions last the longest!

CXXII.

Man's Love is never a steady stream, or constant force. He, so to speak, packs it away in the presence of other "Business," and gives it an airing now and again; but woman reverses all that, and loves right straight along from the start, every day and all the time, provided she loves at all. Whatever she may be about, no matter what, her love is the sole theme of her life, the only occupation of her mind; and she takes good care to give it air every hour of the day; and a fair return, in kind, amply repays her for many an hour of mortal anguish. If she fails to get it, God help her! for her life is but a lingering, painful, torturous death. It is even so with man. If he loves, — as I have loved, My God! — and after long months of toil awakens to find his idol but a phantom; that he has been embalming a doll in

172

his own heart and loving it, but getting no return, what wonder that madness comes, and the wild beating of his heart and throbbing of his temples drive him to the brink of ruin, until he stands toppling on the cliff's of suicide, doubtful whether to leap or not; and only saved by the Omnipotent hand of the interfering God!

CXXIII.

Lust ties man to the outer walls of human life, and keeps him there a prisoner feeding upon the poorest of husks. But Love frees him from many a gyve and thrall; gives him the freedom of God's gardens of joy; feeds him with the bread of life; opens the gates of heaven; and admits him to the companionship of celestial Verities and divinest life and truth. Without love we are, indeed, poor hermits in the world!

CXXIV.

People plunge headlong into perdition and social gehenna by rushing into each other's arms *too often!* Passional excess generates disease; Love cures them; and all the kidney difficulties and nervous disorders extant are but the physical expression of the morbid and unhealthy states of the love-natures of their respective victims.

Those who love can never prostitute themselves or each other, in any way.

It is just as impossible to kindle fire with ice as to long deceive a soul that loves. But, ah, God, *how* terrible is the awakening to the fact that all this time you have been lavishing your heart's best treasures on a dead stock! Then — in *her* case, comes leucor-rhœa or gravid uterus, — not physical ailments, but the outward sign that there's love trouble in the soul, and love the only remedy. In *his* case insanity more or less pronounced, and enduring.

CXXV.

There are periods when love insists upon passional moods. It is its natural appeasement. If riot yielded to, a frightful train of ills are sure to follow, and madness may end the cruel scene.

CXXVI.

Jealousy quite as often springs from magnetic incompatibility and impotence as from love-estrayal; and it brings on heart-pain, dyspepsia, liver and Bright's disease, prostatic, urethral, vaginal, ovarian, and other fatal troubles, long before the allotted span of years run out.

CXXVII.

Doctors tell us that *actual marriage* will cure some diseases of woman. But a diseased woman is not fit for it; and *actual marriage* in diseased states of either party is — monstrous! The doctrine is nonsense, pure and simple. Magnetism may do, *?narriage* no! But facts are facts, and the thing occurs. If love underlie it, well and good; if not, then not. It is disastrous. But if good results follow, it is Affection that works the miracle, nothing coarser! And more wives are injured in that manner than sextons can find spades to dig graves for!

That is a very poor sort of love which always exacts but never gives!" She prated of Love all day long, and neglected by one single act to prove her truth," is the story of many a man's life. "He says he loves me—but just look at me; does love waste one as I am wasted? My God! Let this bitter cup pass from me!" is the daily cry of millions of "Married" *women!* I'm tired and sick of dead babies! They ought to fill out the term of three-score years and ten; but they don't; and those who escape the sewers, sinks, drains, and being carried out with the tides, or being snugly put away in a cigar-box and stuck in a hole in the garden, are mighty uncertain of a safe deliverance from measles, scarlatina, croup, paregoric, or Mrs. Winslow's soothing syrup! Ah, but isn't it a soother?— soothing many a one to a sleep that knows no waking! But these dead ones are not all the offspring of the riff-raff, or hard-handed servitors at labor's shrine; but many a hundred of them might lay claim to aristocratic lineage;

Possibly one of the most notorious sex magicians was none other than the beast himself, Aleister Crowley. Needing no introduction here, Crowley was a ritual magician who studied with the Golden Dawn and later took over control of the O.T.O. Crowley introduced practices of sex magic to the masses with his highly controversial publications, which got him into some trouble with the occult organizations he was involved with. Crowley's discussions on sex magic had a very wide range, gowing from exploration of Hermetic implications, to purley ritual magic, to a kind of "prosperity wish fulfilling" type of style, rather like practices advocated in Rhonda Byrne's *The Secret* to aquire possessions, only Crowley used different methods.

For Crowley, the focus of the intention and prayer during climax strayed into all kinds of various areas, and unlike Randolph, who he no doubt drew a great deal from, did not restrict his wishes to love alone. In his work; *The Paris Working,* Crowley describes some of his attempts to experiment with using different prayers in sex magic, such as wishing for specific sums of money. He would also use the climax to invoke different Egyptian deities and call upon various gods and planets. In this way, Crowley was more as the type of erotic manipulator described above, who in knowing the influence of the erotic was able to try and direct it according to his will.

In his work, *Energized Enthusiasm, A Note on Theurgy,* Crowley explores the creative power involved in the sex act and describes how nothing short of pure genius may be extracted from it:

> The divine consciousness which is reflected and refracted in the works of Genius feeds upon a certain secretion, as I believe. This secretion is analogous to semen, but not identical with it. There are but few men and fewer women, those women being invariably androgyne, who possess it at any time in any quantity.
>
> So closely is this secretion connected with the sexual economy that it appears to me at times as if it might be a by-product of that process which generates semen. That some form of this doctrine has been generally accepted is shown in the prohibitions of all religions. Sanctity has been assumed to depend on chastity, and chastity has nearly always been interpreted as abstinence. But I doubt whether the relation is so simple as this would imply; for example, I find in myself that manifestations of mental creative force always concur with some abnormal condition of the physical powers of generation. But it is not the case that long periods of chastity, on the one hand, or excess of orgies, on the other, are favourable to its manifestation or even to its formation.
>
> I know myself, and in me it is extremely strong; its results are astounding. For example, I wrote "Tannhauser," complete from conception to execution, in sixty-seven consecutive hours. I was unconscious of the fall of nights and days, even after stopping; nor was there any reaction of fatigue. This work was written when I was twenty-four years old, immediately on the completion of an orgie which would normally have tired me out.

Often and often have I noticed that sexual satisfaction so-called has left me dissatisfied and unfatigued, and let loose the floods of verse which have disgraced my career.

Yet, on the contrary, a period of chastity has sometimes fortified me for a great outburst. This is far from being invariably the case. At the conclusion of the K 2 expedition, after five months of chastity, I did no work whatever, barring very few odd lyrics, for months afterwards.

I may mention the year 1911. At this time I was living, in excellent good health, with the woman whom I loved. Her health was, however, variable, and we were both constantly worried. The weather was continuously fine and hot. For a period of about three months I hardly missed a morning; always on waking I burst out with a new idea which had to be written down. The total energy of my being was very high. My weight was 10 stone 8 lb., which had been my fighting weight when I was ten years younger. We walked some twenty miles daily through hilly forest. The actual amount of MSS. written at this time is astounding; their variety is even more so; of their excellence I will not speak.

The Greeks say that there are three methods of discharging the genial secretion of which I have spoken. They thought perhaps that their methods tended to secrete it, but this I do not believe altogether, or without a qualm. For the manifestation of force implies force, and this force must have come from somewhere.

Easier I find it to say "subconsciousness" and "secretion" than to postulate an external reservoir, to extend my connotation of "man" than to invent "God." However, parsimony apart, I find it in my experience that it is useless to flog a tired horse. There are times when I am absolutely bereft of even one drop of this elixir. Nothing will restore it, neither rest in bed, nor drugs, nor exercise. On the other hand, sometimes when after a severe spell of work I have been dropping with physical fatigue, perhaps sprawling on the floor, too tired to move hand or foot, the occurrence of an idea has restored me to perfect intensity of energy, and the working out of the idea has actually got rid of the aforesaid physical fatigue, although it involved a great additional labour.

Exactly parallel (nowhere meeting) is the case of mania. A madman may struggle against six trained athletes for hours, and show no sign of fatigue. Then he will suddenly collapse, but at a second's notice from the irritable idea will resume the struggle as fresh as ever.

Until we discovered "unconscious muscular action" and its effects, it was rational to suppose such a man "possessed of a devil"; and the difference between the madman and the genius is not in the quantity but in the quality of their work. Genius is organized, madness chaotic. Often the organization of genius is on original lines, and ill-balanced and ignorant medicine-men mistake it for disorder.

Time has shown that Whistler and Gauguin "kept rules" as well as the masters whom they were supposed to be upsetting.

IV

The Greeks say that there are three methods of discharging the Lyden Jar of Genius. These three methods they assign to three Gods. These three Gods are Dionysus, Apollo, Aphrodite. In English: wine, woman and song.

Now it would be a great mistake to imagine that the Greeks were recommending a visit to a brothel. As well condemn the High Mass at St. Peter's on the strength of having witnessed a Protestant revival meeting. Disorder is always a parody of order, because there is no archetypal disorder that it might resemble. Owen Seaman can parody a poet; nobody can parody Owen Seaman. A critic is a bundle of impressions; there is no ego behind it. All photographs are essentially alike; the works of all good painters essentially differ.

Some writers suppose that in the ancient rites of Eleusis the High Priest publicly copulated with the High Priestess. Were this so, it would be no more "indecent" than it is "blasphemous" for the priest to make bread and wine into the body and blood of God. True, the Protestants say that it is blasphemous; but a Protestant is one to whom all things sacred are profane, whose mind being all filth can see nothing in the sexual act but a crime or a jest, whose only facial gestures are the sneer and the leer. Protestantism is the excrement of human thought, and accordingly in Protestant countries art, if it exist at all, only exists to revolt. Let us return from this unsavoury allusion to our consideration of the methods of the Greeks.

V

Agree then that it does not follow from the fact that wine, woman and song make the sailor's tavern that these ingredients must necessarily concoct a hell-broth.

There are some people so simple as to think that, when they have proved the religious instinct to be a mere efflorescence of the sex-instinct, they have destroyed religion.

We should rather consider that the sailor's tavern gives him his only glimpse of heaven, just as the destructive criticism of the phallicists has only proved sex to be a sacrament. Consciousness, says the materialist, axe in hand, is a function of the brain. He has only re-formulated the old saying, "Your bodies are the temples of the Holy Ghost."!

Now sex is justly hallowed in this sense, that it is the eternal fire of the race. Huxley admitted that "some of the lower animalculae are in a sense immortal," because they go on reproducing eternally by fission, and however often you divide "x" by 2 there is always something left. But he never seems to have seen that mankind is immortal in exactly the same sense, and goes on reproducing itself with similar characteristics through the ages, changed by circumstance indeed, but always identical in itself. But the spiritual flower of this process is that at the moment of discharge a physical ecstasy occurs, a spasm analogous to the mental spasm which meditation gives. And further, in the sacramental and ceremonial use of the sexual act, the divine consciousness may be attained.

The sexual act being then a sacrament, it remains to consider in what respect this limits the employment of the organs. First, it is obviously legitimate to employ them for their natural physical purpose. But if it be allowable to use them ceremonially for a religious purpose, we shall find the act hedged about with many restrictions.

For in this case the organs become holy. It matters little to mere propagation that men should be vicious; the most debauched roue might and almost certainly would beget more healthy children than a semi-sexed prude. So the so-called "moral" restraints are not based on reason; thus they are neglected.

But admit its religious function, and one may at once lay down that the act must not be profaned. It must not be undertaken lightly and foolishly without excuse.

It may be undertaken for the direct object of continuing the race.

It may be undertaken in obedience to real passion; for passion, as the name implies, is rather inspired by a force of divine strength and beauty without the will of the individual, often even against it.

It is the casual or habitual --- what Christ called "idle" --- use or rather abuse of these forces which constitutes their profanation. It will further be obvious that, if the act in itself is to be the sacrament in a religious ceremony, this act must be accomplished solely for the love of God.

All personal considerations must be banished utterly. Just as any priest can perform the miracle of transubstantiation, so can any man, possessing the necessary qualifications, perform this other miracle, whose nature must form the subject of a subsequent discussion. Personal aims being destroyed, it is "a fortiori" necessary to neglect social and other similar considerations.

Physical strength and beauty are necessary and desirable for aesthetic reasons, the attention of the worshippers being liable to distraction if the celebrants are ugly, deformed, or incompetent.

I need hardly emphasize the necessity for the strictest self-control and concentration on their part. As it would be blasphemy to enjoy the gross taste of the wine of the sacrament, so must the celebrant suppress even the minutest manifestation of animal pleasure.

Of the qualifying tests there is no necessity to speak; it is sufficient to say that the adepts have always known how to secure efficiency.

Needless also to insist on a similar quality in the assistants; the sexual excitement must be suppressed and transformed into its religious equivalent.

VII

With these preliminaries settle in order to guard against foreseen criticisms of those Protestants who, God having made them a little lower than the Angels, have made themselves a great deal lower than the beasts by their consistently bestial interpretation of all things human and divine, we may consider first the triune nature of these ancient methods of energizing enthusiasm.

Music has two parts; tone or pitch, and rhythm. The latter quality associates it with the dance, and that part of dancing which is not rhythm is sex. Now that part of sex which is not a form of the dance, animal movement, is intoxication of the soul, which connects it with wine. Further identities will suggest themselves to the student.

By the use of the three methods in one the whole being of man may thus be stimulated.

The music will create a general harmony of the brain, leading it in its own paths; the wine affords a general stimulus of the animal nature; and the sex-excitement elevates the moral nature of the man by its close analogy with the highest ecstasy. It remains, however, always for him to make the final transmutation. Unless he have the special secretion which I have postulated, the result will be commonplace.

So consonant is this system with the nature of man that it is exactly parodied and profaned not only in the sailor's tavern, but in the society ball. Here, for the lowest natures the result is drunkenness, disease and death; for the middle natures a gradual blunting of the finer feelings; for the higher, an exhilaration amounting at the best to the foundation of a life-long love.

If these Society "rites" are properly performed, there should be no exhaustion. After a ball, one should feel the need of a long walk in the young morning air. The weariness or boredom, the headache or somnolence, are Nature's warnings.

VIII

Now the purpose of such a ball, the moral attitude on entering, seems to me to be of supreme importance. If you go with the idea of killing time, you are rather killing yourself. Baudelaire speaks of the first period of love when the boy kisses the trees of the wood, rather than kiss nothing. At the age of thirty-six I found myself at Pompeii, passionately kissing that great grave statue of a woman that stands in the avenue of the tombs. Even now, as I wake in the morning, I sometimes fall to kissing my own arms.

It is with such a feeling that one should go to a ball, and with such a feeling intensified, purified and exalted, that one should leave it. If this be so, how much more if one go with the direct religious purpose burning in one's whole being! Beethoven roaring at the sunrise is no strange spectacle to me, who shout with joy and wonder, when I understand (without which one cannot really be said ever to see) a blade of grass. I fall upon my knees in speechless adoration at the moon; I hide my eyes in holy awe from a good Van Gogh.

Imagine then a ball in which the music is the choir celestial, the wine the wine of the Graal, or that of the Sabbath of the Adepts, and one's partner the Infinite and Eternal One, the True and Living God Most High!

Go even to a common ball --- the Moulin de la Galette will serve even the least of my magicians --- with your whole soul aflame within you, and your whole will concentrated on these ...ansubstantiations, and tell me what miracle takes place! It is the hate of, the distaste for, life that sends one to the ball when one is old; when one is young one is on springs until the hour falls; but the love of God, which is the only true love, diminishes not with age; it grows deeper and intenser with every satisfaction. It seems as if in the noblest men this secretion constantly increases --- which certainly suggests an external reservoir --- so that age loses all its bitterness. We find "Brother Lawrence," Nicholas Herman of Lorraine, at the age of eighty in continuous enjoyment of union with God. Buddha at an equal age would run up and down the Eight High Trances like an acrobat on a ladder; stories not too dissimilar are told of Bishop Berkeley. Many persons have not attained union at all until middle age, and then have rarely lost it.

It is true that genius in the ordinary sense of the word has nearly always showed itself in the young. Perhaps we should regard such cases as Nicholas Herman as cases of acquired genius. Now I am certainly of opinion that genius can be acquired, or, in the alternative, that it is an almost universal possession. Its rarity may be attributed to the crushing influence of a corrupted society. It is rare to meet a youth without high ideals, generous thoughts, a sense of holiness, of his own importance, which, being interpreted, is, of his own identity with God. Three years in the world, and he is a bank clerk or even a government official. Only those who intuitively understand from early boyhood that they must stand out, and who have the incredible courage and endurance to do so in the face of all that tyranny, callousness, and the scorn of inferiors can do; only these arrive at manhood uncontaminated.

Every serious or spiritual thought Is made a jest; poets are thought "soft" and "cowardly," apparently because they are the only boys with a will of their own and courage to hold out against the whole school, boys and masters in league as once were Pilate and Herod; honour is replaced by expediency, holiness by hypocrisy. Even where we find thoroughly good seed sprouting in favourable ground, too often is there a frittering away of the forces. Facile encouragement of a poet or painter is far worse for him than any amount of opposition.

Here again the sex question (S.Q. so-called by Tolstoyans, chastity-mongers, nut-fooders, and such who talk and think of nothing else) intrudes its horrid head. I believe that every boy is originally conscious of sex as sacred. But he does not know what it is. With infinite diffidence he asks. The master replies with holy horror; the boy with a low leer, a furtive laugh, perhaps worse.

I am inclined to agree with the Head Master of Eton that paederastic passions among schoolboys "do no harm"; further, I think them the only redeeming feature of sexual life at public schools.

The Hindoos are wiser. At the well-watched hour of puberty the boy is prepared as for a sacrament; he is led to a duly consecrated temple, and there by a wise and holy woman, skilled in the art, and devoted to this end, he is ini??ated with all solemnity into the mystery of life.

The act is thus declared religious, sacred, impersonal, utterly apart from amorism and eroticism and animalism and sentimentalism and all the other vilenesses that Protestantism has made of it. The Catholic Church did, I believe, to some extent preserve the Pagan tradition. Marriage is a sacrament.<<Of course there has been a school of devilish ananders that has held the act in itself to be "Wicked." Of such blasphemers of Nature let no further word be said.>> But in the attempt to deprive the act of all accretions which would profane it, the Fathers of the Church added in spite of themselves other accretions which profaned it more. They tied it to property and inheritance. They wished it to serve both God and Mammon.

Rightly restraining the priest, who should employ his whole energy in the miracle of the Mass, they found their counsel a counsel of perfection. The magical tradition was in part lost; the priest could not do what was expected of him, and the unexpended portion of his energy turned sour. Hence the thoughts of priests, like the thoughts of modern faddists, revolved eternally around the S.Q.

The main idea in this work was to emphasize the important amount of creative force involved in the sexual act. Crowley was trying to communicate that if we are but able to harness, instead of expend this force we might be more productive.

This concept of actually using Sexual Attraction under the same law of attraction we have mentioned in so many other areas is an important one indeed, since it drives so many of our actions at various points in our lives. It is certainly better to become familiar with this force, rather than to be unconsciously driven by it into ruin.

The magical force of influence, through love, through the erotic, through sway can be seen as a manipulation, it is true. However, Once we may understand that Love comes from our own hearts as well, that we are participators in the show, that we are not simply swept up in the flames we have a faint glimmer of fascinating hope to come into the position of the magician ourselves. When we align with our own desires sent from heaven, the magician loses power over us as we in turn become the influence we have previously succumbed to by coming to live inside ourselves rather than lusting after the hearts of others.

{Section Six}

WHY SOME SECRETS SHOULD BE KEPT

Give not that which is holy unto the dogs, neither cast ye your pearls before swine, lest they trample them under their feet, and turn again and rend you.

—Matthew 7:6, King James translation

Many secrets impair the quality of our lives and empower scurrilous rascals. But the truth is, some secrets are kept for the safety of the human race, like poisons and matches are hidden from children. The book *The Secret* attempts to convince the reader that they have control over the universe with their thoughts. Whether or not this is true, let us take a moment to consider the ramifications of this statement. Author Rhonda Byrne suggests we use this control to get anything we wish for. Is there no downside to this idea? Are there no wishes that people might make which could cause harm to others? What about a child molester or rapist? What if he got everything he could ever imagine?

Let's examine the sad story of C.W. Leadbeater (1854–1934), one of the most celebrated authors of the Theosophical movement. He was accused of pederasty in 1906, and many more accusations followed. Leadbeater resigned before an investigation was begun by the Theosophical society, and he was never prosecuted for the charges. Years later, Leadbeater would go on to kidnap the famous spiritual leader Krishnamurti when he was just a young boy, though the boy was able to escape with the help of his parents.[118] These actions came from a man who warned against the misuse of one's mind's powers over another. We now read his words with a certain degree of irony.

> Everyone knows that a man who has at his disposal a large amount of steam power or electrical power can do useful work and produce definite results; but few people know that every man has at his disposal a certain amount of this other and higher power, and that with that he can produce results just as definite and just as real. As matters stand at present in the physical world, only a few can become rich by their means; but it is a prominent feature of the vivid interest of the unseen side of life that

---

118 Vernon, Ronald, *Star in the East: Krishnamurti—The Invention of a Messiah.*

> every human being, rich or poor, old or young, has already at his
> disposal no inconsiderable proportion of its forces. And therefore
> the riches of these higher powers are within the reach of all . . . .
> The possession of power always means responsibility; so in order to
> avoid doing harm unintentionally, and in order to utilize thoroughly
> these magnificent possibilities, it will clearly be well for us to learn all
> that we can on this subject.[119]

A perfect example of the dangerous nature of the illusion of control comes to us through the biblical story of Solomon, the king of the Jews. As the story goes, Solomon was presented with the opportunity to have anything he wanted as a gift from God. He chose ultimate wisdom. A seemingly altruistic decision. However, as his life progressed, Solomon utilized that wisdom to acquire more and more power over the spirit world and demonic entities. Summoning all manner of demons, and ordering them to do his biding, Solomon was confident that he was wise enough to hold dominion over them. He even used demons as slaves to help construct the first temple of the Jews. Alas, even Solomon himself was not wise enough to wield such power for long. His loss of control came with the king of demons, Asmodeus. According to the classical Rabbis, one day Asmodeus was captured by Solomon using a powerful ring he was given by God. The ring forced Asmodeus to remain in Solomon's service. Solomon one day asked Asmodeus what could make demons powerful over man, and Asmodeus asked to be freed and given the ring so that he could demonstrate; Solomon agreed and immediately Asmodeus threw the ring into the sea where it was swallowed by a fish. Asmodeus then swallowed the king, stood up fully with one wing touching heaven and the other earth, and spat out Solomon to a distance of 400 miles. Solomon did eventually regain the ring after much hardship, but this did little to prevent the final outcome of his control over the demons spiraling into chaos. In the apocryphal literature[120], Solomon dies in sin, forsaken by God and overrun by demons. Solomon died propped up, trying to trick the demons into thinking he was still alive so that he could die in peace and escape:

119 Leadbeater, C.W., *The Power and Use of Thought.*
120 De Penitentia Adae

Certain Rabbinic writings state that, feeling his strength fail, he sought God to conceal his death so long as the works he had undertaken by the help of demons should be unfinished. Accordingly, he remained upon his knees in prayer, leaning on his staff, and the demons, believing him to be alive continued their work. The Koran adds that a crawling reptile was the first to learn the news of his death; the beast gnawed the staff which supported the dead Solomon and thereupon the corpse collapsed. The demons then ceased to work.[121]

If the wisest man in the world could not hold such secrets with impunity, what chance do the rest of us have?

Thus I, Solomon, had power over the spirits of the earth, and of the air, and of the water, and made them serve me; and my kingdom was exalted, and there was peace in my days. But when I became mighty my heart was lifted up, and I committed foolishness; And forthwith my glory departed from me, and I forgot my wisdom, and became weak and foolish in my mind; and the heathen woman compelled me to build temples to the false gods, to Baal, and Remphan, and Moloch; and my spirit was darkened within me, and I became a byword among men and demons. Therefore have I written this testament, that men might remember me, and think of their latter end as well as of their beginning.[122]

We may find another example of the dangers involved in knowing some secrets in the famous story of Rabbi Loew and the Golem. This story is the prototype for many that followed, including Mary Shelley's *Frankenstein*. According to Jewish tradition, the name of God carries with it all the powers of creation itself. To utter the divine name, also known as the Tetragammaton, is to hold creative power over the world.

"Ahima'ats tells us of the magical miracles performed by Ahron of Bagdad, the merkabah mystic, and by Rabbi Hananel, who brought dead men back to life for a time by wedging a piece of parchment

121 De Givory, Grillot. ND. *Witchcraft Magic and Alchemy*, Bonanza Books, New York, pgs 98-99.
122 James, M.R.1913. Old Testament Legends Longmans, Green and Co.

with the name of God under their tongue or sewing it into the flesh of their right arm. When the name is removed the body falls back lifeless... The magicians of Egypt, who made creatures, were acquainted through the demons or some other artifice with the order of the merkabah and took dust under the feet of the order and created what they wished. But the scholars knew the secret of the merkabah... and spoke the name of God over it, and it was created. In this way Micah made the Golden calf that could dance."[123]

There are many legends in Jewish folklore of individuals who took this most powerful name of God and inscribed it upon a piece of paper and then placed it into the mouth of a man they had fashioned out of clay. This clay man was known as the Golem, and just as God made Adam out of mud, so the Rabbi's attempted to mimic God in his creation of man;

"For obviously, a man who creates a golem is in some sense competing with God's creation of Adam; in such an act the creative power of man enters into a relationship, whether of emulation or antagonism, with the creative power of God."[124]

Needless to say, these attempts at becoming on par with the creator always went horribly wrong. The story of the Golem first appeared in print in 1847 in a collection of Jewish tales entitled *Galerie der Sippurim*, published by Wolf Pascheles of Prague. Rabbi Judah Loew of Prague created a golem to defend the Prague ghetto of Josefov from Anti-Semitic attacks. Once the Golem was created however, he just wouldn't follow orders properly (kind of like when you make a child, they don't listen to you either). The Golem kept growing and started killing not only the people it was supposed to, it started killing everyone. In some versions of the story, the golem even turns on Rabbi Loew himself, who is forced to defend his life from his own creation which no longer obeys him. This is the lesson of utilizing forces of the universe, we may initiate them, but our control of where they go through time is where Chaos mathematics come into play.

It is most important to remember that even the most highly trained initiates, say Tantrik Tibetan Buddhists, who have been studying

---

123 Scholem, Gershom. 1996. *On the Kabbalah and its Symbolism*. Schocken pg. 182
124 Ibid.

their craft since childhood everyday, day in day out, still become over-whelmed when dealing with the forces of the universe in a Shamanic nature. There is a reason, believe it or not, that the Jews require a certain age and level of knowledge of the Torah before one is allowed to study Kabbalah. Much preparation is necessary to learn of some secrets.

> "Let a divine being approach you! It may be nothing or everything. Nothing, if you meet it in the frame of mind in which you confront everyday things. Everything, if you are prepared and attuned to it. What it is in itself is a matter which does not concern you; the point is whether it leaves you as you were or makes a different man of you. But this depends solely on you. You must have been prepared by the education and development of the most intimate forces of your personality so that what the divine is able to evoke may be kindled and released in you. What is brought to you depends upon the reception you prepare for it."[125]

It would be foolish to pick up a gun and expect to just know how it works, wielding the laws of the Universe require a little bit of training lest they go off haphazardly. We must above all hold the greatest respect for these secrets and understand that they affect not only ourselves when we discover and tamper with them, but the entire world. For we are but the world in microcosm and each one of our actions can affect not only ourselves, but everyone we are connected to. The child with the matches can burn not only himself, but can set ablaze an entire neighborhood. The secret is that your thoughts do not only determine your life, your success and your well being, they determine the well being of the entire universe. If you believe for one moment that "You are God" as *The Secret* suggests, take a moment to consider that implication not only for you as an individual, but also consider your role as God as it pertains to all the other people, animals and minerals sharing this space with you. That should be a sobering realization that we all keep in mind every minute of every day. Our individual success, when attained magically, comes only as the result of someone else's failure. When one God wins, another one crumbles. All things must come from something, nothing comes from nothing. If you choose to abuse the law of attraction by utilizing it to acquire untold riches, or Love, be assured somewhere in the world there is an equal and opposite reaction.

---

125   Steiner, Rudolph. 1997. *Christianity as Mystical Fact*. Steiner Books.

We find it is this issue of *control* that is the key when circumnavigating this information. Manly Hall suggests that *The Secret's* type of wish-casting has a darker side that is often overlooked and ignored:

> Though the demonism of the Middle Ages seems to have disappeared, there is abundant evidence that in many forms of modern thought—especially the so-called "prosperity" psychology, "willpower-building" metaphysics, and systems of "high-pressure" salesmanship—black magic has merely passed through a metamorphosis, and although its name be changed, its nature remains the same.[126]

We may find an example of the dangers involved in wielding secret knowledge in the story of Rabbi Loew and the Golem. This tale is the prototype for many that followed, including Mary Shelley's *Frankenstein*. According to Jewish tradition, the name of God carries with it all the powers of creation itself. To utter the divine name, also known as the Tetragrammaton, is to hold creative power over the world.

> *Ahima'ats* tells us of the magical miracles performed by Ahron of Bagdad, the *merkabah* mystic, and by Rabbi Hananel, who brought dead men back to life for a time by wedging a piece of parchment with the name of God under their tongue or sewing it into the flesh of their right arm. When the name is removed the body falls back lifeless . . . . The magicians of Egypt, who made creatures, were acquainted through the demons or some other artifice with the order of the *merkabah* and took dust under the feet of the order and created what they wished. But the scholars knew the secret of the *merkabah* . . . and spoke the name of God over it, and it was created. In this way Micah made the Golden Calf that could dance."[127]

Jewish folklore tells about individuals who took this most powerful name of God and inscribed it upon a piece of paper, which they placed it into the mouth of a man they had fashioned out of clay. This clay man was known as the Golem, and just as God made Adam out of mud, so the Rabbi's attempted to mimic God

---

126 Hall, Manly P., *The Secret Teachings of All Ages.*
127 Scholem, Gershom, *On the Kabbalah and its Symbolism.*

in his creation of man, for obviously, a man who creates a golem is in some sense competing with God's creation of Adam; in such an act the creative power of man enters into a relationship, whether of emulation or antagonism, with the creative power of God.[128]

The story of the Golem first appeared in print in 1847 in a collection of Jewish tales entitled *Galerie der Sippurim*. Rabbi Judah Loew of Prague created a Golem to defend the Prague ghetto of Josefov from Anti-Semitic attacks. But the Golem kept growing and started killing innocents, even turning on Rabbi Loew himself, who was forced to defend his life from his own creation which would no longer obey him.

There exists in this world many things that we do not understand, and events that science cannot explain. We may have brief glimpses of the mysterious spirit world on various occasions throughout our lives. People are naturally attracted to the idea of taking control of our lives and the lives of others, and taking charge of our destinies. But where do we draw the line when utilizing spiritual forces for our own good, or what we perceive to be the good of others?

> Many cases that come along relating to psychic problems have their origin in the individual's desperate desire to grow . . . . In his desire to grow, he is usually looking for some kind of shortcut. He is looking for some kind of a mysterious key that will open for him an understanding or insight otherwise not available. So he is really seeking just a little but selfishly . . . . He assumes the ends justifies the means . . . that the esoteric truths of life are some kind of secret and that it is possible to find the key, buy it, steal it . . . and that by means of this key we can suddenly "unlock the shut door of the palace to the king.[129]

This is not to say that none of us should explore our connection to the laws of the universe. But we must understand the nature of what it is we are doing, we must be conscious of our actions, and just because we *can* do something, doesn't mean we *should* do it.

> Hermes, however, in his "about the inner door," doth depreciate this magic, even declaring that: The spiritual man. The man who knows

---

128 Ibid.
129 Hall, Manly P., *Unseen Forces that Affect Our Lives.*

himself, should not accomplish any thing by means of magic, e'en though he think it a good thing, nor should he force necessity, but suffer her to take her course, according to her nature and decree; he should progress by seeking only the knowledge of himself and God, to gain the Trinity that none can name, and let Fate do whate'er she will to her own clay—that is the body.[130]

It is nice to think that once we come under the realization that we are God, we would begin a noble life; however, the first thought in most people's minds is more like "How can I get back at all the people who have hurt me?" or "How can I get what I deserve, without working for it?"

The secrecy surrounding the science has been due to the mental and moral unpreparedness for it on the part of those content to live the normal life of the world. Save under glyph and figure, cryptic memorials and allegories, the details of the experimental process of regeneration could never be made public, nor can they now . . . . And why? Because, apart from the privacy inevitably attaching to sacrosanctities, it involves perils personal and general; it lays open the most secret recesses and properties of the human organism, stripping bare the quivering roots of the physical and psychic life; it leads into contact with magnetic forces of terrific potency from the knowledge and effects of which we are at present providentially sheltered and safeguarded by the grossness of our sense-bodies and the limitations those impose upon us until such time as we become fitted to function in independence of them.[131]

As discussed in this book, the natural forces and laws outlined in Hermetic philosophy may be used very effectively to heal the diseases which human beings create in their minds. They can be used to aide the development of humanity and free our souls of suffering. But we must remember the rule, *as above so below*. Like all things that heal, these teachings also have the power to harm. Says Dion Fortune in *Psychic Self Defense*:

130 Zosimos, as quoted in G..R.S. Mead, *Thrice Greatest Hermes*.
131 Atwood, Mary Anne. 1918. A Suggestive Inquiry into the Hermetic Mystery. J.M. Watkins: London.

> The essence of a psychic attack is to be found in the principles and
> operations of telepathic suggestion . . . . Suggestion is of three
> kinds: Auto Suggestion, Conscious Suggestion and Hypnotic Sug-
> gestion . . . . Suggestion does not make its appeal to consciousness,
> but aims at laying its hands upon the springs of action in the subcon-
> sciousness and manipulating them from there.

Perhaps Mary Baker Eddy was not so crazy in her assertions that she was under psychic attack. Malicious Mesmerists and hypnotists have become well-known over the course of history. Probably the most famous of these was a fictional character, one based on several real people who were perpetrating their swindles at the time of his invention.

The name Svengali, immortalized in George Du Maurier's bestselling novel *Trilby* (1894), shall be forever pictured when imagining the evil hypnotist. At the time the book was written, hypnotist stage shows were all the rage, and traveling hypnotists and Mesmerists (like Phineas Quimby) drew large crowds. In *Trilby*, Svengali is a middle-aged, dirty, unattractive and snake-like musician. Despite his unseemly appearance, he manages to convince, by way of hypnotism, a young beautiful girl, Trilby, to become his associate. Svengali then hypnotizes her further, so that she becomes a great singer, while he lives off her income and seduces her at his whim. The hypnotism Svengali performs is identical to that of the Mesmerists.

The same year that *Trilby* was published, a woman was actually killed by mental suggestion:

> In 1894, a hypnotist, Franz Neukomm, also made European news.
> Ella first was hypnotized by two doctors who were hired by a "rela-
> tive" to treat her for a "nervous ailment." Their power of suggestion
> temporarily suppressed the symptoms, but then she got even worse.
> Neukomm happened to be passing through, and her relative took
> Ella to be mesmerized by him. He also achieved an effective cure
> of her problem. Neukomm then saw opportunity knocking. He con-
> vinced Ella's relative that the somnambulist girl might again relapse
> in the absence of his hypnotic influence and therefore should remain
> in his care. He would look after her without charge. Her relative then

abandoned Ella to Neukomm. Thereafter, she traveled with the hypnotist as his medium . . . . During each show, Neukomm invited an ailing volunteer from the audience up on stage. Then he would hypnotize Ella and give her a suggestion to place herself in the mind of the patient and provide information about his or her state of health. The night that Ella died, Neukomm, to increase the audience's sense of drama, had changed his hypnotic instructions in a small, but significant way. He told Ella, "Your soul will leave your body in order to enter that of the patient." Imperious master Neukomm deepened her trance, and firmly repeated the "leave your body" command . . . . Ella Salamon died. The postmortem stated that heart failure, caused by Neukomm's hypnotic suggestion, was the probable cause of her death. Neukomm was charged with manslaughter and found guilty. Ella's death was similar to what anthropologists call "voodoo" death, death by suggestion.[132]

Audiences of the time seemed to delight in the practitioner being able to get his victim to do whatever was commanded—from standing on top of a person suspended between two chairs to making someone bark like a dog. It was these early shows that inspired a form of scientific mind control and the study of utilizing the hypnotic state for coercion. The term "mind control" tends to refer to various techniques designed to subvert an individual's control of their own behavior, emotions, or decisions. The jump from using hypnosis for healing purposes to that of controlling another's mind is really not a very difficult one to make:

The next step . . . was the beginning to use these techniques deliberately for purpose of mind control. And essentially the first steps are taken by A.R. Luria in his institute in Moscow. Luria reasoned that if you can get people to have false confessions with hypnosis, you probably could build affective complexes on those false confessions. In other words, you could not only get people to report things that never happened, you could get them to experience the entire range of emotions affiliated with those events.[133]

---

132 Ibid.
133 Scheflin, Dr. Alan, "The History of Mind Control: What We Can Prove and What We Can't," from CKLN FM (88.1 in Toronto).

The laws of the universe as laid out in the Hermetic teachings have been throughout the course of history. If the law of attraction is true, consider the possible consequences of their haphazard and unconsidered use.

What is the best way to make use of these principles? Why not shoot for the moon in your aspirations? ✳

Make thou thyself to grow to the same stature as the greatness which transcends all measure; leap forth from every Body; transcend all Time; become eternity; and then shalt thou know God. Conceiving nothing is impossible unto thyself, think thyself deathless and able to know all—all arts, all sciences, the way of every life. Become more lofty than all height, and lower than all depth. Collect into thyself all senses of all creatures—of fire and water, dry and moist. Think that thou art at the same time in every place—in earth, in sea, in sky; not yet begotten, in the womb, young, old, and dead, in after death conditions. And if thou knowest all things at once—times, places, doings, qualities, and quantities; thou canst know God.[134]

---

134 Hermes Trismegistus, as quoted in G.R.S. Mead, *Thrice Greatest Hermes*

{Bibliography}

Abdul-Sâhib Al-Hasani Al-'âmili. 1980. *The Prophets, Their Lives and Their Stories*. Al-Alfain Bookshop, Kuwait.

Ancient Wisdom and Secret Sects (Mysteries of the Unknown). 1989. Time Life Education.

Atkinson, William Walker. 2006. *Thought Vibration: The Law of Attraction in the Thought World*. BN Publishing.

Atwood, Mary Anne. 1918. *A Suggestive Inquiry into the Hermetic Mystery*. J.M. Watkins, London.

Baker, Carolyn. 2007, *"The Secret": Creating a Culture of Cheerfulness as Rome Burns*. Blog, "The Daily Scare".

Barrett, Francis. 1967. *The Magus*. University Books.

Bauckham, Richard. 1985. *The Fall of the Angels as the Source of Philosophy in Hermias and Clement of Alexandria Vigiliae Christianae*, Vol. 39, No. 4. pp. 313-330 doi:10.2307/1583769

Bergier, Jacques. and Louis Pauwels, 1960. *The Morning of the Magicians*. Stein and Day, New York.

Binet, A., and C. Féré. 1888. *Animal Magnetism*. Appleton and Co., New York.

Blavatsky, H.P. 1886. *The Secret Doctrine*, Vol. 1. Theosophical University Press, California.

Bloch, Chayim. 1925. *The Golem: Legends of the Ghetto of Prague*. Translated from the German by Harry Schneiderman

"Book of the Bee," Syr. ed., pp. 50-53; Eng. ed., pp. 50-52. citation as given in Jewish Encyclopedia.

Brooks, Dennis Scott. 1991. *Paradise Lost and the Commented Epic*. University of Nebraska: Lincoln.

Brodeur, Claude, PhD. 1997. *The New Thought Movement in America*. Societas Rosicruciana in Canada.

Brown, Peter. 2003. *The Rise of Western Christendom*, 2nd Ed. Blackwell Publishing, Massachssetts.

Byrne, Rhonda. 2006. *The Secret*, Atria Books / Beyond Words, New York, NY.

Carmichael, Mary, and Radford Benjamin. *Secrets and Lies*. Special Report from the Committee for Skeptical Inquiry. From csicop.org.

Carroll, Robert. Todd. 2003. *The Skeptic's Dictionary*. John Wilcy & Sons, Inc., New Jersey.

Cavendish, Richard. 1983. *"Grail", Man, Myth & Magic, An Illustrated Encyclopedia of the Supernatural*, Vol. 9. Marshall Cavendish Corp.

Case, Paul Foster. 1936. *To Our Members*. The Wheel of Life, Autumn Equinox.

The Catholic Encyclopedia, Vol. I. 1907. Robert Appleton Company, New York. Nihil Obstat, March 1, 1907. Remy Lafort, S.T.D., Censor. Imprimatur. +John Cardinal Farley, Archbishop of New York

Collins, Andrew. 2001. *From the Ashes of Angels: The Forbidden Legacy of a Fallen Race*. Bear and Co.

Clymer, R. Swinburne. M.D., 1954. *Occult Science*. Philosophical Publishing Co.

Dauphin, C.M. 1999. "From Apollo and Asclepius to Christ: Pilgrimage and Healing at the Temple and Episcopal Basilica at Dor." *Liber Annuus* 49.

Davidson, Gustav. 1967. *A Dictionary of Angels, Including the Fallen Angels*. The Free Press.

De Givory, Grillot. ND. *Witchcraft, Magic and Alchemy*. Bonanza Books, New York.

Delcourt, Marie. 1992. *Hermaphrodite*. Presses Universitaires, France.

Diogenes Laertius. 1925. *Lives of Eminent Philosophers*. Leob Classical Library. V 4-5

Dobbs, Betty Jo Teeter. 1983. *The Foundations of Newton's Alchemy: or, 'The Hunting of the Greene Lyon'*. Cambridge University Press.

Donnelley, Ignatius. 1976. *Atlantis: The Antediluvian World*. Dover Publications Inc., New York.

Dresser, Horatio. 1921. *The Quimby Manuscripts*. Thomas Y. Crowel Co., New York.

Eddy, Mary Baker. 1994. *Science and Health With a Key to the Scriptures*. Writings of Mary Baker Eddy publishers.

Edinger, Edward F. 1985. *Anatomy of the Psyche: Alchemical Symbolism and Psychotherapy*. Open Court Publishing Company.

Eliade, Mircea. 1979. *The Two and the One*. University of Chicago Press.

Emery, Carla. 1998. *Secret, Don't Tell: The Encyclopedia of Hypnotism*. Acorn Hill Publishing.

Etheridge, J.W. 1862. *Targum Pseudo-Jonathan and Onkelos to the Pentateuco*. London.

Everard, John. 1650. *The Divine Pymander in XVII Books*. London.

Farnell, Lewis R. 1896. *The Cults of the Greek States*, vol I, part I. Oxford University Press.

Farrar, Janet and Stewart. 1987. *The Life and Times of a Modern Witch*. Phoenix Publishing Company, Arizona.

Faivre, Antoine. 1995. *The Eternal Hermes*. Phanes Press.

Faivre, Antoine, and Jacob Needleman, eds. 1992. *Modern Esoteric Spirituality*. Crossroad, New York.

Fiebag, Johannes and Peter. 1989. *The Discovery of the Grail*, trans. George Sassoon. Goldmann, Müenchen, Germany.

Fillmore, Charles. 1986. *Metaphysical Bible Dictionary*. Unity School of Christianity.

Fortune, Dion. 1993. *The Magical Battle of Britain*. Sun Chalice Books.

Fortune, Dion. 2001. *Psychic Self Defense*. Weiser Books.

Fr. K. X°. 2002. *Hermes Mercurius Trismegistus: A Treatise Preliminary to the Study of the Hermetic Philosophy*. S.R.I.A.

Fuller, Robert C. 1982. *Mesmerism and the American Cure of Souls*. University of Pennsylvania Press, Philadelphia.

Fuller, Robert C. 1987. *"Mesmerism and the Birth of Psychology"*, from *Pseudo-Science and Society in Nineteenth-Century America*, Arthur Wrobel, Ed. University Press of Kentucky.

Gardiner, Phillip. 2006. *Secrets of the Serpent: In Search of the Sacred Past*. Reality Press.

Ginzberg, Louis. 1909. *The Legends of the Jews*. Jewish Publication Society of America, Philadelphia.

Gottlieb, Klein. 1898. *Bidrag Till Israels Religion Historia*. Stockholm.

Greer, John Michael. 2003. *New Encyclopedia of the Occult*. Llewellyn Publications.

Griffith, F.L., and Herbert Thompson. 1904. *The Demotic Magical Papyrus of London and Leiden*. H. Grevel & Co., London.

Hall, Manly P. 1928. *The Secret Teachings of All Ages*. H.S. Crocker & Co., New York.

Hall, Manly P. 1929. *Lectures on Ancient Philosophy: An Introduction to the Study and Application of Rational Procedure*. The Hall Publishing Company, Los Angeles.

Hall, Manly P. 1992. *Unseen Forces that Affect Our Lives*. Philosophical Research Society.

Hall, Manly P. 1996. *The Hermetic Marriage*. Philosophical Research Society.

Hall, Manly P. 2003. *The Secret Teachings of All Ages*. Putnam Tarcher, New York.

Hancock, Graham. 1993. *The Sign and the Seal*. Touchstone.

Hanegraaff, Hendrik H. *"What's Wrong With The Faith Movement—Part One: E. W. Kenyon and the Twelve Apostles of Another Gospel"*. Christian Research Journal, Winter 1993.

Harrison, Jane E. 1921. *Epilegomena to the Study of Greek Religion*. Cambridge University Press.

Hartmann, Franz. 1887. *The Life of Philippus Theophrastus Bombast of Hohenheim, Known by the Name of Paracelsus, and of the Substance of His Teachings*. George Redway, London.

Hauck, Dennis William. 1999. *The Emerald Tablet: Alchemy of Personal Transformation*. Penguin, New York.

Heidenreich, Alfred. 1980. *Healing in the Gospels.* Floris Books.

Hilkey, Judy. 1997. *Character is Capital: Success Manuals and Manhood in Gilded AgeAmerica.* The University of North Carolina Press, Chapel Hill, NC.

Hill, Napoleon. 2004. *Think and Grow Rich! The Original Version, Re stored and Revised.* Aventine Press, Clemson, SC.

Hirsch, Emil G., and Wilhelm Bacher. 2002. *Tables of the Law* from Jewish Encyclopedia.com.

Holmes, Ernest. 1967. *Creative Mind and Success.* Dodd Mead and Company.

Holmes, Ernest. 1980. *Seminar Lectures.* Science of Mind Publications.

Holmes, Ernest. 1992. *Ideas of Power.* Holmes papers, vol. 3. DeVorss.

Incognito, Magus. 1949. *The Secret Doctrine of The Rosicrucians.* Yoga Publication Society, Des Plaines, IL.

James, Julian. 2000. *The Origin of Consciousness in the Breakdown of the Bicameral Mind.* Mariner Books

James, M.R. 1913. *Old Testament Legends.* Longmans, Green and Co.

Jasnow, Richard and Karl-Th. Zauzich. 2005. *The Ancient Egyptian Book of Thoth: A Demotic Discourse on Knowledge and Pendant to the Classical Hermetica. Volume 1: Text. Volume 2: Plates.* Harrassowitz, Wiesbaden, Germany.

Jayne, Walter Addison, M.D. 1925. *The Healing Gods of Ancient Civilizations.* Yale University Press, London.

Jennings, Hargrave. 1889. *Ophiolatreia.* Privately Printed

Jennings, Jesse. 2002. *The Essential Ernest Holmes.* Tarcher.

King, Chris. 2004. *Sexual Paradox.* Lulu press.

Kingsford, Anna. 1893. *Dreams and Dream-Verses.* (38:1) George Redway, London.

Kingsley, Peter. 2000. *From Poimandres to Jacob Bohme.* Brill Academic Publishers

Kenealy, E.Y. 1878. *The Book of Enoch.* London

Landman, Isaac., ed. 1943. *The Universal Jewish Encyclopedia*, vol. 9. Jewish Publication Society, New York.

Latz, Dr. Gottfried. 1869. *The Secret of the Emerald Tablet,* trans. Dennis William Hauck. *Die Alchemie,* Bonn, Germany.

Leadbeater, C.W. 1961. *The Power and Use of Thought.* The Theosophical Publishing House, Madras, India.

Leadbeater, C.W., and Annie Besant. 1969. *Thought Forms.* Quest Books.

Leitch, Aaron. 2003. *The Egyptian Creation Epic Harmonized From Various Versions of the Mythos.* Theology Website.

Le Plongeon, Augustus. 1996. *Origin of the Egyptians.* Philosophical Research Society.

Lewis, Spencer, 1978. *Rosicrucian Manual.* Supreme Grand Lodge of AMORC, San Jose, CA.

Ley, Willy. 1947. *"Pseudoscience in Naziland"*. Astounding Science Fiction.

Livergood, Norman D. 2003. *The Perennial Tradition*. Dandelion Books, LLC.

Lutyens, Mary. 1997. *Krishnamurti: The Years of Awakening*. Shambhala.

Mackenzie, Donald. 1907. *Egyptian Myth and Legend*. Gresham Publishing Co., London.

Maitland, Edward. 1905. *The Bible's Own Account of Itself*. The Ruskin Press, Birmingham, Alabama.

Magre, Maurice. 1997. *Magicians, Seers, and Mystics*. Kessinger Publications.

Marrs, Jim. 2001. *Rule By Secrecy*. Harper Collins, New York.

McKenna, Terence. 1992. *The Archaic Revival* Harper: San Francisco

Mead, G.R.S. 1964. *Thrice Greatest Hermes*. J.M. Watkins.

Mead, G.R.S. 2001. *Thrice Greatest Hermes*. Weiser Books.

Mead, G.R.S. 2004. *The Corpus Hermeticum, IX*. On Thought and Sense. Kessinger.

Melanson, Terry. 2007. *Oprah Winfrey, New Thought, "The Secret" and the "New Alchemy"*. From ConspiracyArchive.com

Melton, J. Gordon. 1992. *Encyclopedic Handbook of Cults in America*. Garland Publishing.

Merkur, Dan. 1999. *Stages of Ascension in Hermetic Rebirth. Esoterica* I

Mesmer, Franz Anton. 1779. *Mesmerism*. Macdonald, London.

Michas, Peter A. 1997. *The Rod of an Almond Tree in God's Master Plan*. WinePress Publishing.

The Rev. Dr. Miller. 2001. *Cults and Cultism in America*. Orthodox Tradition, Vol. XVIII

Montenegro, Marcia. 1999. *The Serpent in Egypt and in the Bible: Evil, Power, and Healing*. Cana, Arlington, Virginia.

Morenz, Seigfreid. 1992. *Egyptian Religion*. Cornell University Press.

Muhlestein, Kerry. 2002. *The Book of Breathings in its Place*. Review of Michael D. Rhodes. *The Hor Book of Breathings: A Translation and Commentary*. FARMS, Provo, Utah.

Mulford, Prentice. 1889. *Prentice Mulford's Story*. Kessinger.

Mulford, Prentice. 1908. *Thoughts are Things*. G. Bell and Sons, Ltd, London.

Munkdar, Balaji. 1983. *The Cult of the Serpent: An Interdisciplinary Survey of its Manifestations and Origins*. State University of New York Press, Albany.

Murphy, Joseph. 1966. *Your Infinite Power to be Rich*. Prentice Hall, Paramus, NJ.

Nautilus: Magazine of New Thought, October, 1925. (Edited by Elizabeth Towne and William E. Towne).

New Thought: An Organ of Optimism, October, 1907. (Edited by Franklin L. Berry and Louis Radford Wells.)

Pike, General Albert. 1871. *Morals and Dogma*. Supreme Council of the 33rd Degree, Charleston.

Price, Robert M. 2000. *Deconstructing Jesus.* Prometheus Books.

Podmore, Frank. 1909. *Mesmerism and Christian Science: A Short History of Mental Healing.* Philadelphia, Pennsylvania.

Ponder, Catherine. 1962. *The Dynamic Laws of Prosperity.* Prentice-Hall / DeVorss, Marina Del Rey, CA.

Prinke. Rafal T. 1984. *Early Symbolism of the Rosy Cross.* The Hermetic Journal, 25, 11-15.

Quimby, Phineas. 1921. *Circular to the Sick,* republished in *The Quimby Manuscripts.* Thomas Y. Crowell Co., New York.

Quimby, Phineas Parkhurst. 1862. *The Portland Advertiser.*

Quimby, Phineas Parkhurst. 1862. *Defense Against an Accusation of Comparing Myself to Christ.* Self published pamphlet.

Randall, John Herman, Jr. 1970. *Hellenistic Ways of Deliverance and the Making of the Christian Synthesis.* Columbia University Press, New York.

Ranke-Heinmann, Uta. 1992. *Putting Away Childish Things: The Virgin Birth, the Empty Tomb, and Other Fairy Tales You Don't Need to Believe to Have a Living Faith.* Harper, San Francisco.

Rebisse, Christian. 2003. *Rosicrucian History and Mysteries.* A.M.O.R.C. *Rejuvenation* (formerly *New Thought*), December 1922. (Edited by Sydney B. Flower.)

Richardson, Alan. 1991. *The Magical Life of Dion Fortune.* Aquarian Press.

Roberts, J. M. 1892. *Antiquity Unveiled: Ancient Voices from the Spirit Realms Proving Christianity to Be of Heathen Origin* Kessinger.

Robinson, James M., ed. 1988. *The Nag Hammadi Library in English,* 3rd ed. Harper & Row, San Francisco.

Rubenstein, Richard E. 1999. *When Jesus Became God: The Epic Fight Over Christ's Divinity in the Last Days of Rome.* Harcourt.

Rutter, Gordon. 2004. *Magic Goes to War.* Fortean Times.

Scheflin, Dr. Alan. 1995. *The History of Mind Control: What We Can Prove and What We Can't.* Dallas, Texas. From the Ryerson Mind Control Series on CKLN FM (88.1 in Toronto).

Scholem, Gershom. 1996. *On the Kabbalah and its Symbolism.* Schocken.

Schuchard, Marsha Keith. 2006. *Why Mrs. Blake Cried: William Blake and the Sexual Basis of Spiritual Vision.* Century.

Schure, Edouard. 1961. *The Great Initiates: A Study of the Secret History of Religions.* St. George Books, New York.

Sharpe, Samuel. 1879. *Egyptian Mythology and Egyptian Christianity.* J.R. Smith, London.

Sitchin, Zecharia. 1999. *When Time Began.* Harper.

Skolnik, Fred., ed. 2006. *Encyclopaedia Judaica,* vol. 14. Macmillan.

Smith, M.R. 2003. *Yoga in America, What Went Wrong?* Morningside School of Yoga and Physical Culture, Syracuse, New York.

Stead, Christopher. 1994. *Philosophy in Christian Antiquity*. Cambridge University Press, New York.

Steele, R., and D.W. Singer. 1928. *"The Emerald Table"*. Proceedings of the Royal Society of Medicine, vol. 21.

Steiner, Rudolph. 1997. *Christianity as Mystical Fact*. Steiner Books. *Success Unlimited Magazine*, September, 1972. (Edited by W. Clement Stone.)

Symonds, John, and Kenneth Grant. 1989. *The Confessions of Aleister Crowley*, Bantam Books.

Synkellos, George. 2002. *Ecloga Chronographica*. Oxford University Press.*Thought: Boiled-Down Stuff for Thinking People; A Magazine of Practical Psychology*, 1910. Organ of the National Optimistic League. (Edited by Sheldon Leavitt.)

Three Initiates, The. *The Kybalion. A Study of the Hermetic Philosophy of Ancient Egypt and Greece*. 1912. The Yogi Publication Society, Chicago IL.

Trismegistus, Hermes Mercurious. 1871. (Edited by Paschal Beverly Randolph.) *Divine Pymander, Also The Asiatic Mystery, The Smaragdine Table and the Song of Brahm*. Reprinted by Yogi Publication Society, Des Plaines, Illinois.

Trobridge, George. 1969. *Swedenborg: Life and Teaching*. Swedenborg Foundation, New York, NY.

Tucker, Ruth. 1989. *Another Gospel*. Zondervan Publishing.

Turcan, Robert. 1996. *The Cults of the Roman Empire*. Oxford England.

Twain, Mark. 1993. *Christian Science*. Prometheus Books.

Vernon, Ronald. 2001. *Star in the East: Krishnamurti—The Invention of a Messiah*. Palgrave Macmillan.

Warren, Dr. Lee. 1996. *Angels*. May/June *Plim Report*.

Wattles, Wallace. 2007. *The Science of Getting Rich*. Destiny Books.

Weigall, Arthur. 1976. *The Paganism in Our Christianity*. Gordon Press.

Weinberg, Judy. 1976. "All You Ever Wanted to Know About Lilith". *LILITH* Magazine.

Werner, Uwe. 1999. *Anthroposophen in der Zeit des Nationalsozialismus*. Munich, Germany.

Whitty, Michael. 1918. *Editorials. AZOTH*, vol. 2, number 5.

Wilson, Colin. 1975. *Mysterious Powers*. The Danbury Press, London.

processmediainc.com